TENNESSEE WILDFLOWERS

J. Kent Preyer

NAPOLEON BLUE PRESS

TENNESSEE WILDFLOWERS

J. Kent Preyer

Copyright © 2014 by J. Kent Preyer
All Rights Reserved

Cover Art Copyright © 2014 by Rebecca Preyer

Cover Author Photograph Copyright © 2014 by Robin Cradles

Cover Design: Sarah Wynes

This book is a work of fiction. Names, characters, places, and incidents are the product of the author's imagination or are used fictitiously, and any resemblance to actual persons, living or dead, events, or locals is entirely coincidental.

All rights reserved. This book was self published by the author J. Kent Preyer under Napoleon Blue Press. No part of this book may be reproduced in any form by any means in any form whatsoever without the express permission of the author. This includes reprints, excerpts, photocopying, recording, or any future means of reproducing text.

Published in the United States of America
First Edition 2014
Napoleon Blue Press
ISBN: 978-0-9903850-5-9

This book is dedicated to

Helen Louise Green Preyer
&
Herbert Austin Preyer
Mom and Dad

TENNESSEE WILDFLOWERS

COME ON OVER HERE, SIT A SPELL, and I'll tell you a true story. When I was just a little sprig, I'd be walking to school and I'd pass a gangly old fella in coveralls sitting on a wooden fence. Much to my surprise, that man sat there every single day, hitting himself in the head with a hammer. Whack! Whack! Whack! One day, I walked up to that old-timer and asked him, "Hey Mister, why do you hit yourself in the head with a hammer over and over?" The man stopped, and placed the hammer in his lap. He peered down at me. A look of utter peace flooded over his face. He said, "Because, young man, it feels so good when I stop."

- Oft' told tale in the hills of Tennessee

To you, I am nothing more than a fox like a hundred thousand other foxes. But if you tame me, then we shall need each other. To me, you will be unique in all the world. To you, I shall be unique in all the world...
— Antoine de Saint-Exupéry
The Little Prince

The truth will set you free, but first it will make you miserable.
— James A. Garfield

JJ AND JOSH

AUGUST, 1999

1

How do I tell my son something I know is going to break his heart?

A man and a young boy stood together gazing into a full-length antique bronze dressing mirror. A strong Canadian cold front had blown in the night before and the master bedroom they were in felt damp and chilly. Normally this late in the summer Nashville would be hot and clammy, so much so that your whole body hung onto exhaustion even after you'd found the salvation of air conditioning. But today this Antebellum-style home, a stately manor that had twice been featured in *Southern Living* magazine, felt drearily cold throughout.

Earlier the house had been showered with hail for over thirty minutes. It left a blanket of white pearls covering the roof and freshly cut green lawn. Now, an icy rain was falling from the dark clouds in a heavy downpour. The house creaked and groaned in the stronger gusts of wind and occasionally a shrill whistle would find its way through the old structure. Those who were sensitive to the more ethereal dimensions of life would have also sensed that the house today was burdened with a kind of poignant sadness.

Outside, on the long driveway by a large blooming magnolia tree, a black limousine sat idling in the downpour. The driver was concerned because he knew his passengers were running very late. But the house was locked and no one inside was answering the doors or the phones, so there was little he could do but wait.

JJ Fletcher stood back from the mirror to get a full view of himself. He was a dashing man in his late twenties, a well-bred, well-built Tennessee gentleman and a proud descendent of tobacco plantation owners. Even though there was nearly four thousand acres of rich productive farm land owned by the Fletcher family, JJ spent most of his time as a practicing attorney. He was also the only son of Tennessee's enormously popular governor Cowboy Fletcher. Neither he nor his father spent enough time among the tobacco fields to have calloused hands anymore, but they would still personally oversee the large farming operation from planting to harvest. In the summer, due to this part-time farming and weekly afternoons on the golf course JJ's skin saw enough sunshine to sustain an ample farmer's tan. He had wavy champagne-blond hair and beamy white teeth; and when he walked into a room he would turn heads like a movie star. His bold self-assuredness won over most folks. *He could charm the warts off a toad*, his Grandma Hazel would often declare about her easy-on-the-eyes grandson. As one might expect, not everyone was on board. JJ Fletcher's unblinking confidence and his chiseled good looks outright nauseated some people. But JJ rarely noticed.

At the moment his confidence had staggered a bit. Oddly, an image of Mae West popped into his mind. He remembered hearing that the actress once said: *He who hesitates is last.*

Or was it Lost?

His son Josh was always closer to his mother and he had always been amazed, even sometimes a tad resentful, that the two had such a special, symbiotic connection. The alliance had been there from day one in the hospital (even for JJ on that amazing day), but the mother and son merger grew even more pronounced when Josh learned to speak. Little J and his momma would talk, laugh and play for hours. JJ would sometimes come home to find them both sound asleep among a pile of toys, stuffed animals and books. And yes, the green-eyed monster would be there. Why not be jealous? Before Josh's birth his beautiful wife used to be waiting for him when he got home, in a white silk slip, two glasses of wine in hand, ready to play grown-up games.

When JJ was being honest with himself he knew it was only fair for him to take responsibility for his part in his wife getting pregnant and the concluding birth of their son. There had been a fairly well established link. On the other hand, they hadn't planned on having children. Well, he hadn't anyway. JJ always suspected his wife may have been a behind-the-scenes operator to get in the *family way* because she was so completely overjoyed when the doctor confirmed the news, which for him had been a not-so-joyous bombshell. JJ didn't really like toddlers of any kind. They were too grabby and always seemed to be covered with chocolate and dirt.

Whether his wife deliberately missed a pill, actually forgot, or was one of the five to six percent who got pregnant anyway was irrelevant now. They had a son. And now that Josh was growing up and developing his own personality, JJ actually enjoyed coming home from a long day at work and seeing them asleep together. The image of the woman he had courted and won in college and the son he had sired both conked out on the floor in front of the sofa was nearly as satisfying as any self-indulgent welcome he had gotten a few years earlier. JJ suspected this change was due to in part to something called becoming an adult.

JJ watched as Josh struggled with his necktie. JJ had found a plain navy blue tie for Josh to wear but the boy insisted on a red one with little Buzz Lightyears on the front. JJ decided it wasn't worth debating. Not today.

Even at six years Josh had a vigorous need to earn his father's approval, and making a perfect Winsor knot was undeniably a male gender milestone that fell into this category. His sweet, bright face kept becoming more excited as he came close, but the tie only became more contorted with every adjustment.

"Are you ready for me to try, Son?"

Josh dropped his hands. JJ knelt down and straightened the tie. They both stood back and took another look in the mirror. They were eye-catching in their freshly pressed suits.

JJ hadn't even known that Josh had a suit to wear until he found it in a dry cleaning bag in the back of the boy's closet. His wife had probably gotten it for a family photograph, or maybe a wedding she took Josh to that JJ had missed. There had been a couple of events he had not attended recently because of work. Whatever the suit had been for, she could never have imagined that soon her son would be wearing it for the reason he had it on today.

Now. Tell him, now.

JJ had turned his cell phone off and unplugged the land line yesterday. Laptops were closed, televisions and computers were off throughout the house. He had not put on his watch and had stopped looking at clocks. JJ's secretary from his law office, Byrdie - a loyal, sparkplug of a woman of Japanese and Italian decent - normally kept JJ brilliantly organized and right on schedule. If she were here now she would be in a state of pure, frenzied madness because of JJ's procrastination. But JJ had locked Byrdie out of the house two days ago. Not just Byrdie, JJ had successfully blocked out most of the world for the past two days.

It was no surprise that the blare of the limousine horn from outside nearly jolted JJ out of his cowboy boots. He had been jumping at shadows all morning. JJ sighed, pulled himself together, then took a look down at his feet.

If I'm jumping out of my boots, at least they're damned fine-looking ones.

JJ had considered not wearing them, but his wife had bought the Tres Outlaws cowboy boots for his twenty-sixth birthday, and that had only been three months ago. He knew she must have spent a lot of time thinking about what a great gift the hand-made boots would be for him, and they were. Wearing them today in her memory was the very least he could do.

I think I'll have a drink of that George Dickel first. I'm certain that limousine outside has a bottle.

JJ buttoned up Josh's suit jacket.

I'll tell him everything on the way over.

"Are those made out of alligators?" Josh asked as he looked quizzically at JJ's boots.

"Yes, Son," JJ answered, "they sure are."

JJ immediately noticed Josh's face become ashen.

He remembered that Josh had seen the live alligators at the Nashville Zoo at Grassmere and had gone on and on about how much he liked them. He had several books about the reptiles and owned a much watched DVD called, *Tales from the Wild: Gus the Alligator.*

JJ quickly modified his answer, shooting for a soothing tone: "They don't hurt the alligators at all. I promise you, Son."

JJ had no idea how the alligators his boots were made from met their doom. He imagined they were shot through the head on some barely regulated alligator farm at the Texas/Mexico border, but he was not about to tell that to his six-year-old son.

When JJ found out he was having a boy, he envisioned days of teaching him important things in life – how to know when a tobacco leaf was ready for harvesting, how to shoot straight, how to drive a truck, how to smoke a cigar and drink good Tennessee whiskey, and other such time-honored *manly* things. Over these past six years his doubts confronted him. JJ himself had never in his life, not once, been concerned about how cowboy boots were made, leather, alligator or otherwise.

But Josh clearly was distraught, and by the look on his small face he was not consoled much by JJ's assurance that alligator boot making was a benevolent operation.

It seemed there was always an underlying barrier between them. The lack of the father-son bond was an unidentifiable, intangible dichotomy. JJ thought, *he's my son, my flesh, my DNA, MYSELF! And yet I am at odds with some fundamental part of who he is.*

Sometimes JJ felt this boundary between them was the size of the Smokey Mountains.

It was a concern that Josh, young as he was, felt many times as well. He did not understand this gigantic, god-like figure that towered over him, who spoke too loudly and crudely, smelled of cigarette and cigar smoke, coffee, and a musky sweet odor. (Josh would later learn the odor was called Stetson cologne.) His father would sometimes even make his mother cry. Still, after she cried, the two would both whisper and hold hands, and then suddenly his momma was happy again. Why on earth she liked him so much was extremely difficult to grasp. At least twice a week his daddy would cook dinner and the food was almost never like his momma's. The unbearably boring TV news, weather, and football, baseball and – the biggest yawn-inducer – golf, were all JJ seemed to be interested in watching, and he would never let anyone change the channel. The car radio was an especially cruel torment where Josh was forced to suffer through ear-covering racket that his father explained had crazy names, like Bon Jovi, ZZ Top, Lynard Skynard, Alabama or – his daddy's favorite – KISS! At home, JJ would slide his feet out of his boots and plunk them on the coffee table. He'd say every single time: "These old barking dogs are tired." Josh noticed they were not just tired, but sometimes smelled truly stinky.

JJ looked into the mirror again. It was just the two of them now and there was no more holding the outside world at bay. This awareness engulfed JJ. In that precise moment of profound realization, JJ asked, he prayed, with a perfect, silent, singular intention, "God, please help me remove this damned wall between me and my son."

Once again the limousine horn blasted. The jarring noise caused JJ to jump again and forget all about his plea. JJ did not forget that he wished to be closer to his son. That would be on his mind for many years to come. But his exact prayer was lost to him.

Of the two in that equation – JJ and the Infinite Power he had addressed in his moment of pure, sincere intention – it was only JJ who had forgotten.

As measured in the earthly realm it would seem an especially long time, but the answer for JJ would one day come.

2

The parking lot of the Valentine Funeral Home was at full capacity. The two story columned mansion had been remodeled in 1922 into a magnificent Southern gothic mortuary. The upstairs portion served as the Valentine family home. The funeral home was one of the largest in Nashville, but today it could barely accommodate the unusually large amount of visitors that were arriving.

Great sycamore trees lined the long white pea gravel drive where cars were parked in improvised spaces. The guests of the funeral home, who were having to walk an unanticipated long distance under umbrellas and raincoats, were mostly commenting about the severe summer storm and wishing they had worn more appropriate shoes. If you were talking to someone from the Tennessee hills, or they had family from those parts, they would tell you that rain during a funeral was always a sign the soul they were coming to say their respects to was favored by God, and that he or she had died much too soon.

Today, the rain was falling in sheets.

* * *

Inside the funeral chapel, the large crowd was filling the seats. The viewing had attracted a very distinguished flood of mourners, as well as the press. Candles burned in brass candle holders along the walls and candelabras at the front on either side of the casket. The overwhelming fragrance of roses and carnations - as well as a keen sense of apprehension - hung in the air.

A reporter from the local Channel 2 News station, a man with salt and pepper hair slicked back with Vitalis, was standing next to the news camera and crew near the back of the room. His daughter, a sixteen-year-old intern named Rebecca C. Hooper, held the camera steadily directed at her father. She had earlier done his makeup and picked out his suit. Because of the fervent dreams she held of the day when she would be in his place, in front of the camera, she watched and memorized his every move. The security guard for the funeral home kept a close eye on the notoriously brazen reporter making certain he didn't make any attempt to come any closer to the grieving family.

It was an open casket. The deceased was an attractive young woman with luminous, wavy hair framing her lightly freckled face. Her elegant mahogany casket was surrounded by mountains of flower arrangements.

Greeting the last of a line of mourners, standing near the casket, were the heavy-hearted deceased woman's parents. He was a well-respected judge. She was the president of the Nashville chapter of The Red Cross. They were an impressive couple in most any setting. Today though, much of the room's attention was on the couple standing adjacent to them, the woman in the casket's in-laws.

That would be Cowboy and Petula Fletcher. Cowboy was the current governor of Tennessee. He was in his mid-fifties, an imposing and distinguished man, woozy and ruddy from a life of too many cigars and alcoholic beverages. He could stand to lose about fifty pounds and perspired a lot more these days than he did in his youth, especially now, in the suffocating worsted wool suit coat his wife had chosen for him. By his side was his wife, a tightly wound, frosty, woman in her late forties wearing a stylish Chanel black pant suit. She was once Miss Tennessee and still retained the poise, if not the refinement, that came with that honor. Her exact date of birth, and the fact that her parents had been woefully poor bootleggers from the hills of Tennessee near the small town of Muddy Pond, were no longer a part of the public record. A team of lawyers from Saint

Louis, Missouri eradicated those problematic details for Petula Fletcher many years ago. Nor was it widely known that her elderly daddy and momma were hidden away in a trailer park near Barstow, California. Petula embodied the remnants of a true to life Southern Belle seldom seen these days, and she lived her life by the Southern adage:

Keep your hair light and your past dark.

Though superfluous, Petula blotted her eyes with a white linen handkerchief. It wasn't that she hadn't loved her daughter-in-law that real tears were not presenting themselves. Petula had been elated when JJ brought his future wife home. She was sweet, intelligent, and had a family background of outstanding reputation. Cowboy was extremely fond of his daughter-in-law as well - he had needed four additional Old Fashioneds over and above his usual morning intake just to show up for her funeral today. The trouble was that Petula could only see events and people in relation to their potential political gain. As sad as this unexpected death had been to Petula, it was exactly the kind of family tragedy that would secure a tidy victory for her husband in his upcoming November election. Petula knew a well-established fact: To win over the heart of a Southerner, nothing holds a candle to unexpected, unbearable family misfortune.

Cowboy's opponent, a wealthy and unexpectedly shrewd businesswoman from Memphis, had been making this re-election much more challenging than they had experienced in the past. The businesswoman's campaign had released and flooded the prime-time media market with a television ad that Petula felt crossed the lines of Tennessee political decency, and it had made her blood boil. The ad featured old footage of Cowboy Fletcher riding a horse in a 4th of July parade surrounded by Shriners clowns. A strong persuasive male voice listed off the usual laundry list of slanted political allegations and then the ad ended with the man's voice delivering the renowned Texas idiom, clearly taking a swipe at the governor's name: "Cowboy Fletcher is all hat and no cattle." The ad had a consequential impact on some of the Tennessee electorate and the businesswoman's poll numbers had gone up a game-changing six points.

So today, as Petula looked out among the unprecedented crowd of mourners (voters) and imagined all the sympathetic, well-wishing viewers watching from their living rooms all across Tennessee, the primary emotion Petula felt was acute, retaliatory, relief.

I hope you're watching your TV set too, you malicious Memphis she-wolf trying to steal my husband's political dreams.

Petula gave an illusory dab in her eyes again, and imagined poll numbers rising in favor of Cowboy Fletcher like a balloon released from the hand of a Shriner's clown.

The organist, Ruby Billingsley, played the popular spiritual hymn "Just a Closer Walk with Thee" on a Hammond C-3. Ruby's close friends described the nearly sixty-year-old, high-spirited woman as "colorful and sweet." Though others were more likely to characterize her as "daffy and dangerously scatterbrained." The truth probably rested somewhere in the middle. Adorning Ruby's front dress pocket was a small brooch made of pink sapphires designed into the likeness of a pig.

Petula was endeavoring to maintain the veneer of tranquility as she listened to Ruby's uneven, and somewhat inappropriately up-tempo, church hymn. Suddenly, she zeroed in on an odd sight. A mason jar with a jumble of wildflowers had been placed among the other tasteful flower arrangements.

How did that happen without me seeing it?

Petula whisked her handkerchief into her crocodile Coco Chanel clutch, sidled over to the flower arrangements and picked up the Mason jar. She headed straight toward Vernon Valentine, the professionally somber funeral home owner standing near an exit door. Both of Vernon's parents had passed a few years back. They had left the family business to the only child of their six kids interested in keeping the family business going, Vernon.

(Vernon Valentine – now in his mid-seventies – and Cowboy's now deceased daddy, Hal Fletcher, had been best friends from childhood. One of Vernon's and Hal's teenage adventures was still legendary today in the annals of Nashville lore - but that infamous story will have to wait until later in the story.)

As Petula approached the gentleman-in-charge with the offending jar of flowers, Vernon silently questioned her intentions with a quizzical look. Then he quickly understood her objective with her disapproving look back. He scrupulously took the Mason jar and disappeared through the exit, and Petula returned to Cowboy's side.

She checked her watch and fiddled with her pearl necklace. "I would go and call him again, but it seems he's turned all his phones off," she whispered to Cowboy through her linen handkerchief. "Of all things, why does he have to be late today?"

Cowboy didn't offer her a glance, just eyed the crowd languidly and replied back softly, "Don't make a scene, Pet. My head is already splitting."

* * *

Outside the Valentine Funeral Home a limousine pulled to a stop at the front entrance.

Inside the limousine JJ stared at Josh, who was totally absorbed in his new Game Boy. JJ had considered asking the driver to continue on. He wasn't sure where, but he imagined maybe across Mississippi, Louisiana, Texas and then crossing over into Mexico might be a good escape route. JJ was a strong man who could face any challenge with remarkable confidence, but death had proved to be an unbearable adversary, one that he had no resources inside to pull from. When his Grandpa Hal had died many years ago he never honestly accepted or dealt with the much-loved family member's death. Until now his life had been fairly seamless, even blessed; a bachelor's degree in agriculture, law school where he met his wife, a job right away at the firm of his choice, and then the partnership. He always felt like a lucky man.

There had been one tiny bump early on. It was his high school junior year, and he had fallen for a girl. Her name had been Ruth-Adele Holloway, and JJ thought she was the prettiest girl he'd ever seen. She was a pure country redhead and wild as a peach orchard boar. She was a sophomore who had transferred to Hillsboro High School the year before from one of the several small schools that were closing up in the hills around Nashville at the time. He first saw her on the school campus lawn. She was sitting alone under a scarred old oak tree reading a book, the autobiography of Loretta Lynn, *Coal Miner's Daughter*. JJ fell instantly. He asked Ruth-Adele out on a date three times. She gave him an unambiguous and brutal "No!" twice. But the third time was the charm. After that first date they both fell crazy in love.

They were a fiery pair, one of those unique, combustible couples who caused everyone to look twice and who rarely noticed anyone else was even watching. They were scarcely ever seen apart. She lived way up in Armadillo, an old lumber town that had dried up when the mill was closed, so JJ had to drive nearly forty miles to get her in his Ford pickup for their dates. But he would have driven four hundred more if he had needed to.

As first-loves often were, it had been intense and single-minded. It had never occurred to either one of them who might be observing their activities, and who might not approve of what was being observed. The relationship had come to an abrupt end for reasons JJ didn't understand at the time. (That would come later.) It stumped him. It was the only thing in his life that didn't seem to roll out effortlessly for him. He'd thought he would never love, or more to the point, lust like that again.

But he had. He met a girl on his debate team his second year of law school. She was sexy and smart and he couldn't take his eyes off her. When he proposed to her at Jimmy Kelly's Steakhouse Restaurant two years later, he was in love with his whole heart. He didn't know a man could be any happier than that.

Later, a day did come along that had made him happier. The day his son was born and he saw the boy's face for the first time. Not much on earth could beat coming eye-to-eye with your own new baby. It transcended all reasonable understanding. JJ saw the blue eyes of his son, Josh, and instantly understood the meaning of the word *worship*. He had said to his wife, "You know how I don't normally like children or babies of any kind, but this really is different. It's as if all three of our hearts were one and the same, beating together. Can you feel that?"

She did.

The limo driver opened the darkened passenger door and JJ stepped out. News photographers appeared as if from nowhere and their cameras began flashing. Josh descended from the car after JJ, the boy stood close behind his father's legs daunted by the looming columns of the mortuary and the flashing camera lights. They were well under the covered roof, but the raindrops were whisking right through, the cold water stinging their eyes.

Josh had a bad feeling.

It was the same kind of feeling emanating from his stomach that he had experienced about a year ago at Dollywood. That had been when his Grandma Petula was pressuring him to get onto a roller coaster ride called THE BLAZING FURY. She kept reassuring him that there was nothing to be scared about. "You're going to love it, Little J, and you'll be begging me to bring you back all day." He did not love it. He had barfed up his corndog and watermelon slushy, and his head felt like it was swirling for the next three days. From that experience he had concluded that adults – by and large, a certain grandmother - were not to be trusted.

JJ noticed his son's worried eyes and took his hand.

God, his hand is so small and fragile.

He had told Josh everything. Well, a version of everything. At least it was the truth. Okay, it was a version of the truth. Josh had barely looked up from his hand held computer game and JJ knew he had no idea what he was trying to explain to the boy.

How do you explain death to a six-year-old when you yourself didn't even understand it?

His wife would have called it artful evasion, and added, "The apple hasn't fallen far from the tree." This would have been a reference to JJ coming from a long line of politicians. She hadn't really liked politicians much, but had nonetheless predicted JJ would one day follow in his father's footsteps and run for political office, maybe even make the run for governor. Even though she would never live to see it, her prediction would prove to be an accurate one.

JJ wondered how she would have handled it, if reality had been somehow altered. What if fate (*the cowardly monster that it was*, JJ thought) had chosen a different series of events that led to his wife standing here today instead of him? No doubt she would have handled things a whole hell of a lot better than he had. As he stared at the looming doors in front of him, JJ wished that fate had chosen those other events. He wished it intensely. But it wasn't so, and he had to step forward with his son, holding tightly to his small hand, and open the door.

* * *

Inside the chapel, JJ and Josh entered the back of the room as the crowd and cameras turned to witness the most anticipated guests. Petula offered a disapproving glance at her watch. Ruby Billingsley had to strain from her organ bench to see JJ and her face blushed with delight, which she quickly tried to hide. You weren't supposed to feel delight at a funeral after all. She never had children herself and being a distant relation of the Fletchers she had always imagined JJ as the son she never had. She thought, as she struggled to see JJ and Josh enter, *and that little son of his is turning out to be as cute as a bug's ear as well!*

JJ and Josh walked past the sympathetic guests to the front. Josh was being careful to shy away from the eyes of the onlookers. He had never understood why they stared at him with such intrusive eyes. For Josh the walk to the front seemed like miles before they got passed all the aisles of people. And *the people* weren't acting normal. Some were crying and clasping his daddy's hand as they passed. They even reached out for him, but he pulled away just in time. Josh breathed a sigh of relief to have them all safely behind him.

JJ's secretary, Byrdie, sat in the front row. JJ stopped as she stood and gave him a heartfelt hug. Byrdie took his hand. She whispered, "She is wearing her rose bracelet. I knew she'd want to have it with her." JJ wasn't sure what Byrdie was referring to, but he smiled and nodded.

JJ noticed his Grandma Hazel sitting next to Byrdie with his Aunt Jewell. He gave them both a quick hug. Jewell held Josh's hand for a moment and smiled at the young man. "Everything will be okay, you precious little boy," Jewell said. "Not today, but in time. That's what time is for." Josh didn't know what she was talking about, but he really liked his Great Aunt Jewell and smiled back.

"Can I sit with you, Auntie Jewell?" Josh asked.

"You can come back and sit with me. I would love that," she replied. She thoughtfully squeezed his hand. "This is important so listen to your Great Aunt Jewell." She waited for his busy young eyes to rest on hers. She finally let go of his hand and placed her unsteady, frail palm on his chest. "You listen for your momma here. *Here* in your heart." She gave a graceful nod to Josh. "She'll be watching over you for the rest of your life."

Josh didn't understand what she was talking about. But he smiled at her. He thought his great aunt was beautiful.

JJ took Josh and walked over to his parents.

Petula and JJ hugged. Then JJ hugged his father.

Petula bent down to Josh and adjusted his tie. "How's my Little J?"

"Okay, I guess," Josh replied.

"I like your tie."

"It's Buzz Lightyear."

"I see that." Petula caressed Josh's face.

JJ walked over to hug his wife's parents and they consoled him in a tearful embrace, then looked around for their grandson. They saw that Josh had ventured over to the mahogany box. They all watched the little boy looking up. It was a touching moment they would never forget.

JJ hesitated. He braced himself. He could hear his Grandpa Hal's voice. JJ thought of the congenial older gentleman expounding on about some folk saying that had something to do with facing the adverse consequences of your actions: "It's time to grasp the nettle," Grandpa Hal was fond of saying, with a shake of his silver-stemmed, cherry wood pipe. It sounded about right. JJ went to the wall where an empty chair awaited and then slid it over to Josh. He then took in a brave, deep breath, and lifted his son up on the chair to see.

Josh stared at his mother's face. Most people in the room watching the boy imagined he must have been feeling sadness, but they were wrong.

Josh felt utter confusion.

This isn't anything at all like what Daddy was telling me in the car ride over here.

The reporter, excited and eager, motioned for his equally enthusiastic daughter Rebecca to zoom the camera in closer to the scene playing out up by the casket. He quietly reported, "Governor Fletcher's grandson, Josh, has stepped up to say goodbye to his mother. What a brave little boy, and what a personal and private moment. Let's watch!"

Josh wasn't sure what was being expected of him. Everyone was looking in his direction, in a bizarre, sympathetic gaze!

And his momma was not herself – *literally*.

He wasn't even sure who it was laying in what looked like a too-narrow, cushiony white bed. It had a lid that was half closed over the bottom half of her body. That made no sense what-so-ever.

This is worse than the roller coaster. Way worse.

He reached into his suit pocket and pulled out a little brown and white hamster. He held his pet up close to his face. "Gumbo, what is all this going on here?"

Petula stepped up to JJ and leaned into his ear. "He's going to really miss his momma...but maybe you can hasten him up a little?"

JJ turned and nodded to his mother, then lightly pushed her back. He could handle this. And that strong perfume she was wearing was too much. He knew she had the fragrance delivered from French Polynesia: "Because the Tahitian Vanilla is more pure at the source," she always said. The pungent smell of it had always made him keep his mother at least two feet or more at bay.

He bent over to Josh. "It's time to say goodbye."

"Bye, Momma," Josh said.

"She said goodbye," JJ told him.

"I didn't hear anything."

"She whispered it, Son."

"Gumbo didn't hear anything either."

"I told you not to bring Gumbo."

"Why are all these people here?"

"They're friends of your momma's. Now step on down. Everyone here is expecting a good little boy."

"I'm not doing anything until you tell Gumbo and me what's going on."

"It's like I explained in the car."

"You didn't say anything about all these people in the car...or this weird bed."

"Just get down for me."

"No."

"This isn't the place to argue with me, just do what I say, right now." JJ took a firm hold on his son's arm and Josh lost his grip on the hamster. Gumbo leapt from his hand into the casket. It quickly scurried next to his mother's dead body and ran under the closed lower lid.

Petula produced the handkerchief again and wiped her forehead. "For the love of Saint Peter," she said quietly, keeping the handkerchief in place. From under the lace of the fine Irish linen held to her head she looked out at the seated guests to see what they were doing. Their heads were turning to one another – Whispering! And that ridiculous reporter was leering intently at JJ and Josh mouthing words she couldn't hear into his microphone. She suddenly became deeply worried about what his take on the evening news was going to be. He had never been one of those reporters she could count on to do the right thing.

JJ had reached his limit. He sat Josh on the floor, then reached over and lifted the bottom lid of the coffin. He looked around until he could find the hamster. It was trying to hide under his dead wife's right foot. JJ grabbed it, then turned to his son. As he dropped the lower lid closed, he said to Josh, "Take the critter and put it in your pocket!"

Josh, tight lipped, took Gumbo and placed him in his suit jacket pocket. Petula exhaled a deep sigh of relief.

JJ looked at his wife. Then he saw the rose bracelet on the wrist of her hand, crossed on top of her other hand on her chest. It had rubies set in white gold roses and it was one of his wife's favorite pieces of jewelry. After they had been robbed several years ago, his wife had put the bracelet in their safety deposit box. JJ had completely forgotten about it and how Byrdie had gotten possession of it from the Tennessee Community Bank was anybody's guess, but that was what Byrdie was best at, the details. JJ looked around at Byrdie and gave her a knowing nod. Byrdie smiled back, using a handkerchief to wipe a tear from her eye.

He looked back in the casket. It occurred to him that this was the last time he would ever see his wife's face. And her voice, he would never hear that again either. He loved the sound of her voice. It reminded him of a mandolin. It had an even, gentle, calming effect on him. Of course, there would be photographs and the recordings he would find here and there, but those were just imitations and would be no consolation. He knew, whatever it was, that magical wonder his wife had brought into his life, it was gone. And it was never coming back.

A photographer stepped past the security and knelt down for a picture. "Governor, can we get a photograph of the family for *The Tennessean?*"

Petula quickly grabbed Cowboy's suit coat and pulled it down taught, straightening the shoulders. As she motioned for JJ and Josh to move in she turned on a somber face for the camera, hoping the others would take her cue and prepare for a professional photograph that was bound to be on the front page of tomorrow's newspaper.

Josh shouted, "She's not going on a trip! Momma doesn't even have her purse!"

JJ was stunned. He stared into Josh's accusing eyes.

Jesus Christ, that was the loudest voice I've ever heard in my life. JJ thought. He wondered how his son had even made it.

"She never wore lipstick that color," Josh continued, yelling even louder. "I don't think it's even really Momma!"

TENNESSEE WILDFLOWERS

Every face and ear in the room was fine tuned to the front. Every eyebrow lifted. You could have cut the thick astonished tension in the room with a knife.

Petula grabbed JJ's arm. "JJ, please tell me you explained this to him before you brought him here."

JJ defended himself: "I tried, Momma. I just didn't know what to say."

"You lied to me!" Josh yelled out enraged again. Josh kicked JJ in the shin as hard as he could, making sure to aim high, right above the top of the *murdered* alligator skin cowboy boots.

JJ groped forward and groaned with pain, the throbbing in his leg shot right up to join the corresponding pain in his heart, watering up his eyes and causing him to clutch his leg.

Petula was horrified. Cowboy rubbed his temples in anguish.

Josh stood firm, irate, but somewhat satisfied with his well-placed shin-kicking.

Ruby Billingsley, endeavoring to draw some attention away from the inopportune scene near the casket, increased the volume of "How Great Thou Art" to a crowd-distressing level.

FLASH!

The photographer snapped the shot, a photo of privileged family dysfunction captured forever for the archives.

And, as fate (and the senior editor at the paper who didn't particularly like Governor Cowboy Fletcher) would have it, that *was* the photograph the newspaper ran on the front page of the next day's edition of *The Tennessean*.

3

In Josh's upstairs bedroom, Gumbo raced zealously inside his squeaky wheel in the small cage sitting on Josh's writing desk. The room was adorned in an African safari theme: stuffed animals – tigers, zebras, elephants; safari accessories – khaki ensembles, safari hat, a butterfly net; zebra striped rugs on the hardwood floor. On the walls were jungle scenes painted with wild creatures staring out of the dark green foliage. The ceiling fan doubled for a propeller of a plane painted to look like a young boy was flying right down into the bedroom zooming off onto some exciting adventure.

The rain outside had died down considerably, but the old house still held a shivery chill that made it difficult to stay warm. Josh was sitting on his bed, snug in his red long-john pajamas and oversized wool socks. He was speaking animatedly to a worn-out stuffed monkey propped up on a fluffy pillow. The cotton plush toy had been a constant companion for Josh over the years, so frayed some stuffing was falling out in places and it only had one button eye left. It was a story familiar to them both:

"Rattlesnake Calliope would sit out on her front porch in her rocking chair with a fishing pole in her hand and the bait - a little field mouse. She'd tie the end of the fishing line to the tail of that little mouse." Josh held up a make-believe fishing pole and pretended to cast it into an imaginary sky. "Then from her front porch she'd fling that squeaking little mouse way, way out into the high grass on the hillside. The mouse would come to a landing out in the rocks and grass - where something was waiting." Josh imagined the mouse sailing off in the sky, its little mouse paws extended out in frightened horror as the tiny rodent fell down into a rocky ravine. Josh looked to confirm that his stuffed monkey appeared suitably terrified as well. *He did.* Glancing over at his hamster, Josh said, "Gumbo, don't listen to this next part." Josh looked back to the monkey. "A rattlesnake hiding in the rocks would leap out and grab the mouse with the fangs in his mouth. Then the snake would be hooked and ready to reel in for the catch."

JJ, tie now gone, top buttons undone, stepped quietly into the room. JJ's leg was still hurting, although a little less now because the pain killers he took were kicking in. Josh's well-planted kick left a skinned shin surrounded by a quickly darkening bruise and when JJ poured rubbing alcohol on it earlier he had cursed six ways to Sunday.

JJ smiled. He recognized the story Josh was telling.

Unaware that his father entered his room, Josh continued relaying his tale to the tattered monkey: "Rattlesnake Calliope would reel that mean old snake right upon the front porch, and oh, it would be a fierce battle. Her eyes, which were the color of Bluebell flowers, and the hot red eyes of the snake would meet. Rattlesnake Calliope wasn't afraid of that snake in the least. She would wrangle that creepy snake around his neck with her bare hands. Then she would throw it into a big cast iron cooking kettle with all the other rattlers she had captured that day."

JJ had no real idea how Josh was taking his mother's death. In the limousine on the ride back from the funeral home Josh had held onto JJ and cried so hard JJ had felt the warm tears soak right through his shirt. The reception after the funeral had been at the governor's mansion. There, Josh had talked with other kids his age and even played outside in the gardens. Now he seemed to be relating this old story, a favorite bedtime tale that his momma often told him, with a kind of glee. It was likely shock. This was Josh's first close experience with death and JJ was sure the boy would have some very sad days and nights ahead of him.

They both would.

Josh was short of breath. He coughed and wheezed a little, but continued, "...and then she'd make stew. There was always a pot of rattlesnake stew for a passer-by at Calliope's house. And on Sunday there would be two pots...because..." Josh was suddenly stumped, he couldn't remember the next part.

JJ stepped up and Josh turned around. JJ said, "On Sunday there would be two pots because when the Lord gives you a gift you're obliged to share your rewards with others."

Josh smiled and nodded. "I want to meet Rattlesnake Calliope."

"I know your momma told you that story," JJ replied.

"Momma said she met Rattlesnake Calliope when she was in the woods picking wildflowers and she was going to take me to see her. I want to know what rattlesnake stew tastes like." Josh beamed.

JJ said, "Now Son, Rattlesnake Calliope isn't a real person. She's just what we call a Tennessee Tall Tale."

Josh was visibly disappointed. JJ joined him on the bed.

"But Momma said she ate some of her stew."

JJ sighed. "I know what she said. She was just teasing you. She teased me with the same story."

Josh was skeptical. He knew his daddy didn't know everything. He had heard his momma say so on many occasions.

JJ said, "Listen, I'm really sorry about what happened today at your momma's funeral. I was wrong. I should have told you the truth. The whole truth."

Josh took out his asthma inhaler and tried to use it.

"It's empty," Josh said.

"It's empty?" JJ was alarmed. "Lord Almighty. Don't move. I'll take care of it." JJ stood up, completely lost as to what to do next. He looked at Josh's puzzled face. "I'll go call the doctor." JJ hoped Josh would offer up a clue of some kind.

Josh did. "They're in the drawer…over there," Josh said struggling to catch his breath, pointing at the dresser. JJ went to the drawer and pulled it open. There they were. Two unopened inhalers. He took one from its box and stepped over and gave it to Josh.

Josh inhaled deeply from the device. And after a few moments they were both breathing a lot easier.

JJ brushed through his son's wavy hair with his fingers. "From now on I'm going to try really hard not to screw up being your daddy. I promise you, okay."

Josh replied, "Okay."

JJ looked at his son's sad eyes. His beautiful boy. The last thing Petula said to him this afternoon was: "Be strong for your son. He needs you to show him how a man handles this kind of thing." His mother's advice was rarely something he paid close attention to, as there was always so much of it, but JJ thought – *This time Momma is likely right.*

JJ temporarily shoved the vast, bleak sadness away, and said, "Hey, Son, I think we should go downstairs together and raid the freezer for some ice cream."

Josh said, "It's kind of cold."

JJ replied, "I don't believe it's ever too cold for ice cream."

Josh thought it over. "I guess not."

Josh jumped up, grabbed the stuffed monkey, then joined his father to leave.

JJ said, "I think I can still make a root beer float, how's that sound?"

"Okay," Josh said.

"Okay," JJ echoed back.

Inside, JJ felt unbearable solitude.

So this is our life now? From three to just us two.

JJ forced a smile back onto his face, and took Josh's hand and they exited the room. They walked down the faintly lit hallway.

Josh whispered very quietly into his monkey's fuzzy velvety cotton ear, "Pretend you didn't hear what Daddy said. She *is* real."

And think not you can direct the course of love, for love, if it finds you worthy, directs your course.
        - KAHLIL GIBRAN

Love is a serious mental disease.
        - PLATO

THE BRAINS GOD GAVE YOU

Fifteen Years Later

1

The trees wrapping throughout the suburban streets of Nashville were fiery with fall colors. Leaves of red, orange and yellow dotted the tree line above and flowed over the well-manicured lawns; many raked into neat piles.

A fleshy-pink flat nose poked through one of the leaf-hills, snorted and sniffed the air. She picked up the scent of her master. It was a replete mixture of fragrant rose skin lotion, baked apples, Downy fabric softener, and the unmistakable aromas of anger and wholesale frustration. Her morning escape, and current secret leaf-pile hideaway, had resulted in the desired effects from her human master.

This was about as exciting as your day ever gets when you're a pig.

* * *

Not far away, JJ Fletcher was jogging with two able-bodied Secret Service agents flanking him on either side, all in high-end track suits.

JJ, in his early forties, still possessed his substantial good looks, but was graying a little at the temples and had the beginnings of crow's feet around the corners of his eyes. JJ had never noticed, but others had, and his PR firm had been touching up his photographs for a while (including air brushing his slightly uneven nose) in preparation for his second run for governor coming up next year.

Along the jogging route were more Secret Service agents talking into their micro Bluetooth earpieces, looking for any potential threats to the governor. *Danger ahead* was a "10-30"; the code word "Parrot" signaled an *unidentified person or object*.

One of the Secret Service agents, Noah Applegarth, a rookie, fresh out of the training academy over in Cannon County, was about fifty yards ahead of JJ. Noah had deep brown Mediterranean eyes and an engagingly-sweet face. He spied an impending threat coming from a neighborhood lawn. "We have a code...a code...?" He squinted and tried to identify the strange creature bounding down the paved road toward him. Whatever it was, it was leaving a small wake of swirling leaves in its path. Noah listened-in more closely – *yes, it was making strange grunting sounds!* The young agent, eyes wide now, blinked several times to clear his vision, *My God!* he thought, *It's wearing a little summer hat.*

Great! My first day on the job and I have this already! He keyed his radio ear piece. "10-30! Code 10-30! We have a Parrot! I need back up. The Parrot is approaching the security perimeter at a high rate of speed!"

The young Secret Service agent sprinted ahead, unsnapping the leather flap covering his Walther PPK 7.65mm, and then stopped. The identity of the target finally became clear, and a wave of relief washed over Noah. He took a breath as his body quit slamming his circulatory system with adrenaline. He ran ahead, swooped in and tackled the small pink pig. The little hat went flying. The agent rolled onto the sidewalk, the little swine tightly grasped in his arms. Noah spoke into his radio ear piece, "The Parrot has been identified and immobilized."

JJ jogged up and strained to see what had interrupted his morning run. The two agents ahead of him slowly approached the area that

Noah had secured. They all eyed the pint-sized beast in his arms. One of the agents giggled. JJ said, "Agent Applegarth, first day on the job and you have already neutralized a threat."

"Yes, sir," Noah replied, not sure if he should be proud or embarrassed, as the pig nuzzled his face for a quick kiss.

Ruby Billingsley veered around the corner from the street up ahead - still quite agile for being in her early seventies - scouting all the underbrush in every direction, quickly approaching hysteria. She had a large overcoat pulled on top of her baby-blue housecoat and had lost one of her matching fuzzy house slippers. She yelled, "Minnie Sarah Ophelia Pearl, if you don't get back here right now…" Ruby saw the Secret Service agent grasping her pet pig and then began waving frantically. The pig grunted and squealed at the sight of her owner, and Agent Applegarth had to hold on tight to keep her from squirming away.

"Gee willikers, what kind of trouble have you gotten into now little girl? Mister, don't hurt her, she's just a tender-hearted little pig, and she don't bite."

JJ saw Ruby and pushed through the protective agents waving exuberantly. "Good morning, Mrs. Billingsley!"

Ruby's face lit up. "Good morning, Governor Fletcher!"

JJ motioned for Noah, still on the ground, to give the pet pig back to Ruby. JJ said, "You look lovely this morning, Mrs. Billingsley. Is that a new hair color?"

Ruby touched her hair proudly. "How sweet of you to notice."

Noah struggled to his feet and handed the pig, all of twenty pounds, over to Ruby. He picked up the little hat, eyed it with curiosity for a moment. A little price tag hung from the hat marked at $1.98. He smiled, and gave the hat to Ruby.

Ruby said, "Minnie Pearl would never harm Governor Fletcher. Why, I've known him my whole life. Both our families are descendants from the Irish province of Ulster." She waved Minnie's hoof. "Wave hello to the handsome governor."

JJ smiled. "Well it sure is a pleasure to run into you, but these broad-shouldered brutes here have me on a tight schedule." JJ began to jog backwards. He often ran into his constituents and knew how to keep moving along.

"Don't mind me," said Ruby. "Just say hello to your momma, and tell her I'll see her at the Veterans' Biscuits for the Brave Breakfast on Saturday." She placed the little hat on her pet pig's head, securing the elastic band under its chin. She yelled back to JJ, "I'm bringing five cases of my legendary blackstrap molasses. I'll save a jar for you, Governor."

"Make it three!" JJ replied. He waved and continued jogging along the route with the dutiful agents bounding on ahead in search of more potential danger.

In truth, although the Secret Service agents were the best trained in the world and served with the highest level of duty and honor, nothing they gleaned in their training camp manuals could have helped them protect JJ Fletcher from what was lying ahead.

* * *

In the same suburban neighborhood, no more than a half mile away, another jogger was out enjoying the resplendent fall morning. Her breath was steady and her heart rate purred in perfect rhythm. She slid steadily along, focused, feeling the power of her body utterly absorbed in the moment. She had learned from her personal trainers this was called *being in the zone*. She often felt exactly the same way on stage. She was listening to her cherry red SanDisk Clip MP3 player and singing along to one of her favorites, Michael Jackson's "Dirty Diana".

She was in a sparkling red jogging suit, a matching head scarf and sunglasses. She was being paced by two muscular, tanned men in gray sweats with reflective sunglasses covering their eyes and cutting edge communications equipment fixed in their ears. Most celebrities of her caliber received threats that could be considered serious a dozen or so times a year and this international superstar was no exception, thus the extra security. In reality, the closest she ever came to any real danger was when a man wearing absolutely nothing but his cowboy boots and his Fruit of the Loom briefs shoved her to the ground during a music video she was shooting at The Parthenon replica in Nashville's Centennial Park. Police identified him as a local wino and concluded the reason he had pushed her so violently was simply because he was drunk again, saw the craft services cart, and was extremely hungry. She had the assault charges against the man dropped and even paid for him to have an extended stay at Cumberland Heights Alcohol Addiction Treatment Center.

Even so, a person could never be too careful. Her scarf and sunglasses were a half-hearted attempt at staying off the radar. Yet, in spite of her efforts, this fiery, bewitchingly glamorous woman could never be off anyone's radar.

Kitty Stardust had essentially been unable to hide from anyone since she stepped onto the stage of the Grand Ole Opry at the age of nineteen. It was Tuesday Night Amateur Hour. The bustling crowd was noisy and not terribly interested in whatever was occurring on stage. They were there for the headliners that came out at eight o'clock. They had arrived hours early to ensure they got the best seats and to catch up on any juicy Opry celebrity gossip. Suddenly, the crowd began to quiet down and take note of a new voice pouring out of the large speaker cabinets on either side of the Opry stage. Before the first chorus of the song even began, the clamorous hubbub in the room had transformed into a stunned revered stillness. They were hearing a unique, full voice of perfect pitch and range, resonant and lusty with life. It also possessed that Opry-essential dash of twang. To their amazement it was coming out of a red haired, big busted, twig of a girl wearing an emerald green glittering rhinestone-covered dress.

A silver-haired woman in the fourth row wearing a white blouse and red bolo tie turned to her husband and whispered, "She's no bigger than a bar of soap after a week's wash...but holy mackerel...what a voice!" Her husband nodded in agreement.

The young woman on stage sang a song made famous by her idol, a woman she had never met, someone she believed had been a goddess and graciously had come down to bless the earth with her beautiful voice. Patsy Cline.

Kitty had found the green rhinestone-covered dress at a second hand store on Forrest Avenue earlier that week and paid the entire contents of her pocketbook to own it for herself. When she arrived back home and tried it on, her mother Estella-Jeanne said, "Go back upstairs young lady and put on a proper Opry dress. Did you bother to look in the mirror? You are not wearing that getup. It starts far too late and it ends way too soon!"

When Kitty stood unmoving at the bottom of the stairs with a defiant look in her eyes, her momma added what became her basic obligatory pronouncement regarding most of her daughter's professional choices: "Ruth-Adele, if you wear that dress, I swear on your father's grave, it will be the end of your career!"

This dire warning was not unlike the one she had angrily pronounced just that morning. That was when she was met with the news that her daughter had planned to change her given name of Ruth-Adele Holloway to the stage name Kitty Stardust. "Ruth-Adele, if you plan on using that silly, tawdry-sounding name for yourself, I swear on your father's grave, it will be the end of your career!"

But at nineteen, Ruth-Adele Holloway already had good instincts, and knowing that her mother was prone to exaggeration (and noting as well that she didn't have anything resembling a career yet) she ignored her momma's advice and wore the tight-fitting, glittering green dress, and had told the Opry's house announcer to introduce her as Kitty Stardust.

That night she proved her momma wrong. The crowd came quickly to their feet and cheered for an encore. The song she sang was "Walkin' After Midnight". She took a bow, then thanked Patsy Cline up in heaven for inspiring her to sing. Everyone there was very excited. They knew exactly what had just occurred and were full of pride to have been there to witness it in person – the birth of another Grand Ole Opry star!

And to their utter joy, they got their encore.

Now, some 22 years had passed, and every year her career grew with more and more devoted fans all over the world. She had dreamed big in her thrift-store dress under the Opry stage lights, but still she never imagined she would ever be as famous and well-loved as she was today. Her life now had truly become beyond her wildest dreams. As Kitty jogged along, she was feeling grateful for the very good life she'd been blessed with so far.

Among the many accomplishments she had accumulated over the years, she was especially proud of the charity marathon she created called The Critters-In-Crisis Run, which was why she was out training this morning. The event, which raised money to help rescue abandoned animals and find them new homes, was happening in less than a week. And she found out this morning that they had greatly surpassed their fund raising goals. This promised to be the most successful animal charity run ever.

Feeling exuberant, Kitty turned up Michael Jackson and picked up her pace.

Eight blocks ahead, two men were standing in the middle of an intersection. One of them was wearing a vibrant saffron-colored shirt, dark jacket, black jeans and Ray-Ban sunglasses. He was an exquisitely sculpted handsome man in his mid-thirties and looked shamelessly fit. His name was Rhashan Robinson, Kitty Stardust's Head-of-Security. He was being confronted by a much shorter bald man in an immaculate gray suit and tie, also wearing Ray-Bans, Agent Derek Cooper. Although Derek was smaller, his arms and legs bulged like tree trunks from under his suit, a suit purchased at a two-for-one sale from the Men's Warehouse deliberately chosen a size too small for the tight and awe-inspiring effect. It did cause admiration from many, but it had no effect on Rhashan. He was not impressed in the least by this chest thumping twit, and was extremely irritated that he had come across Agent Cooper on what otherwise was turning out to be a very tranquil morning. Rhashan was at a stage in life where he relished a pleasant morning such as the one he had been having. Until now.

Rhashan Robinson moved from Jamaica with his mother when he was ten. She had left a bad husband in Kingston in search of a better life in Memphis, Tennessee. She found a much better job at Brenner's Shoe Factory, an employer that didn't require a lot in the way of legal documentation. But she found a much worse husband at a blues bar on Beale Street. Rhashan tried on many occasions to save his mother from her increasingly violent domestic life, but she refused to accept his help. To escape the futile life his mother had chosen, Rhashan joined the Navy on his eighteenth birthday. After experiencing a life threatening bullet wound to his shoulder in the Persian Gulf and receiving a Distinguished Service Medal, he moved to Nashville. He secured a few security-related jobs and eventually acquired a permanent position with On-Guard-Security Inc., a company providing security guards for the Nashville area which often included some of the regions more famous Country Western stars.

It came as a complete surprise when Kitty Stardust had asked Rhashan to come to her home after he had done a routine On-Guard-Security Inc. assignment for an engagement of hers. The job had been a normal music concert assignment. He met her for only a few moments an hour before the show where he was briefed by her manager. Ms. Stardust had gotten a death threat a week earlier and they were taking routine precautions.

The concert went without a hitch. Her fans were a fairly well behaved bunch. None appeared to have any homicidal intentions. His job included seeing Ms. Stardust to her home in her private limousine, which he did. He had finished his assignment early enough to go to The Waffle House for a midnight breakfast, take his Basset Hound, Coltrane, out for a much appreciated walk, and be in bed by two o'clock. He didn't even believe Kitty had asked his name the entire time, and thought she had not noticed him much at all.

Kitty had noticed him. She liked his quiet no-nonsense, earnest demeanor, and she had a feeling that he was just the man she was looking for. Her career was taking off a little more quickly than she had expected and she needed someone to fill a full time security post. She felt certain she could trust Rhashan Robinson. After doing some security checking of her own, she had called him and asked him to come by her home for dinner.

At her home, when she offered him the position as her Head-of-Security, he had turned her down outright. He liked his present job and wasn't looking for any changes. But Kitty surprised him with a traditional Jamaican dinner; jerk chicken, black beans and rice, fried plantain, and bottles of Ting soda with banana fritters for dessert. He had been impressed. She had taken the time to consider his heritage, and had cooked the entire meal herself. He hadn't had banana fritters that good since his mother had made them back in the kitchen of their tiny apartment on Mount Olive Road in Memphis. At that point he would have been a fool to say anything but yes. And Rhashan was no fool.

Kitty's instincts had been right. No one had been more loyal to her than Rhashan Robinson. That had been more than twelve years, two managers, and four agents ago, and Rhashan was still the one by her side protecting and watching over her. He still kept an apartment on 8th Avenue in Midtown, but when Kitty purchased the 160 acres south of Nashville and built Stardust Ranch, Rhashan and Coltrane had moved into one of the four guest homes. Most of his free time was spent there tending to the many farm animals, including twelve Appaloosas, seven alpacas, and so many stray dogs, cats and fowl that an accurate count of them would be nearly impossible. Kitty had become someone who was much more than an employer for him. She was a trustworthy friend, and she felt exactly the same way about Rhashan.

Now Rhashan was glaring down at Agent Derek Cooper. The top of the Secret Service agent's head came about nipple high to Rhashan and he noticed that Derek's shaved dome had several razor nicks on it.

"This route was reserved for Kitty Stardust," Rhashan said. "It was secured with the Nashville Police Department two weeks ago."

"This is the governor's route today," replied Derek, puffing out his chest a little more. Rhashan wondered why anyone would wear so much foul-smelling cologne and figured this one had to have been Army for sure.

"My boss is training for a charity marathon. We're on a tight schedule. I'm sure the governor would not mind sharing the road just this one time," Rhashan said, pleading more than he cared to. "She's pretty harmless."

Derek shook his head. "The governor's security protocol is not negotiable, and not debatable. Your employer will have to take a detour today. I'd suggest Old Creek Road."

"My client doesn't do Old Creek Road."

"Then she can wait at Madison Park until the governor has passed through and I have released the area."

"Kitty Stardust has to catch a plane later today. Maybe the governor can take Old Creek Road?"

Derek pulled back his suit jacket exposing his gun secured in its holster. He cocked his head and managed to flex both biceps all in one ostentatious move. "Governor trumps celebrity, so I'm afraid any more discussion with you is entirely a waste of my time."

Rhashan, with much reluctance, conceded. Agent Derek Cooper did rank, and there was nothing he could do about that. Agent Cooper stepped away and turned his back to Rhashan.

Rhashan keyed his radio. "Starwalker Two, Starwalker One here. We have a situation."

Down the street where Kitty was jogging, she noticed her bodyguards motioning to her. One was speaking into his radio. She stopped and pulled out her ear buds.

From the bodyguard's radio Rhashan's voice could be heard: "Tell Kitty we'll have to take a detour up Old Creek Road in order to keep her on schedule today."

Kitty leapt to the bodyguard and grabbed the headset from around his ear. She held it to her mouth and yelled, "Rhashan! Rhashan! This has better be a ludicrous attempt at a joke!"

Rhashan replied back through the radio: "It's no joke."

Kitty threw the radio headset back to the bodyguard and took off jogging in fast, extended, resolute strides.

Rhashan peered down the street to see Kitty coming his way, the bodyguards were racing right behind her. The look on her face was clear, even from a distance. Rhashan braced himself.

As he waited, he listened in on Agent Derek Cooper's conversation. Derek was now about five yards away talking into his radio.

"I read," said Derek. "Operation Morning Run is terminated."

Derek turned toward Rhashan and yelled, "Hey Goliath! There's been a change in plans. It looks like the roads of Nashville are back open for Ms. Starlight."

Derek quickly turned and ran full stride in the opposite direction from where Kitty was coming.

Rhashan yelled to Derek loud enough for him to hear, "It's Stardust...Asshole!"

Rhashan watched in the direction where Derek was running. He saw a black limousine pull up and park. Two people quickly exited the limo and waited. One was an Asian-looking woman (*or possibly Italian,* he thought) and the other was a serious looking stout man with black curly hair and a beard, wearing a dumpy, baggy suit. Rhashan recognized the two from the news as Governor Fletcher's personal assistant and campaign manager. Even at this distance Rhashan could tell they both seemed apprehensive.

Something was up.

Rhashan quickly took out a specialized handheld radio from his belt and started adjusting frequencies. While he was stationed in the Persian Gulf, one of his operational duties at sea was eavesdropping on Iraqi radio chatter. He had continued his interest in radio communication as a hobby after he arrived back in the States and had become quite adept at finding spy frequency bands on his shortwave radio. He had gotten so involved that he had learned Chinese, and some basic German and Russian so he could listen in on conversations all over the world. He had even bought a secondhand radio teletype on eBay and hooked it to his shortwave receiver. He smiled. It had been easy to find the frequency JJ's security were using. He listened closely to his radio as Kitty stormed up to his side.

"Rhashan! Rhashan! I am not jogging up Old Creek Road! It goes behind that strip mall!" she yelled.

Rhashan nodded. "Yep."

Kitty continued, "It's nothing but potholes, broken glass and smelly dumpsters. You might as well have me running through a minefield!"

"Yep."

The other bodyguards arrived and waited.

Kitty added, "Remember the last time, Rhashan? That garbage behind the strip mall smelled up to high heaven and the doctor said it could have been responsible for the chronic sinus infection I got. It practically destroyed my vocal cords," she exaggerated.

Rhashan nodded.

Kitty realized Rhashan was not listening to her at all. He was only nodding at her pauses. She hated it when he just nodded. It made her imagine she talked way too much. Her momma talked way too much.

"What in blue blazes are you listening to?" she asked him.

"Check this out, Miss Kitty." Rhashan motioned for Kitty to look in the direction of the limousine parked far down the street.

By now JJ and his Secret Service agents had arrived to join the personal assistant and the campaign manager. Kitty and Rhashan looked at the entourage gathered around the limousine. At first it occurred to Kitty that these people, whoever they were, had been why Rhashan had to alter her jogging route. She angrily examined who it might be...then she suddenly realized it was Governor JJ Fletcher.

Dear God, JJ Fletcher!

The sight was a sizeable shock. It took a moment to steady herself. One of the bodyguards noticed and took her arm, and asked her if she was alright. She mumbled something to him that sounded like gibberish, even to her own ears.

Kitty recognized the two people talking to JJ. It was Byrdie Mirabelli, JJ's personal assistant, and Elliot Pendleton, his campaign manager. JJ looked very distressed by whatever they were saying.

What on earth were they telling him?

JJ unexpectedly turned away from the tense conversation and glanced over in Kitty's direction. He did a double take. Their eyes locked. It was as if an electric current stretched, quivered, and turned white hot through the air between them like a crackling lightning bolt.

Kitty's mind suddenly filled with memories of another time and place. She heard the sound of cheers and an announcer's voice revealing that the Hillsboro High School Burros had just scored a touchdown bringing the score to fourteen and seven in the home team's favor. She was standing under the bleachers and quickly looked out through the seats and saw the Burro mascot leaping up and down; the cheerleading team proudly danced around in the green and yellow team colors. She looked back to the boy standing in front of her, an irresistible young stud in tight Wrangler jeans and a worn-out, black KISS T-shirt. He had a wavy blond mane of hair, pure tanned skin, a nose slightly too large for his face (leaning slightly to the left from an accident he had at the age of thirteen involving a stubborn horse and a fence post). His translucent blue eyes stared longingly. One side of his soft lips curled up in a demure smile. Kitty was clearly overcome in a high school crush, and was weak from the lingering kiss the boy had just given her.

Kitty wore a leather jacket over a halter top and a wrap-around skirt. She was holding a box of popcorn and a cup of iced Coke. The boy, a seventeen-year-old JJ Fletcher, was holding a bottle of Jack Daniel's. He took the cup from Kitty and poured the whiskey over the ice and Coke inside. He smiled a goofy, alcohol impaired smile, and looked into Kitty's eyes. He handed the cup back to her. Her body was slight next to his. Her red hair was tied back in a ponytail and her lightly sunkissed skin was moist from the warm, humid night. They both were sultry and sweaty, and smelled strongly of Cutter mosquito repellent. Kitty reached for the Jack Daniel's, instead of the cup, and swigged the whiskey straight from the bottle without the slightest flinch. She handed the JD back to JJ with her own sexually unambiguous smile.

JJ bent in and kissed Kitty and wrapped his arms around her waist to pull her closer. Kitty spilled her popcorn to the ground. One of her red converse tennis shoes went up onto a toe, then the foot twisted up and around. For her, it was like flying and falling all at the same time. The sound of the football game became muddled. She closed her eyes and the smell of whiskey and Lucky Strike cigarettes from JJ's warm breath encircled her like a spellbinding drug. All she heard was the sound of JJ's raspy voice, whispering in her ear: "I am completely in love with you Ruth-Adele Holloway."

"Kitty!" It was Rhashan. "Kitty! Can you hear me? Are you okay?"

Kitty looked at Rhashan. Her memories of the past were quickly whisked away and she realized one of her new bright red Nikes was twisted up into the same position as that night long ago when she was fifteen and had snuck under the bleachers at the Hillsboro High School football game with JJ Fletcher.

She quickly put her foot back flat on the ground. She forced herself to stand firm and steady.

Get a grip on yourself, for crying out loud!

Kitty looked to see if JJ was still staring back at her, but he was gone. He had been shoved inside the limousine. Byrdie was the last to get in the car, and the door slammed closed behind her.

"They came to get the governor because of his father," Rhashan explained. "He's had some kind of a medical emergency." Rhashan dialed the radio to clear up some intermittent static.

"Cowboy?" Kitty asked.

"Yes, Miss Kitty. He's been taken to Centennial Medical Center." Rhashan listened to crackling voices that Kitty couldn't make out. "It was a brain hemorrhage," he finally said to her.

"Brain hemorrhage?" Kitty was openly shocked.

JJ's father, Cowboy, had always reminded Kitty of a loud carnival barker. She had met him on several occasions over the years, and it had seemed to her that he had always been more interested in sizing up her boobs and ass than anything meaningful about her.

"Cowboy was in the Gulf of Mexico deep sea fishing. He was on his sport yacht when, they're saying, he collapsed right on the deck," Rhashan said.

"Lordy!" Kitty said as she watched the limousine turn around and drive in the opposite direction, disappearing behind a large row of cypress hedge.

"Cowboy is in surgery right now. The doctor is attempting to relieve the pressure on his brain," Rhashan said.

"Well, that is some news," Kitty replied after a moment of reflection. "I just didn't know that JJ Fletcher or his father even had one of those."

"A fishing yacht?" Rhashan asked.

Kitty replied, "A brain!"

Rhashan smiled, and nodded. He knew part of Kitty and JJ's history together, but he had heard Kitty say many times over the past few years that she had purged and all but forgotten that period of her life, and he had taken her at her word.

Kitty said, "Well folks, I've stood here and completely lost my target heart rate."

This normally would have been true after a runner took a short break from concentrated exercise, but in this case Kitty's pulse had not decreased at all. In fact it was at least 10 beats higher than her target rate, and her heart had been pounding in her chest at this distressing velocity from the moment she had laid eyes on JJ Fletcher. It had been many years since she had last had any contact with JJ and she was certain she had fully eradicated him from her mind, and more importantly, her heart. But her brain and its associated nervous system had betrayed her. Her body was adrift in unruly physiological changes and defiant chemical reactions.

Kitty checked her pulse.

What in Sam Hill?

Kitty wondered briefly if she might be having a heart attack. But she knew better. Her biological heart was in good health.

Kitty pushed her sunglasses closer to her eyes and had to accept the truth. JJ Fletcher was not purged completely from her system. And that, for Kitty Stardust, was shocking, unwelcome news.

2

Cowboy Fletcher's face was pallid, his body peacefully still. He was in a hospital bed in a private intensive care unit at Centennial Medical Center in Nashville. A bulky white bandage enveloped the upper portion of his head. A myriad of tubes and wires connected to his upper body were monitoring his volatile, but stabilized, physical condition. The right side of his face had a stark droop because he had survived a hemorrhage in the left hemisphere of his brain. Due to an IV of morphine being released at regular intervals, Cowboy seemed to be resting peacefully. He appeared completely unaware that his wife, Petula, JJ, and a doctor had gathered at the side of his bed, all in a highly apprehensive mood.

The surgery had been a daunting four hour ordeal. And for Petula the anxiety and trauma began much earlier. At 11:23 P.M. the night before, Rosalita, the housekeeper, had jolted Petula awake from a deep Valium and Mint Julep induced sleep with the news that there was a man on the phone who needed to speak to her right away. There was a critical medical emergency involving Cowboy. At first Petula thought the call must be some kind of a hoax, but when the caller identified himself she knew the troubling news was undoubtedly true.

Corky Dinger was an old college buddy of Cowboy's, an oil tycoon that Petula could barely tolerate. She thought he was an idiot. Even Cowboy himself often commented: "Corky couldn't pour piss out of a boot if the instructions were written on the heel." Even so, about twice a year Corky would show up with a wallet stuffed full of cash and the two men would run off together on some adolescence-salvaging adventure. They'd be gone for days, or even weeks. At least in this current precarious situation Corky had done the right thing and called Petula. For that she was thankful.

Petula had not slept at all since Corky's phone call, and with the desperation of "the crisis" as well as the long stressful hours of Cowboy's surgery, there had been no time for Petula's quite extensive makeup routine. Here in the hospital room she looked bone-tired. Her Jon Renau wig was an unwieldy mess, her bare face was a spectral pale, and she had no discernible eyebrows. JJ, looking over-fatigued himself, was wearing the jogging suit he had on when he was alerted to his father's condition earlier that morning.

JJ and Petula had their eyes fixed on a very serious looking Dr. Kulkami, the hospital's Chief Neurosurgeon, a graduate of Madras Medical College in Chennai, India. He was a cordial, distinguished man. At the moment the doctor's dark eyes did not appear encouraging and Petula analyzed him with a penetrating glare.

JJ said, "My daddy is as strong as an ox. You just tell us what we can do to help him."

Dr. Kulkami replied, "The surgery went very well. Mr. Fletcher is stabilized. Now we just have to wait and see."

JJ nodded. He had hoped for more details, and a more optimistic prognosis, but Dr. Kulkami appeared to be the kind of doctor who kept to the routine facts, and maintained a professional distance.

Petula took an obstinate step closer to Dr. Kulkami and pointed at JJ. "My son here is the governor. And the man over there in that bed is a former governor of Tennessee. You probably are not aware of that because you're not from this country." Petula looked knowingly at Dr. Kulkami's name tag. JJ looked with knowing concern at Petula. She continued, "I know you doctors nowa-days like to cut corners on your patients to please all the hospital shareholders. My husband plays golf regularly with those shareholders, so let me make one thing perfectly clear; I've already spoken to Cowboy's personal physician, Dr. Maxwell Hadley. He's vacationing in Bora Bora at the moment, but he'll be in touch with you by phone. You do know of him, don't you?"

The vacant look in Dr. Kulkami's eyes remained unchanged and he didn't respond; he didn't feel the need.

Petula's body had endured a vast amount of stress, coffee, cigarettes, prescription medications and straight whiskey in the preceding twelve hours, and it all had reached a volatile point. Her eyes appeared delirious, as if she might snap, or perhaps she already had snapped. "I expect my husband to get the best possible treatment available while he's here at your hospital. And I am holding you personally responsible for seeing that *that* is precisely what he gets," Petula said, taking in a determined breath. "And if he does not get the best possible treatment, or God forbid he gets one of those hospital-acquired infections so prevalent in these places, or worse, some snooping reporter manages to get a photograph of Cowboy in this disparaging state, you'll find your hospital buried in a mountain of litigation. And as for you, doctor, you'll be lucky to find a job treating prostitutes in Calcutta. Do I make myself clear?"

JJ swiftly took Dr. Kulkami by the arm and directed him away from his momma, which was fine by her. She was through with the doctor anyway. Petula grabbed her sizable Coco Chanel handbag and began rummaging around inside.

JJ said to Dr. Kulkami, in a calm, friendly tone, "I think what my dear momma's trying to say is that we are completely confident your hospital will give Daddy the best possible care."

JJ and Dr. Kulkami looked over to Petula, who had plucked a perfume atomizer from her purse and was spraying it in every direction of the room. The doctor was concerned. This concern was genuine, at least in the clinical way in which he felt concern for most people. He was often heralded as the best neurosurgeon in Tennessee and over time, as his self-worth had inflated, he had come to see the general public as an unstable pool of brains in critical need of the many mood stabilizing medications he had the authority to prescribe. "If you need, I can write your mother a prescription," he said to JJ, producing a prescription pad from his white coat pocket.

JJ responded quickly, "Oh Lord...Lordy no! Thank you, Doctor."

"It's no problem for me." Dr. Kulkami said, holding tight to his prescription pad and pen as if he fully expected JJ would be reconsidering.

JJ continued, "But my momma is right, in a way. The partners of this hospital are close political supporters of the governor's office, and I am sure they would agree my daddy has more than earned his spot at the front of the line."

After a moment, Dr. Kulkami replied, "I treat all my patients with the same pristine care, Mister Governor of Tennessee." Dr. Kulkami turned toward Petula. "But I'll be sure to place a call to my mother and have her keep a copy of the Calcutta want ads set aside for me, just in case I fail to meet your expectations."

Dr. Kulkami exited and let the door close behind him. Petula waved him off with a flip of her hand. "What this room needs is some decent lighting," she said. "Put a call in to Byrdie and have her pick a lamp up at Bradford's Furniture. The light in here could suck the life out of a perfectly healthy person."

JJ nodded. "I'll do that, Momma." He walked over to the bed and looked at Cowboy's motionless face. He said, "Daddy, what were you doing in the Gulf of Mexico? Fishing? Dr. Hadley warned you that you had to slow down now. Why don't you ever listen?"

Petula opened her handbag again and shuffled through several prescription bottles until she located one that looked promising. She looked at Cowboy. "He's a stubborn old fool and has always done whatever he wants." She looked at the bottle and read the label. "Take one per day. I better have four." Petula grabbed a can of diet Pepsi from a tray table and swallowed the handful of pills with a gulp.

Petula had a sudden thought. "You did remember to call Josh, didn't you JJ? He needs to be here, in case—" Petula stopped cold, and became dewy-eyed. She straightened Cowboy's hospital gown. "*In case* your father never opens those old foolish eyes and tells me how much he loves me again."

JJ said, "I placed a call to the Peace Corps office. Josh will be calling me as soon as they can get a message to him. Apparently there's no phone reception where he is right now."

"Oh, dear Jesus. How has it come to this? My grandson is irretrievable in some God forsaken place in the middle of Timbuktu, while my husband is just lying here in this hospital, preparing to meet his great reward."

"Don't talk like that, Momma. Daddy may be able to hear every word you're saying."

"Were you not paying attention, JJ?"

"The doctor said we need to wait and see."

"I don't care what he said, I could see it in the way that doctor was looking at me."

"He's just Indian, Momma."

Petula shook her head. "He may be some kind of foreigner, but it was all I could see when I looked in his eyes. It was like looking into the eyes of the Grim Reaper."

Cowboy's eyes opened.

JJ noticed, and he jumped to Cowboy's side and took his daddy's hand. "Daddy?"

Petula was stunned. She saw Cowboy's eyes searching around the room until he focused on her face.

"Cowboy?" Petula leaned in closer to him. "Can you hear me?"

Cowboy's left brow furrowed and his left hand began to twitch. JJ and Petula watched, trying to understand what he needed. His hand made a motion like he was writing with a pen.

JJ hit a button above the bed and spoke into an intercom: "Nurse, we need the doctor right now! My daddy opened his eyes!"

Petula spoke loud and directly: "It's your wife, Petula. Can you see my face? Can you hear me, Cowboy? You're in a hospital in Nashville."

JJ leaned over the bed. It appeared his father recognized him. "It's a miracle, Momma."

Petula continued to speak loudly. "Do you remember what happened? You were on your sport yacht. You were fishing, in the Gulf of Mexico."

Cowboy kept motioning with his hand. Petula noticed, but kept speaking firmly to Cowboy: "The sport yacht, Cowboy. You had a brain hemorrhage. On your yacht. Am I making myself clear?"

"I think he wants to write something, Momma. Look at his hand." JJ reached for a piece of paper and pen from the bed stand drawer and placed the pen in Cowboy's hand.

Dr. Kulkami and a nurse rushed in.

JJ looked up. "His eyes are open. I think he understands us."

Dr. Kulkami leaned over the bed and shined a penlight into Cowboy's eyes. "He's responding. This is good. This is quite good. Mr. Fletcher, can you hear my voice?"

JJ said, "He's written something on a piece of paper."

Petula took the note, quickly glanced it over. She held it up where they could all see.

The nurse squinted, and read it aloud in a sharp staccato, "Stop all the damn yelling!"

Even with his limited facial and hand movements Cowboy appeared happy that he had successfully communicated to the outside world.

Dr. Kulkami said, "Sometimes trauma to the brain can cause personality changes."

JJ replied, "Apparently not in this case, Doctor."

Petula squeezed Cowboy's hand. "Darlin', I couldn't imagine my world without you in it. These doctors here had you pegged for the morgue downstairs, but not me. They don't know what I know." Petula began to cry. *Real live tears.* "...I know...Cowboy...a Fletcher never gives up."

3

Josh Fletcher had gotten as comfortable as anyone could be expected to in the window seat of a British Airways Boeing 747. The announcement made by the pilot a few hours earlier said they were over the Atlantic, but Josh could only see a vast eerie darkness below. Looking up, there was a clear view of a moonless night and he noted that the stars were a heck of a lot brighter than normal here at a cruising altitude of 32,000 feet. The Milky Way looked like an iridescent cloud of white pixie dust someone had scattered into a black pool and some stars were so brilliant they shined like fireflies on a dark summer night.

A few years ago, Josh had been lucky enough to attend a lecture by Stephen Hawking at the American Museum of Science where the renowned theoretical physicist and cosmologist reflected on the possibility of life elsewhere in the universe. As Josh looked out the cabin window, he marveled at the idea. It was easy to imagine he was coming back home to earth after a long visit deep into space.

Which, he thought, was a fairly accurate way to look at it. For nearly two years Josh had been in a small village in Africa that was as different from Nashville, Tennessee as any distant alien planet would likely be.

Josh, at twenty-one years, looked a lot like his father did at that age; an engaging, attractive young man. He had a strong chin, now with a few days of stubble, and a slightly large nose. Glasses covered wistful, light eyes. "They're the color of Blue Delphiniums," his mother had often said when he was a small boy. Tufts of blond hair generously tousled out from under a well-worn baseball cap with the South African Cricket Team logo sewn onto it. In a white linen shirt and jeans Josh was lean and well-muscled with an earthy tan from working for many months outdoors, often in a sweltering heat. For the past two years, he was helping construct a water supply and delivery system for the people of New Xade, a remote village in Botswana.

Now he was seated next to an elderly Canadian woman who, it was quickly established, had been visiting Africa as well. The half-done crochet baby blanket she was working on rested on her lap and she was now snoring. Although the snoring was considerably loud and unpleasant, Josh would not have woken her for all the gold in Fort Knox - because then she might resume talking.

Josh had learned, with no eliciting what-so-ever, that the snoring woman's husband had refused to travel for any of their fifty-one years of marriage. But he died three months ago. Now, she was making up for lost time in spades. Every embellished story she told Josh was followed by an animated: "Have you ever heard of such a thing?" followed then by: "It simply took one's breath away!" The quad bike ride across the Kalahari, the trek up the side of Mount Kilimanjaro, the elephant ride to witness the migration of the zebras, the motorboat outing to experience the mist of Victoria Falls! Josh thought she was theatrical and a genuine character, but when the miniature bottles of red wine the airline attendant kept bringing her overtook the old woman and she fell asleep, the end of the storytelling was a merciful relief.

TENNESSEE WILDFLOWERS

Other than the ceaseless vibration of the woman's soft palate, the airliner was fairly peaceful. This gave Josh some time to collect his thoughts. Josh's Peace Corps assignment was only cut short by two weeks, but it forced him to relegate the last of his packing to his friends. They promised to send the bulk of his belongings and souvenirs home for him, but even so, the rush to get ready for the trip home had been grueling.

His going away party had been a quick gathering of close friends and co-workers. They drank lala-palm wine and had bowls of fried mopane worms, with onions and a spicy chili sauce. Most of the party guests had barbecued crocodile steaks, which Josh had gracefully declined. He didn't eat meat in the first place, but there were additional grounds; Josh had a hazy recollection of a video he had as a child called, *Tales from the Wild: Gus the Alligator*, and for him, crocodiles were too closely related for comfort. Eating them just seemed wrong.

The dancing and drinking had gone on well into the morning. At some point Josh had collapsed into an oversized hammock with his two closest friends, Kasia and Mosi. Snug in the hammock, they had fallen into a drunken, peaceful slumber. A few hours later, a rooster crowing from the farmhouse next door woke the three up, or Josh would have missed his bus. They quickly gathered Josh's bags and the three of them walked to the bus stop together.

The bus stop was merely a wooden bench on the side of the dirt road, a familiar spot for Josh as his primary mode of transportation for the past two years had been the blue and yellow painted Volkswagen transporter bus. The short walk this morning had been uncharacteristically quiet and somber.

Kasia had been one of the first people Josh met when he arrived in Africa. She was an attractive woman in her twenties who wore dresses and patterned scarves on her head that were ablaze in bright colors, and she was always swathed in an amazing display of jewelry she made herself. Kasia's parents owned the small hovel Josh had lived in during his stay in New Xade. He and Kasia had become inseparable over the past two years. They would often stay up talking until late in the night and fall asleep together much to the dismay of her parents. They were worried their only daughter would marry the blue-eyed, white boy, and run off with him to America!

Mosi he met later at a bar called The Hideaway in Ghanzi, a nearby small town. The skinny young man in dreadlocks with an infectious smile was supposedly employed by the bar owner to serve drinks, but it was often unclear if he was an employee or one of the patrons.

That first night together, Josh, Kasia and Mosi drank Kaffir beer and smoked some weed around a campfire behind the bar. The three danced and laughed until the bar closed and the owner shooed them home with a disapproving shake of his head.

The next day the three friends had unbearable hangovers and Kasia's mother helped them recover with honey, bananas and an herbal concoction of morogo leaves, ginger, and other unidentifiable root-based components. The hot drink was bitter and tasted like licorice. To Josh's surprise it had worked. It was miraculous, and they all three were able to drink copious amounts of beer again the very next night.

The three of them became close from the first night together at The Hideaway. Josh and Kasia would often make the trip in to Ghanzi to meet Mosi. They'd go out drinking and dancing. Often they would stay at Mosi's tiny, tin-roofed apartment or all three would go back to New Xade and sleep in Josh's small one-room shanty. Across the room from his cot bed Josh would sometimes hear his two, usually sloshed, friends having sex inside a sleeping bag he had provided for them. In Mosi's apartment at least there was a separate room where Josh could sleep, out of earshot, on a small sofa. Several times they invited Josh to join them, but he always declined.

Josh was the blond, blue-eyed stranger in a strange land which drew a great deal of carnal curiosity in this remote area of Africa. Many a young woman made concerted, brazen attempts to get Josh Fletcher into their bed. Still, Josh never had sex with any of them, often much to their frustrated disappointment.

Josh, Kasia and Mosi arrived at the small bench at the bus stop. They sat down and then all three openly sobbed like children. Kasia's body shook with her tears. Josh had found that African people don't contain their emotions in the same way he had learned to do as a young man raised in Tennessee. It was a regional trait that Josh had assimilated thoroughly. They remained locked arm-in-arm, weeping, until the bus driver honked the horn and gave them all three a surly, impatient look.

When Josh waved goodbye from the back window of the tiny bus, Kasia and Mosi ran after it. This image of his friends running in their bare feet down the dirt road, throwing him kisses, was heartbreaking, and it became seared into his memory. It would remain with him for the rest of his life.

Josh continued wiping tears away for the entire bus ride to the small airport outside of Ghanzi. There he hopped a short flight on a single engine plane to the airport in Cape Town. He had to fly to London and switch flights at Heathrow with another long delay. Yanked from the calm, easygoing life he had grown fond of in New Xade, he was more dead-tired than he had been in a very long time, and when he finally got to his seat on the flight headed for Chicago O'Hare, he nearly collapsed from exhaustion.

Then, as luck would have it, he had to hear about the innumerable expeditions of his Canadian seat neighbor. His backside ached from the cramped seating and the hopelessly non-invigorating shaft of air from the tiny fan above him was making his throat burn. It even felt like his asthma, which had subsided in Africa, was returning. Josh wished he could sleep, or even just relax, but he couldn't.

The call that his Grandpa Cowboy was seriously ill had been a shock. Death was something Josh had not faced since he was six and his mother had passed away. JJ had indicated in his phone conversation with Josh that his grandfather's illness warranted him cutting his Peace Corps assignment short, which had frightened him. On the other hand, Josh knew his family had a practice of erring on the side of the tragic and over-dramatic, so it was entirely possible his grandfather's situation was not as dire as his daddy had made it sound. Josh decided that with the unimaginable hours ahead of him, it would be preferable not to dwell on this subject until he arrived home and had all the facts.

Back at the London airport Josh had done something he hadn't done in recent memory and paid full price for an actual hardback book. It was Stephen King's latest, a whopping one with lots of characters which he thought should keep him busy for the lengthy flight, so he turned on the minuscule beam of light above his head and tried to read. It didn't work. His mind had a different agenda.

Someone other than family was desperately waiting for Josh to arrive back home.

It was the middle of the night in Nashville and Josh imagined this person could be sound asleep in a warm comfortable bed; which sounded unimaginably pleasing to him at the moment. More likely, though, this would not be the case and this person would be wide awake, restless and anxious.

Just like me. Josh thought.

It had been over six months since they had seen each other in the flesh.

Six months is a hell of a long time when you're crazy in love.

4

In Belle Meade, an exclusive, affluent neighborhood of Nashville, far off the main street, a thirty-two room mansion was mostly dark. It was hidden behind giant weeping willow trees and centuries old grandfather oaks. Six massive columns stood tall and lordly in front of the Antebellum home, made of solid limestone quarried from the very property the house stood on.

Much like her great nephew, Josh Fletcher, Jewell Whitecotton was having trouble sleeping. She was not miles away sailing through the faraway night sky like Josh, but was instead in the basement of her home in Belle Meade. And unlike Josh, her mind was not flooded with thoughts from events or people from the present day, or the recent past for that matter. The neurons in her brain had long since lost their ability to be preoccupied with such things. This was due to microscopic breaks and lesions throughout her cerebral cortex. Her numerous doctors had been treating Jewell with antiplatelet drugs and some experimental medications, standard treatments for her condition, but nothing they had tried had had any medically verifiable results. Jewell's brain now only seemed to retain memories that were generated forty years or further in the past. But that was just what the doctors believed. The truth was Jewell knew a hell of a lot more than they ever thought she did. Frankly, Jewell couldn't give a rat's ass what those needle prodding, pill pushing, quacks thought anymore. Not even her caretaker, who watched over nearly every move she made, knew she had quit taking most of their pills a long time ago. Jewell had become a seasoned master of the fake pill swallow. Nashville's sewer system was where most of them actually ended up.

At the moment she was desperately trying to find a box of canned yams. She needed three of the cans for a Thanksgiving dinner her mother, Hazel, had planned in 1951 when Jewell was just fourteen..

If you want your dinner to be top-drawer, begin preparations four days before!

Jewell could see her mother Hazel's face as clear as day. Her eyes would be glittering with excitement. In the Fletcher house, Thanksgiving was one of the biggest dinner events of the year, almost more elaborate than Christmas. Jewell treasured helping her mother prepare for the guests.

Choose your dress right away, there may be alterations to do. Set out the table linens, check the bedding in the guest rooms and the guest towels in the restrooms. You may have to run down to Macy's for anything that is stained or doesn't match. Send the knives out for sharpening. Ben Franklin's Five and Dime has wonderful Thanksgiving decorations and knick-knacks. Woolworth's has Brach's candies for the children, and get extra for the adults too. Order the Turkey from Donny Potterman's Butcher Shop. Give Donny a big tip and he'll set aside the most robust turkey for you!

Donny Potterman's Butcher Shop closed in 1966, after Donny had died from congestive heart failure right on the floor of the butcher shop in front of a horrified Maxine Hayes with her five pounds of ground chuck still clenched tightly in his hands. Ben Franklin was now a bar. The Woolworth's building was demolished over a decade ago. The Macy's building had been converted into a paint gun amusement center. These facts had been explained to Jewell dozens of times, but within moments the exchange was lost to her. The doctors insisted that it was important to keep trying, so family and friends continued their efforts to help her hang on to the present-day, no matter how futile it appeared to be.

Jewell's last completely unmarred memory was on December 26th 1972. That was the day she heard that President Harry S. Truman had died. It was the final, fully realized memory Jewell's deteriorating brain could grasp onto, and so it held to it fairly securely. The past president was 88. It was pneumonia that had taken him. Walter Cronkite had delivered the terrible news.

The real Christmas tree that Jewell had put up was still twinkling with its multi-colored lights. The gifts were all gone and the wrapping paper was cleared away. Her husband Fritz was sleeping on the sofa and Jewell was in the kitchen cooking up some French toast in a cast iron skillet. On the television, a Bing Crosby movie marathon was interrupted with the news. Jewell stepped from the kitchen and sat next to Fritz, and took his hand. She could still recall how warm and safe his hand felt as she cried. Fritz felt like crying too, but men didn't do that back in his day.

Jewell loved Harry Truman. Her husband Fritz was from Independence, Missouri. Fritz's father had hosted political fundraisers several times while the Truman's were in the White House, and the families remained friends when the president returned to Independence after leaving office. Their homes on North Delaware Avenue were only a few blocks from each other.

On four occasions Jewell had met the 33rd president of the United States. President Truman had been exceptionally friendly, down to earth and folksy. Bess was a bit reserved and quiet, but she always called Jewell by her name, and this made quite an impression on Jewell. Fritz and Jewell received a Christmas card from the Truman family every year, and Jewell would proudly display it on her fireplace mantle. This tradition continued until Bess passed in 1982 at the age of 97, at the time, the oldest living First Lady in US history.

TENNESSEE WILDFLOWERS

When Walter Cronkite finished the story about the life, and death, of Harry S. Truman, Fritz took Jewell in his arms and said, "My dear Jewell, the world just lost a good man. A very good man."

Jewell asked Fritz a question that day, and his answer made her realize she had married the world's most perfect man.

"Should we go to the funeral?" she'd asked.

He looked at her as if the question was outlandishly absurd. "Whether it is a wedding or a funeral, it is never a question of whether to go. You always attend. That's what good people do."

Jewell Fletcher became Jewell Whitecotton on Saturday, June 23, 1956. Fritz Whitecotton was 32, Jewell was 19. Even though their daughter was marrying a notable, well-respected Kansas City businessman, Hal and Hazel Fletcher were so opposed to this union they refused to attend the wedding ceremony.

Hazel Fletcher blamed herself for what she believed was her daughter's act of defiance, breaking the conventions of polite society, by marrying a man nearly twice her age! It was, after all, upon her urging that Jewell had moved from Nashville to attend Stevens College, an all-girl school in Columbia, Missouri, over 400 miles away. Hal Fletcher, who held that there were plenty of perfectly fine private schools in Nashville, was in complete agreement.

It's my wife's fault!

Hal would say this quite often to anyone who would listen.

When Jewell left for Columbia, she had just gotten her driver's license. She could barely back the Hudson Commodore her daddy had bought her out of the drive without running over the hedges, or some statuary. Her little brother Jackson's heart broke when she drove away for college. He loved his older sibling. She always had an endless supply of caramels for him in her dress pocket, or a box of Cracker Jacks. Jewell would give him the prize from her box too, every time.

Jewell took Jackson to see *The Adventures of Ichabod and Mr. Toad* at Nashville's Princess Movie Theater just a week before she left. It was a Disney film that (at ten-years-old) he thought he might be too grown-up to see, or be seen going to, but when the black-caped horseman came riding out on the giant screen, WITH NO HEAD!

Jackson was so scared he cried. Jewell promised not to tell anyone, and she never did.

Jewell always seemed so sophisticated and pretty to Jackson. She basically raised him, and life without her hanging around just seemed entirely unimaginable. But she did it. She put her three large mint green Brooks Brothers bags in the trunk of her giant Hudson Commodore, kissed Jackson on the cheek, and told him, "Be a good boy...but not too good." Then she just closed the door, waved goodbye to her family, blew Jackson a kiss, and drove away.

Jackson ran away and climbed into a giant walnut tree where he stayed hidden the rest of the day. Finally, hunger and the cold night air forced him down. He wondered why no one else seemed so profoundly crushed. He thought he saw his mother brush a tear away as she dried the dishes at the kitchen sink later that evening. His dad just sat in his La-Z-Boy and watched *The Ed Sullivan Show* like it was any other night. With Jewell gone it felt like a wonderful, magical spell had been lifted right out of his soul. So he began a new life, one that no longer included an older sister hanging out close by. He never felt completely like a kid ever again. This was eight years before he would drive away to college himself, not Missouri, but Austin, Texas, where Jackson would later acquire the nickname "Cowboy" that would stick with him for the rest of his life.

Jewell's Hudson Commodore was quite a hit at Stevens College. "The Behemoth", it was christened by her college mates. She and her new girlfriends would often lower the top down and drive to Kansas City to shop at The Country Club Plaza. And then at the end of the day they'd head off to eat at the Savoy Hotel, on 9th Street, for dinner.

One evening while the girls were seated at their favorite table discussing menu choices, a gentleman in a dark blue three piece suit stepped up and offered to buy them all drinks. The girls explained they were not old enough for adult beverages. Undaunted, the man modified his offer; he insisted he buy them each a New York steak dinner. He appeared innocent enough, but the girls clearly did not believe it was an appropriate proposition. He was too old and a complete stranger. And not so attractive either.

The funny-looking visitor was tall and spindly, with a thin black mustache (the girls teased Jewell later calling it "the licorice lip tickler"). He was not easily daunted by the wary looks the girls were throwing his way. As the matter of fact, he was so confident and assertive that none of the young women knew how to tactfully tell him that he really had to go away. So steak dinners were ordered all around. As it turned out, it was a fairly enjoyable evening of excellent food and good conversation, and in the end he didn't look so bad anymore.

His name, they soon found out, was Fritz Whitecotton, a local businessman. He had been at work all day and had decided on a whim to go out on the town and enjoy some good company, something he almost never did. They also learned his family founded the Aunt Viv's Canned Food Company (much wealthier than they imagined by looking at him), he was 31 years old (older than they could've imagined at their age), and he rode his bicycle everywhere he could because, he explained, "Exercise is good for your health." (kookier, at that point in American history, than they could have ever imagined).

By the time they were finishing their Baked Alaska and drinking the last of their Cherry Cokes, it was quite apparent that this wealthy businessman was smitten with Jewell Fletcher. When they all stood to leave, he asked Jewell if he could call on her that very next week. Jewell caught the disapproving looks from her girlfriends, but she actually enjoyed the rather odd man (even though he had intruded in on their girls' night out) and she accepted.

How could one date hurt?

The one date turned into many. The Hudson jaunts to Kansas City with her girl chums came to an end. In their place was Fritz driving to Columbia, Missouri every Friday and Saturday evening to pick Jewell up. During those weekends with Fritz, Jewell was treated to hours and hours of wonderful food, drink and conversation. She had never in her life met anyone who seemed to be so tirelessly interested in what she had to say. All week long she would be waiting in anticipation until Friday when Fritz drove up to her dorm in his new white Cadillac Coupe de Ville. She was equally enthusiastic to learn all about him.

Fritz was the son of Theodore Whitecotton, who started Aunt Viv's Canned Foods as a small canning company run out of a small warehouse in Kansas City. The "Viv" in "Aunt Viv's" was actually Theodore's sister Vivian who was more than attractive enough to model for the company's trademarked label. She had a modern face that gave the company logo just the refined look Theodore wanted. (Had Vivian had any inkling that her face would forever be associated with tiny canned frankfurters she would have nixed the idea on the spot.) The company had fair success with green beans, corn, carrots and candied yams. But it was when Theodore decided to include Vienna sausages in the company's manufacturing line that the business took off like a rocket. The sausages were made from a recipe Theodore bought from a local butcher for ten dollars. "Isn't life full of little cockeyed absurdities?" he always said when asked about that absolutely true story.

The Vienna sausages were a colossal success. When Theodore's only son, Fritz, took over the business in 1945 they had grown enough to house a canning factory five times the size of the original one. Their star product was now selling in 39 states as well as in Canada.

By this time Vivian Whitecotton had moved to Stockholm, Sweden and never, *ever* again wore her hair in the genteel style that appeared on her brother's enormously successful canned food label. There was another noble, but extremely personally hurtful, reason Vivian left the U.S. and her family behind for a fresh, new life in Scandinavia, but in those days no one ever spoke of such things.

Five years later (at the time when Fritz was spending 29 cents per gallon to fill up his Cadillac to drive to Columbia every Friday and Saturday nights to meet Jewell) Aunt Viv's Vienna Sausages were in all 50 states and 17 countries. And because of a very fortuitous contract with Uncle Sam, every soldier sent off to fight the war in Korea would find in their war rations packs, right next to their tins of coffee and dehydrated milk, two cans of Aunt Viv's Vienna Sausages.

In 1975 Fritz sold Aunt Viv's Canned Foods to Swanson Foods for a reported $750 million. He made some wise investments in the early eighties and quadrupled his net worth. Fritz was very rich in business, and very rich in love, right up until his untimely death.

Hal and Hazel had, over time, overcome their disapproval of Fritz Whitecotton. They eventually realized that he treated their daughter extremely well and was a pure gentleman. Still, they only visited their daughter twice a year at best. Jewell came to Nashville less than that herself. She missed her momma's big Thanksgiving and Christmas dinners the most. Jewell just couldn't completely forgive her mother. Her parents not attending her wedding had hurt her more deeply than she ever told anyone, even Fritz. But she often reminded herself of it. She vowed to take that memory, and its accompanying heartbreak, with her all the way to her grave. Emotional scars are really not so different than physical scars – always right there where we can easily find them; maybe not in the mirror or with our fingers running over them, but just as real. So, Jewell did as she vowed. She held onto the emotional pain her parents left her with, and she never let it go.

Whether it is a wedding or a funeral, it is never a question of whether to go. You always attend. That's what good people do.

On the rare visits Hal and Hazel made to Kansas City, they had noticed Jewell was becoming forgetful, and even confused enough to excuse herself from conversations on occasion. Even though her parents expressed their concern, Fritz did not tell them Jewell had been diagnosed with a very rare kind of dementia. He only told them she was tired, which is exactly what Jewell told him to say. Hal and Hazel were also completely unaware that Fritz was taking Jewell to see the best doctors his money could buy, and that these doctors had very little to offer in the way of slowing the progression of the disease.

No one knew, not even Jewell, that Fritz had drawn up a will clearly stating his wish that all of his wealth be provided to assure his wife would never spend a day in a nursing facility. Fritz's favorite grandmother had suffered her agonizing last years in one of those hellish places. Fritz's objective to provide a will with his strict instructions was a wise, and unfortunately, prophetic, inclination.

He died in 1987 when his new Cadillac Seville was broadsided by a man evading police in a red Plymouth Duster. The police report later stated that when the Duster hit the Cadillac it was going an estimated 102 miles-per-hour. The driver of the Duster and Fritz died instantly. The man, who was only 21 years old, had stolen forty five dollars from a 7-Eleven at gunpoint. Ironically, as the young thief was leaving the convenience store he grabbed five cans of Aunt Viv's Vienna Sausages. The cans were found inside a blood-soaked paper bag along with the stolen cash.

Fritz Whitecotton's last will and testament was iron clad. Jewell was the sole heir and all the money was explicitly assigned for the condition of her never living a day in a nursing home.

By this time, Hal Fletcher had already passed away and it was up to Hazel and Jewell's younger brother, Cowboy, to make sure Jewell was cared for exactly as the will had stated. It was mutually decided by Hazel, Cowboy, and the attorneys in Kansas City, that it was best to move Jewell to Nashville to live with her mother in her childhood home in the neighborhood of Belle Meade.

Jewell was not visibly aware of any of this. When she was told that her husband had been killed, she didn't appear to have any recognizable emotional response to the news. She was sitting in the front row of folding chairs as her husband was lowered into his grave, but Cowboy noticed his sister seemed more interested in the blackbirds that had crowded into a nearby tree than to the dire activities going on directly in front of her. In truth, just because someone decided to not show their emotions for the whole world to see, didn't mean they were not there.

They were there.

After Hazel died in 2001, Cowboy made certain all of his sister's needs were seen to. Jewell rarely left the house any more. She would become overly frightened if anyone attempted to take her outside for even a short walk. Cowboy was lucky in that his mother's trusted long-time house keeper, a woman who had been with the Fletcher family for thirty-some years, named Georgia True, had offered to stay on and help care for Jewell full time.

Georgia was sound asleep in an upstairs guest bedroom that was essentially now her second home. She had put Jewell to bed hours ago. Georgia had tucked Jewell in her double-deep feather bed, made sure she had taken her medication (not detecting Jewell's masterful fake-swallow) and was falling asleep. Georgia had turned on a low light on in the adjoining bathroom, and then turned the bedroom light off. She had no idea that Jewell would be waking up two hours later to the alarming belief that her mother's Thanksgiving plans were a day behind schedule.

Now a single light bulb illuminated the large basement stacked full of boxes on every side. Most of the boxes were marked with the Aunt Viv's Canned Food logo. When Jewell moved back to Nashville, her mother (who always expected another great depression was looming just around the nation's corner) insisted they bring back with them all the Aunt Viv's inventory that Fritz had stored in the giant storm cellar of their Kansas City home. They took the hundreds of cases of canned food and transferred them to the basement of the house in Belle Meade.

Nearly a third of the boxes had been emptied over the years, but there were still loads of boxes left. Thankfully the 2010 flood had spared their basement or the many cases would have surely been ruined.

Jewell had suddenly become completely lost as to why she was in the basement looking through old dusty boxes of canned food. This experience of becoming suddenly lost was perfectly normal to her. She took a well-deserved seat on a case of Aunt Viv's canned red beans. She had been going through boxes for over an hour and not a single can of yams ever made an appearance, and now she couldn't even imagine what she needed them for anyway.

It was like a spot light that searched *and searched* a theater stage, but it never seemed to find the actor or the prop it was intended to help illuminate. The audience was left alone in the dark, with no plot or even a captivating, swaggering actor to keep them entertained for a while. It was enormously confounding and tiring. In the past Jewell would become so irritated by the confusion and chaos in her head that she would scream out. But she learned early on that when she did that, then busloads of strangers showed up. And they were of no help. They'd poke her with needles again and dump the pills down her throat. Then she really would feel like the nut that got shoved into the fruitcake, and she wouldn't wake up for days. Or who knows, maybe weeks. It had been a world of unrecognizable objects and strangers for a long time now. She had learned it was best to keep that confusing world a quiet one.

She was looking at a meat freezer that had been under most of the boxes she had taken down and gone through. The old thing was completely covered in dust. A hasp and lock on the front was especially corroded. General Electric was printed in rusted, tarnished silver letters across the front. And it looked like it was ready to fall off.

On top of the freezer there still sat a case of Aunt Viv's Vienna Sausages.

I think I'll take one of these cans of Vienna Sausages to the kitchen, get some Saltines, and have a snack.

She walked over to the freezer and ran her hand across the dust on the box. A smiling image appeared. It was Aunt Viv's warm face. Under Aunt Viv's image was the now famous, trademarked, maxim:

WARM MEMORIES IN EVERY CAN!

She noticed the freezer was humming. It was a large sized freezer too. At least seven feet wide and four feet deep. She looked to see that a long black cord was running along the back of the wall to a metal plug box screwed into a two-by-four on the upper portion of the basement ceiling. The muffled, rattling hum of the freezer's old motor sounded tired. She could relate.

When Jewell pulled the box of Vienna sausages toward her it snagged on the hasp. She pulled a little harder to free it, and to her amazement the whole hinged fastener fell crashing to the floor, padlock and all. The hasp had been secured into place more than fifty years ago, and the continuous vibration from the freezer must have finally taken a toll on the old screws.

Maybe there was something in there that might be just the thing to go with a can of Vienna sausages and crackers?

Jewell sat the box of canned food on the floor. She was still sturdy for her age and it was an easy task, but - with all the box moving she had done over the past hour - tomorrow she would be stiff and in a world of pain. And, of course, tomorrow she'd have no idea why.

Jewell pulled open the lid of the freezer and peeked in. The light bulb hung close enough to illuminate where she was looking. At first the frozen misty air created a dense swirling cloud that Jewell couldn't see through. As the warmer air filled the inside of the freezer, the thick white mist lifted over the top edge. It reminded Jewell of how a deep winter fog rolled in over the Tennessee hills.

Jewell blinked at the frosty air rising up from the freezer into her eyes. After a few blinks her eyes cleared up, and it slowly became unmistakable what the freezer had held inside of it for so many years.

"Heavens to Betsy!" Jewell said to herself as the memories flooded in. "Finally, a familiar face!"

> *Let us be thankful for the fools. But for them the rest of us could not succeed.*
> - Mark Twain

AS LUCK WOULD HAVE IT

1

Per Petula's specifications, Byrdie had selected a tasteful Torchiere floor lamp from Bradford's Furniture and its warm light illuminated Cowboy's hospital room in a healthy glow. No longer in intensive care, Cowboy rested peacefully in a private room with a hospital bed fitted with 100% Egyptian cotton sateen bed linens. The sheets on his bed were against hospital policy. It had been a brutal and unpleasant clash of wills, but in the end, Monique, the charge nurse at the time, accepted the breach in policy. Petula would supply the clean set of the prohibited luxury bed linens each morning, or the deal was off - the white starchy hospital sheets, the ones Petula found so intolerable, would be returned. Petula arranged for Nicholson Cleaners to complete this daily task for her using her American Express card.

A small dry erase board was propped on the bed next to Cowboy, who was sleeping deeply. On it was written:
PLEASE BRING CIGARS

In a casual Ely Cattleman Western shirt and Wrangler jeans, JJ sat in a leather chair across the room with his boots propped up on an end table. He was reading a letter. A hospital tray table was piled high with paperwork. Byrdie sat nearby with her MacBook Pro ready for dictation. JJ put the letter aside, and removed his reading glasses.

"I admire the determined efforts of your City Council and I personally feel your request has its merits." JJ gathered his thoughts, then dictated further to Byrdie: "Your proposal is comprehensive and clearly establishes that the Spring Peeper Frogs occupying Hickory River Slough generate mating calls that are well above the limits of your city's noise ordinance. The testimony of your citizens is convincingly heartfelt as well. But upon review, the governor's office cannot legally evoke an executive order to have the Spring Peepers exterminated." JJ looked to Byrdie. "What is that crazy contest of theirs I go to?"

Byrdie looked up from her MacBook. "The Captain of the Cornpile Corn Shucking Showdown."

JJ nodded, recollecting, then continued, "I do thoroughly enjoy your Captain of the Cornpile Corn Shucking event and I look forward to seeing all of you there again next year."

Startling JJ and Byrdie, Petula bolted into the hospital room with two paper cups of coffee in her hands. In full makeup and her Chanel tweed suit pressed, she looked her fashionable best. She slammed the covered coffee cups on a hospital tray and searched the room in frantic twists and turns. "You've got to see this!" she exclaimed. "Oh my God. Oh my God. Byrdie, where is the TV controller?"

Byrdie stood up peevishly. She stepped over to the hospital tray where the TV remote was sitting next to the coffee cups Petula had just set down. She handed it to Petula, who quickly waved it back to her. "Could you, you know, Byrdie?" Petula said. "I can never make those thingamajigs work the TV right."

JJ said, "Momma, Byrdie and I are working." He motioned at the scattered papers beside him.

Byrdie stood waiting, remote in hand.

Petula declared, "JJ, this is important."

"Why always the drama, Momma?"

"Oh, it's warranted this time, JJ. It's big. Channel 2, Byrdie. Channel 2."

JJ motioned for Byrdie to wait. "I'm busier than a borrowed mule, Momma. How big?"

Petula grabbed Cowboy's glasses from the nightstand by his bed. "Biblical!" She poked the glasses onto Cowboy's face. "Wake up, Cowboy. You're going to want to see this." She turned snappishly to Byrdie impatiently pointing to the TV. Byrdie looked to JJ.

"She's got a bee in her bonnet, Byrdie," JJ said. "Let's take a break and have a look."

Byrdie murmured (in her inaudible voice), "A bee in her bonnet? Try bats in her belfry." She pointed the remote at the television hanging in the upper corner of the room and turned it on to Channel 2.

Cowboy opened his drowsy eyes and Petula pointed fervently for him to watch the television, then she anxiously put her hands on her hips to watch.

On the television screen was Linda Chan, a local Nashville anchor. Behind her was a digital image of a man in a suit with thick peppered hair brushed back in a youthful looking blow cut. He looked smart, handsome and confident. It was Don Summerfield, vice president of the United States of America.

A crawl scrolling across the bottom of the screen repeated the message:

...WE WILL BE RETURNING TO THE RYMAN AUDITORIUM'S BROADCAST OF "I CAN HEAR AMERICA SINGING" AFTER THIS BREAKING NEWS...WE WILL BE RETURNING...

"More details are coming in regarding the bizarre and shocking story involving Vice President Don Summerfield." Linda Chan read the words from the teleprompter in her usual exceptionally professional manner, yet the slight disbelief in her eyes could not be concealed. "Rebecca C. Hooper is standing by at Big Frog Mountain Wilderness Area where local police, The National Guard, and a search party of concerned citizens have reportedly located the last of the missing Boy Scouts. Rebecca, what can you tell us about what happened there earlier this evening?"

The television screen cut to Rebecca standing outside. Powerful floodlights illuminated the dark woods behind her. She was sexy, thin, and exuded an intelligent, professional persona. (And she was the highest rated reporter in Nashville, since she replaced her now retired father.) Rebecca was standing in a cleared area where military style tents were set up and emergency teams of rescue workers fluttered about clutching flashlights and coffee. Rebecca reported, "Thank you, Linda. The last missing Boy Scout was located just moments ago. I am here in the Cherokee National Forest in a cleared area set up as a temporary trauma treatment facility. Big Frog Mountain is directly behind me. That is where the Boy Scouts had been camping earlier tonight."

Rebecca moved toward a tent where an EMT escorted a frightened Boy Scout with ratty hair and a dirty tear-stained face inside. Rebecca continued, "The Boy Scouts are inside these makeshift medical tents where they are being treated for trauma and minor injuries acquired while having to flee through the woods in terror and darkness. In an exclusive interview, a spokesman for the local police department, who chooses to remain anonymous, has described to me what first set into motion the tragic events earlier tonight. Vice President Don Summerfield and two of his hunting partners were wild boar hunting in this wooded area behind me. It must be said, all hunting in this part of the National Forest is prohibited and how the small hunting party ended up here is not clear. What has been confirmed, is that the vice president was severely intoxicated when he stumbled upon what he reportedly believed was a herd of wild pigs. In the ensuing gunfire a Boy Scout Troop Leader was shot. The victim, an Iraq War Veteran whose young son was among the Boy Scouts camping here, is now in stable condition. The gunshot wound was mainly confined to the victim's buttocks and, at this time, is not considered life threatening."

In Cowboy's hospital room the group stared at the television dumbfounded. JJ remarked, "Maybe they've made a mistake?"

Byrdie had already pulled out her BlackBerry and was quickly scrolling through breaking news stories. She grimaced. "The Huffington Post has the vice president's mug shot up already." She scrolled some more. "Oh my! I just received a Tweet with a photo of the Scout Troop Leader's bullet wound. It's already gone viral on YouTube. H'mm, that is unpleasant."

JJ nodded. Petula picked up the coffee cup from the table and drank. "I hate to be the one to say it," she said, "but Don Summerfield is not going to survive this. Something of this magnitude is not ever going to be turned into a silk purse by any stretch. Not this sow's ear."

On the television screen, Rebecca had moved next to where a tall, attractive, engaging young man in hiking gear was standing. Rebecca took the young man by the shoulder and looked to the camera. "I am here with witness Matt Forrest, who was camping about a half mile from where the terrifying incident occurred. Can you tell us what you heard or saw, Matt?"

"I heard a lot of gunfire, I mean a lot! Then the sound of children screaming and calling out for help. Some were wailing," Matt said, clearly still a little rattled. "It was like a horror movie, or a video game. I called 9-1-1 on my cell, then I went running into the woods to see if I could help out. I found about a dozen of the boys hiding behind some logs, and I took them to an abandoned mine shaft I knew about. We stayed hidden there until I heard the rescue team calling out for us."

"Thank you, Matt. You're a true hero here, on this otherwise tragic and, for the children, nightmarish and terrifying night." Rebecca stepped away from Matt, never breaking eye-contact with the camera. "Miraculously only the Boy Scout troop leader was hit by the negligent boar rifle fire. Unfortunately, the children awoke to the sound of blaring rifle shots and witnessed their leader inexplicably being gunned down in the darkness. It's unimaginable what they must have thought. Once all the boys have been treated and released from here they will be transferred to the trauma center in Chattanooga. Back to you, Linda."

The television cut back to the news desk. Linda Chan reported, "Families of the Boy Scouts are being asked to pick up their children at Chattanooga's Parkridge East Hospital. We will be bringing you up to the minute news coverage of this shocking story as it progresses throughout the night. Now we return you to the Ryman

Auditorium's musical salute to the nation, 'I Can Hear America Screaming'." Linda Chan quickly caught her slip of the tongue, and corrected herself: "I Can Hear America *Singing*."

Byrdie muted the TV, and began to jot notes in her MacBook. "I'll make certain the governor's office makes sympathy calls to all the Boy Scout families, and of course the Boy Scout troop leader. I'll try to arrange a personal visit for you Governor. I'll get a press release ready. These children will need the best post-traumatic stress experts and counselors available as well, and the governor's office can supervise getting that going immediately."

"Thank you, Byrdie," JJ said, then recalled something. "I think there's a picture of me and Don Summerfield in hunting clothes with a dead caribou on the governor's official website."

"I'll remove it immediately," Byrdie said, and quickly got to work on her MacBook to start the ball rolling on her many tasks at hand.

Petula turned to JJ. "You should call Bob."

JJ considered the idea. "I don't think the president of the United States needs to hear from me in the middle of a mess like this."

"Think about it JJ," Petula said. "Don Summerfield's political career ended tonight when he decided it was a good idea to get stewed to the gills and go plundering through a national park with a loaded boar rifle."

JJ thought, and said, "He's going to be crucified."

"That's right." Petula nodded with resolve.

JJ said, "Don't you think it's a little too politically calculating to jockey for a man's job before he's officially lost it?"

"This happened in your state, JJ. All eyes will be on you no matter what. To be blunt, this tragedy could be a very serendipitous stroke of luck for you."

JJ and Petula noticed Cowboy was writing on the dry erase board. He wrote:

CALL THE PRESIDENT

JJ asked, "Shouldn't we consult with Elliot first?"

"He'll be on board JJ. He's a smart man," said Petula. "My grandmother always said, 'When the oven's hot, put your loaf in.'"

JJ looked over to Byrdie. "Byrdie, can you get me the president on the line?"

Byrdie nodded. "Yes sir. Right away."

Petula said, "Next year is an election year. President McKenzie won't need this distraction to linger. I predict by tomorrow morning Don Summerfield will be telling the whole world how sorry he is for shooting a Boy Scout troop leader, one of America's most enduring icons, in the ass. Then he will somberly and regretfully resign from office."

Byrdie stepped up and handed her phone to JJ. "It's the president, Governor."

"That was quick," JJ said, impressed with Byrdie's skills yet again.

Byrdie shook her head. "He called you."

Petula looked besieged with delight.

JJ collected his thoughts, drew in a deep breath, and then took the phone from Byrdie.

"Hello, Mr. President."

2

It was a sunny day at the Nashville International Airport. Skies were cloudless and satin-blue.

Taking Exit 216-A off Interstate 40 East were two Lincoln Town Car limousines. The black government cars - polished to a high shine - merged onto Terminal Drive and followed the signs for International Flights.

Inside the two limousines were Governor JJ Fletcher, his staff, his Secret Service agents, and his mother.

* * *

"I deeply regret what has happened and I cannot express how sorry I am for the family of Lieutenant Richard Tubbs, the Boy Scout troop leader involved in the incident." Vice President Don Summerfield said, as cameras popped and flashed in the press room like Chinese firecrackers. This shocking, but not entirely unexpected, news footage was being broadcast on every television screen, laptop, and iPhones, throughout Nashville's International Airport. It could even be heard as breaking news on AM/FM radio stations.

Those morning travelers who were not stationed in front of a TV set or their laptops here at Nashville's International Airport Arrivals Gate 17, were scurrying up and down the concourse meeting flight schedules or expectantly looking ahead to meet their loved ones. They lugged and heaved their luggage and backpacks; some in shorts and T-shirts, some in sweaters and coats, some in suits. In-flight meals were often extra these days, so many people had resorted to grabbing bagged burgers and fries for their flights from the fast food court, or had purchased greatly overpriced snacks or bottled drinks from the terminal shops.

Many airport travelers had delayed their busy activities to watch the television screens mounted throughout the airport where CNN, Fox News, MSNBC, and other cable channels were available. All were broadcasting the same "Breaking News" story.

On every TV screen was Don Summerfield. He was normally an astute, handsome man, but now he looked disheveled and tired. He stood in front of a plethora of microphones on a stage with two glib, official-looking men in suits behind him. One would guess these men were some of his newly acquired lawyers. The vice president continued, "I am relieved to hear Lieutenant Tubbs will soon be able to walk again and I hope his unfortunate injury won't prevent him from enjoying the outdoor activities I am told he loves so much." He cleared his throat, and persevered. "I further apologize to the families of the young, brave Boy Scouts who witnessed the tragic, and what must have been horrifying, incident. I regret to inform the good people of this nation that I will be resigning from the office of the vice president without delay so the country can continue uninterrupted by my personal crisis."

Don Summerfield quickly glanced at his feet. Whatever he was about to say next had given him pause. His shoulders slumped, he pushed his hand through his sloppy, thick hair. He looked back to the cameras. "Also, in response to the petitions from the National

Office of The Boy Scouts of America, and the public, I will be relinquishing and returning all my Scout Den Leader Badges."

Done with his obligations and stepping back from the microphones, Don Summerfield said, "I'll be taking no questions." He then quickly exited the stage with the suited men on either side of him.

Not watching any of the TV screens, or Internet live-streaming of the news either, was a young man seated near the gate – Dylan Fairway. He was a lanky young stallion in cowboy boots, 22 years old with deep, wise eyes. He was wearing a black leather vest and cowboy hat. His husky, dangling arms were covered with elegant tattoos. Both ears and one eyebrow were pierced. He was holding a stuffed Spider Monkey with a little T-shirt that read: "You My Monkey." He looked to have a bad case of nerves, shifting in his seat and glancing around in purposeless directions.

Dylan was the lead singer in an up and coming Nashville-based band called Napoleon Blue, who were now touring the country. He purchased the stuffed monkey last week from the FAO Schwartz in New York City. He arrived home to Nashville late yesterday. Dylan was so jittery and anxious he was making people who were seated next to him get up and move seats away.

Dylan took his cell phone from his vest pocket. He touched in a phone number.

"Bluebird Café," the sweet-sounding female voice said from the phone. For Dylan it was like heaven to hear the familiar Tennessee long drawl to her words. Nashville was home, and Dylan missed it terribly when he was out on the road. And lately that was not all he'd been missing.

Dylan said, "I want to confirm my dinner reservations for tonight. This is Dylan Fairway."

"We have you down for seven thirty, Dylan," she said. "Table for two."

"Perfect. Thanks, Darlin'. What's your name?"

"Jasmine."

"That's a pretty name. Thanks, Jasmine."

He put the phone back in his pocket and looked again at the computer generated sign on the wall. It read the same as the last time he looked (ten seconds ago):

CHICAGO O'HARE TO NASHVILLE – ON TIME

* * *

Inside the lead limousine were the governor's Secret Service men, Agents Applegarth and Cooper. Inside the car that followed were JJ Fletcher, finishing off a bottle of Ski Citrus Soda, Elliot, speaking into his BlackBerry, Byrdie, reading her MacBook, and Petula, who was applying the last strokes of her Chanel Rouge-Red lipstick, looking over her visage approvingly in her silver hand mirror.

Byrdie announced officially, "I cleared your schedule this evening for the dinner party with Josh. Tomorrow morning you'll be unveiling a new bronze bust of Andrew Jackson at The Hermitage house. I called Dr. Snyder, and she'll be seeing you at eleven thirty. I have a pressed suit ready for your afternoon appearance, where you're the Grand Marshall of the Mule Day Parade."

JJ asked, "What's that for?"

Byrdie replied, unwaveringly, "It's to pay homage to the industrious role the mule played in helping build this country, sir."

JJ shook his head. "No, the doctor appointment."

"Dentist. She's replacing that crown."

"Oh, right." JJ put his hand on his cheek, trying to recall.

Petula indicated she needed Elliot's attention, patting his knee, and he put away his BlackBerry. Elliot bit his lip and looked at JJ with slight trepidation. He knew what she was planning to say, at least some version of it.

Petula said, "JJ, you know how I hate to meddle into your life."

"I do?" JJ asked, dubiously.

"Now just listen. Elliot and I have been talking."

"Stop right there," JJ said, holding up a hand. "I am not doing *Dancing with the Nashville Stars*. I already told Elliot that three times."

"No. Not that, JJ," Elliot explained. "She brought this to my attention last night, and I believe your mother may have an important and valid point."

Byrdie stopped reading her MacBook, dropped her hands into her lap, and mumbled to herself (in her inaudible voice), "Heaven help us. Here comes another one."

Petula quipped, "Did you have something to contribute, Byrdie?" Petula always noticed Byrdie was mumbling, and she found it irksome.

Byrdie answered diplomatically, "I'm just vivaciously waiting to hear what you have to say."

Petula quickly dismissed her by turning away. "Now JJ, with the vice presidential position open and with you the likely choice for the office, we thought that to make you a more attractive contender, you may want to consider getting married."

"Before you answer…" Elliot jumped in. "Keep in mind, Americans, as a rule, prefer, no, *expect*, their leaders to have a spouse, especially the president. And if you become the vice president, and having Bob McKenzie's people just confirm how likely that is, it would never be too soon to look ahead to the main office."

Petula nodded. "I know you say I conspire too much JJ, but it takes a conspiracy to get anything of real importance done in this life."

JJ said succinctly, "I was married."

"That was fifteen years ago," Elliot said. "I know you've seen a few women now and then. You might consider looking more deeply into one of those relationships."

"No, Elliot. Not those women." Petula shook her head. "JJ, there is an elite dating service I have been consulting with. They are a respectable company with the highest references. They will find the perfect woman for a man of your importance. Byrdie can just call them up and schedule you some dates."

Byrdie held up her hands. "I have nothing to do with this, Governor."

JJ stared at Petula and Elliot with speechless disbelief.

"Some of these women are quite successful in their own right," Petula added. "Very good families."

"And quite attractive." Elliot nodded. "Petula has shown me some of their portfolios. I'd even go as far as to say some were smokin'." He held his hands to cup imaginary breasts. "Some of these girls have made very wise investments. We're talking some prime real estate."

Byrdie stared at Elliot with only mild aversion, because frankly, with Elliot, she'd come to expect nothing less.

JJ held his hands up to both Elliot and Petula. "Stop," he said.

"Elliot," Petula interrupted. "We're talking about a future First Lady of the United States of America. Not France. I'm very serious about this. There's no need to be tawdry."

Elliot shrugged his shoulders. "They don't all have to be Barbara Bush."

JJ exploded: "I said stop!" Everyone in the car became quiet and attentive. JJ's Grandpa Hal would have said, "You could have heard a mouse pissing on a ball of cotton." JJ continued, "I want to make something crystal, non-negotiable, and clear. The dating service business and wedding planning activities are officially vetoed. Nixed, forbidden. I'm putting the kibosh on it for all time. No one is to look into this matter further, or by executive order I will have you placed in front of a firing squad and shot."

Petula sighed deeply, defeated for the moment. Elliot shrugged again.

JJ asked Petula, "How's Daddy?"

Petula replied, "I had to hire a new nurse for him this morning."

"Why?" JJ inquired.

"He bit the last one. Well, *ones*," Petula answered. "This time it was because the silly woman kept trying to feed him brussels sprouts."

Everyone in the car nodded.

As the limousines pulled to a stop at the arrival entrance, JJ sat up to see that several press crews, photographers, and reporters were moving toward them. Rebecca C. Hooper was leading that pack.

JJ said, overtly irritated, "I said no press. Josh made me promise."

Elliot shook his head. "It wasn't me this time."

Byrdie added quickly, "I know nothing about this, Governor."

Petula took out her silver hand mirror again and checked her makeup and wig. She pushed some stray hairs into place. "You are the governor of Tennessee, are you not? And your son just endured two exhausting years in the Peace Corps on the other side of the world in some godforsaken country that no one in this car even knows the name of—"

"Botswana," Byrdie replied astutely.

Petula shrugged, and continued, "I spent many a week in the African bush wild game hunting with your father, and I don't recall such a place. If Josh's arrival back home is not even noted by the media, then the whole thing would have been for nothing, and two years of my grandson's life will have just been squandered away. And for what?"

JJ looked at his momma with sincere concern.

Petula put her mirror in her purse and snapped it closed. "You all know I'm right."

If anyone did not know that, they *did* know it was too late to do anything about it now.

The reporters swarmed the limousine like hungry wolves.

* * *

"Flight 287 has landed and will be arriving at gate seventeen."

Dylan looked up, invigorated by the announcement made by a sultry, Southern female voice from some unseen speaker above. He was so beside himself he almost slipped out of the chair. He steadied back in the seat, and then heard a commotion generating somewhere from behind him.

Dylan looked back to see something very troubling. From the concourse, walking at a brisk pace were JJ, Petula, Elliot, two Secret Service agents, several photographers, reporters, and camera crew, all headed straight his way.

"Holy shit," Dylan cried out. He quickly surmised what the clamoring mob was all about, and just as quickly made the determination that there was no clear escape. He threw the stuffed monkey in the seat next to him, and braced himself for what was coming.

Dylan had been told the governor was not able to come to the airport today due to prior commitments. Apparently the commitments had been changed. Now, faced with no other option, Dylan stood up and did his best to appear pleasantly surprised.

"Well, if it isn't Dylan Fairway?" JJ said as he arrived. "I haven't seen you in a coon's age." Seeing Dylan was a real joy for JJ. For one, JJ knew he was a very pleasant boy who had been a great friend to his son, but more to the point, the young man reminded JJ of someone he secretly (and at times not so secretly) had been enamored with for most of his life. *What a coincidence,* JJ thought. *I just saw Kitty out jogging the other morning?*

"How the hell are you stranger?" JJ said, and extended a hand.

"I'm doing really well Governor Fletcher," Dylan replied, giving JJ a firm shake.

Petula glanced over Dylan's tattoos, piercings and grungy attire with a disparaging shake of her head.

JJ said, "You know, you look more and more like your momma every time I see you."

"I keep hearing that." Dylan glanced at Petula. He was raised to be a gentleman so he kindly addressed her, "How are you, Mrs. Fletcher?"

Petula was alarmed the tattooed man would even speak to her. She said, with an aloof tone, "Well, young man, I'll be a lot better when I see my grandbaby back home in one whole piece."

Dylan noted the chilly timbre from her. He replied, "I feel exactly the same, Mrs. Fletcher."

Petula feigned an important conversation with Elliot and quickly stepped away.

JJ, ignoring his mother, said to Dylan, "Josh said you and your momma went over to visit him for a spell."

"Yes, we did, about six months ago."

"It made me feel better knowing someone was checking in on him while he was way over there in..." JJ looked to Byrdie standing next to him for a prompt.

"Botswana," Byrdie said, slightly exasperated.

JJ continued, "What that boy needs is someone to put a tight rein on him. He's got ants in his pants to travel all over God's creation. A fine Tennessee girl is the only thing I know that might keep that boy here in Nashville, where he belongs."

Dylan thought a moment, then said, "Other than one little detail, I could not agree with you more, Governor Fletcher."

JJ smiled, he really was just making conversation when he asked, "And what might that one small detail be?"

Before Dylan could answer, passengers began to file from Gate 17.

Elliot took JJ by the arm and turned his attention away from the gate to face the small gathering of press. "Governor, Ms. Hooper from Channel 2 has a question." Elliot motioned at Rebecca.

"Governor Fletcher," Rebecca inquired. "Now that your son is returning from the Peace Corps, can we assume he is going to follow in the Fletcher family career of choice and jump right into politics?"

"My grandma Hazel, God rest her soul, always said..." JJ replied, with a good natured wink, "...an election to a Fletcher is like a pickup truck passing a yard dog, when he sees one coming, he just runs!" JJ smiled his legendary smile, then added, "But as far as Josh goes, we'll just have to wait and see."

Rebecca nodded, and continued with a more pressing inquiry, "My sources tell me that President McKenzie has contacted your office about the possibility of you replacing Don Summerfield as vice president."

JJ deflected her: "I'm here for my son. He's been gone for two long years and that's all I'm thinking abo—"

Petula interrupted, "You are absolutely right, as usual, Rebecca. President McKenzie has been in contact with our people from the moment the tragedy occurred with Vice President Summerfield, or I guess it is official now, ex–Vice President Summerfield. My son here is far too modest to boast of this well-deserved attention he's getting from the White House. But I'm his momma. I can proudly sing my son's praises for him."

"Momma," JJ said calmly, "there's no reason today can't just be about Jo—"

Elliot interrupted, "President McKenzie has mentioned a short list and we are honored to be at the top of that list." He took out a stack of glistening folders and handed them to various reporters. "Here is our latest press kit. You'll find some excellent photographs of Governor Fletcher and President McKenzie standing together in the Oval Office."

As the eager reporters sifted through the folders, glancing at the photographs, JJ slipped over and whispered to Byrdie, "I don't recall ever being in the Oval Office with Bob McKenzie?"

Byrdie leaned in. "You never actually were," she said with some dismay. "Elliot and your mother photo-shopped those pictures this morning."

JJ sighed. Elliot and Petula were deeply entrenched with the reporters now. He'd have to deal with them later. He stepped back over to Dylan to watch the passengers exiting the gate. "Hey, Dylan, I have a great idea. We're giving Josh a welcome home dinner tonight. If you don't have any plans you should come and join us. Josh would love it if you were there."

Dylan was instantly crushed. "I kind of did have plans."

"Well break them if you can. You are more than welcome. And I know Josh would love to have someone his own age there to talk to." JJ sensed Dylan's hesitation. "No press. You have my word on that," JJ said.

Dylan remembered he'd read somewhere that love was full of unspoken compromises of the heart. He hated shit-quotes like that. But he decided to compromise anyway. *For today.* "Yes sir. It would be a pleasure to join your family." Dylan quickly added, "For dinner...tonight."

JJ smiled. "That would be great. Come by the governor's mansion right after this, and bring a hearty appetite. We're serving up hot chicken, bacon and beans, and cornbread. Can't get more downhome than that for my boy."

Dylan knew that Josh was a vegetarian. Josh had apparently never mentioned that crucial dietary fact to his daddy. There were a lot of things Josh had not mentioned to his daddy. Dylan couldn't exactly blame him. For Josh, talking to his father about sensitive matters, like vegetarianism, was bound to start a heated conflict. And Josh wasn't good with conflict. Dylan imagined he'd be slipping hot chicken, and bacon and beans onto his plate when no one was looking. Luckily, he did have a hearty appetite.

Josh emerged from the gate. He had on a backpack and carried a small handbag. He looked around until he saw Dylan. Josh's face lit up as their eyes met, but the moment was quickly obliterated by the blinding flash of cameras. The crowd moved in, pushing Dylan aside.

JJ jostled to the front. He gave Josh a big hug and a spine-dislodging pat on the back.

JJ said, "Look at you, son. You're grinning like a mule eating briars. It's so good to see you."

Josh had lost sight of Dylan. He looked back at JJ. "Good to see you too, Daddy." Josh turned aside, so the cameras couldn't get a direct shot of him. "I didn't expect you, or all of them..." Josh indicated the reporters.

"Sorry, the circus out there is entirely your grandmother's doing. But as for being here to see you come home, I wasn't about to let business keep me from seeing my one and only son." JJ underscored this with another hearty slap to Josh's back.

Rebecca C. Hooper, who had elbowed her way through, enthusiastically interrupted, "Josh, welcome back to Nashville. Can you tell us what it was like way over there in...?" Rebecca was uncharacteristically lost for words. In a bluster, she looked to her notes.

"BOTSWANA!" Byrdie yelled. The loud outcry drew all the focus her way. "For crying out loud it's not that hard." Byrdie maintained her rant: "It rhymes with 'hot sauna'! It's a small, but not unheard-of, country in Southern Africa! It's easy to find on any map, or just do a Google search. If you did, you'd find an endless supply of interesting facts and probably some nice color pictures!"

"Botswana." Rebecca nodded, as she confirmed it in her notes, and looked away from the slightly wired-up little woman.

Josh said, "I am grateful to have gone...to Botswana." He winked at Byrdie. "It was such a huge honor. It was an extraordinary experience that I will never forget."

Petula turned to Elliot and whispered to him, "We can only pray he hasn't contracted malaria or become a communist."

Elliot added, "Or gotten some topless bush-woman with a bone through her nose pregnant."

"Dear God, Elliot!" Petula punched Elliot in his arm. She seized the moment. Petula thrust herself between Josh and JJ, grabbing Josh and hugging him tightly. "My little grandbaby, thank the Lord you're back on good, old US soil." She smacked him a red lipstick-imprinting kiss on the cheek. She turned arm-in-arm with Josh and JJ. Petula said to the crowd, "We couldn't be more proud of Josh over there, where-ever it was, spreading freedom and protecting all of us from the forces of evil."

Josh looked slightly bewildered. "I didn't—"

Rebecca jumped in. "Josh, can you tell us all about the night your battalion destroyed that cell of extremist rebels? It must have been terrifying. What did it feel like to take those monsters down who wanted to steal away all of our freedoms?"

Josh was totally confused. JJ and Byrdie were equally perplexed. Josh finally said, "I helped build irrigation canals and a water treatment plant."

Petula pulled Josh closer, and shook her head. "My grandson is too proud to speak candidly about his daring, heroic activities abroad. I'm certain he has signed all manner of documents that prevent him from speaking of them anyway. No more prying today. Now let's get some nice photographs of the whole family." Petula bent close to Josh's ear. "I had to tell the media something, for heaven's sakes."

"What about the truth?" Josh asked.

Petula gave Josh a little elbow jab. "Little J, the truth is like a football, you've got to kick it around sometimes to keep the game interesting."

Petula put her arms around her son and grandson, and held on tightly as cameras flashed. Josh asked, "So is there anything else I need to know? Am I scheduled to fly a mission to Mars or am I in the Winter Olympics?"

Petula said, "Don't be silly." She spoke louder now to the crowd. "That's it for today. We have a private dinner to attend for my gorgeous grandson. No press allowed. This boy needs some hearty American food inside his tummy. We can only imagine what he's been eating…in the trenches, over there."

Elliot helped separate the press from JJ, Josh and Petula. "You heard her. That's it for today," Elliot said. "Everyone got a press kit?"

Dylan, who had been watching from a safe distance, looked at the stuffed spider monkey sitting in the airport chair. He reconsidered his earlier decision to abandon the gift, ran back and grabbed it.

The entourage, separated from the press now, moved on down the corridor. Byrdie stepped next to Josh, and said, "Josh, I knew your mother very well, and she would have loved that you were in the Peace Corps. She always wanted to go to Africa."

Josh looked at Byrdie, a little surprised. "Really? I don't think anyone has ever told me that before."

Byrdie nodded confidently. "You remind me of your mother. She would be very proud of you today."

Josh smiled gratefully at Byrdie.

Dylan jogged up and joined them. He handed the stuffed monkey to Josh, who read the shirt and smiled. Josh said quietly to Dylan, "I am so sorry."

Dylan shook his head. "It's okay. They're excited to have you home, just like me." He snuck in closer and whispered, "I can share you for a while. But not too much longer."

"You deserve better," Josh said.

"You can make it up to me later." Dylan gave him a flirtatious smile. "Soldier boy."

3

Nurse Gisele Lutkenhouse said, "Hey there, Cowman, it is approaching high noon." Her voice purred like a sultry kitten: "Wake up sleepyhead."

Cowboy's eyes blinked open, drowsy from prescription medication. He saw the face of an angel. A blonde, Swedish angel.

In Cowboy and Petula's home, an upstairs bedroom had been re-arranged to accommodate a few oxygen tanks, medical monitoring devices, and a high-end hospital bed designed for the home. The bed was electronically adjustable to fine-tune its position for Cowboy's comfort. The room itself was decorated predominantly with expansive oil paintings of past and present Fletchers. Among the family portraits, were a few beloved heroes of Petula's and Cowboy's; George Washington, Abraham Lincoln, and Ronald Reagan. There were also mounted heads, and full bodies, of various wild animals that Cowboy and Petula had tracked and killed on their numerous hunting excursions together.

Gisele Lutkenhouse, RN, was bending over Cowboy's bed. She had the face, body, and bedside instincts of a Playboy Bunny.

Nurses from the Visiting Nurses Association had been exiting the Fletcher residence almost hourly over the past few days. These upset skilled-workers had met with all kinds of bite wounds. Being stroke impaired, biting was Cowboy's best and easiest recourse against his dour caretakers. Many of these women were ranting on about threats of legal action to Petula as she sent them on their way out the front door. And for the life of him, Cowboy could not understand why the profession of being a registered nurse required that a woman (and one man) be *so damn painful-to-look-at*. Cowboy had not spoken these words, of course, but had written them down on his dry erase board several times for Petula to read. So when Nurse Gisele Lutkenhouse walked into the Fletchers' lives just yesterday morning, it had not happened a moment too soon.

Gisele had gotten lost on her way to the Fletcher home. "I had to use my spirit helpers to guide me to your house, and sometimes I misunderstand their psychic symbols." That had been Nurse Gisele Lutkenhouse's explanation to Petula for being fifteen minutes late. Petula, reasonably, was ready to slam the door on the new nurse, and call the VNA and demand an explanation. And suggest they get GPS devices for their nurses. But Petula stopped herself. She took a second look. The luminous Scandinavian face, the platinum blonde hair, the nurse's outfit. *It must have been professionally altered to make space for her curvaceous figure*, Petula thought. And that sultry voice with the Swedish accent. It was if this woman had stepped out of a movie from the fifties starring Elvis Presley, or Dean Martin. This second look gave Petula pause.

Petula had been happy enough with the other nurses. They looked like nurses - nurses that came from Eastern European countries, with pale, sullen faces ready for tedious nurse-related duties. Cowboy, on the other hand, had been very unhappy with these women (and that one man who sweated profusely, had ghoulish eyes, and even gave Petula the creeps). The Fletcher family attorney had told Petula she better quickly find someone Cowboy liked, and moreover, someone he would not sink his teeth into, or they could be tied up in brutal legal proceedings from the Nurses' Union for the next several decades.

Petula stepped back. She kindly invited Nurse Lutkenhouse inside. "Well, I am just glad you finally found us," Petula said to the woman in the eye-popping white uniform. "Come on in out of that dreadful chill."

Petula didn't even bother to look at Nurse Lutkenhouse's references. Petula asked the nurse only one simple question: "Do you have any compelling affinity for brussels sprouts?"

Nurse Lutkenhouse did not.

Nurse Lutkenhouse wiped the corners of Cowboy's mouth with a warm wet towel. "You have two visitors who have just popped in to see you."

Cowboy reached for her breasts. Nurse Lutkenhouse pushed his hand back down. "No, Cowboy. Are you having that dream again where the Titanic is sinking and you think I am your life preserver?"

She said it with her engaging Swedish cadence. She shook her head. "It is your son, and your grandson back from his travels abroad."

JJ and Josh watched from Cowboy's bedside, amazed. Nurse Lutkenhouse straightened Cowboy's pajamas, brushed his hair back, and raised his bed. And it was all in one seamless, and inexplicably erotic, move. Josh was holding a large African mask.

"I will be right over here," Nurse Lutkenhouse said to JJ and Josh, pointing to a chair and table with pill bottles on it. "Cowboy doesn't like for me to get out of his line of vision. He suffers from Separation Anxiety Syndrome, or SAS. He has the Salzburg version which can be very traumatic for patients."

"I didn't realize that," JJ said.

"Psychology was my field of study in my early schooling in Stockholm," Gisele explained. "I thought to make it my focus of study when I was at Oxford. But my father beat into my head rocket scientist, rocket scientist, rocket scientist. So that is what I did. To please my father. But a life in a small laboratory puzzling over chemical formulas and engineering problems, and writing papers for scientific journals had too few rewards." Gisele looked up to the heavens. "Sorry, Daddy. I came to America to pursue my dream of becoming a nurse."

Josh smiled and said, "Well it is a pleasure to meet you Nurse Lutkenhouse. I hope Grandpa hasn't been too much of a handful."

"He is an angel," she said, looking at Cowboy. "I will just be organizing his medications for tomorrow if you need anything."

Nurse Lutkenhouse stepped over to sit at the table. She began to sort through prescription bottles. JJ and Josh watched a moment. Even when she counted pills her body did a little bewitching dance. It *was* mesmerizing. JJ and Josh finally turned back to Cowboy.

"Hi, Grandpa," Josh said.

Cowboy wrote on a dry erase board:
HELLO LITTLE J

"I brought you a gift from Africa." Josh held up the mask. "I thought it might look good with all your animal bodies and heads. The man I bought it from told me an interesting story about it." Cowboy listened intently, as Josh continued, "There was a tribe cursed for many years by a witch doctor from the neighboring tribal clan. Because of the curse, their hunting was futile, the rain stopped, and - the translation is a little off, but the best I could tell - the men in the tribe couldn't get it up anymore." Cowboy nodded, knowingly. Josh went on, "Then a shaman from their tribe carved this mask and placed it at the edge of the village. From that day forward the curse was lifted. The hunts were abundant, it rained again, and the young women were all soon happily giving birth to new babies. The man who gave it to me said the mask had an enchantment placed on it that forced evil spirits to flee in horror."

Cowboy motioned his hand for Josh to bring the mask closer. Josh let him examine it. Cowboy nodded with appreciation, then wrote:

LOOKS LIKE WILLIE NELSON

JJ and Josh both laughed.

Josh said, "I hadn't noticed, but I think maybe so."

JJ said, "I have to agree with Josh. I think it would go with the other things you got in this room, Daddy. And if it frightens off evil spirits, we could probably use some of that."

Nurse Lutkenhouse got up and walked over to look at the mask. "Do you mind if I put it up. I really like it." She looked at Cowboy who was non-committal, then nodded.

Nurse Lutkenhouse took the mask from Josh and held it up to examine it more closely.

Petula propelled through the bedroom door with a handful of get well cards in her hands. "Cowboy, I've sorted through your get well cards again and I've thrown out all the ones who I knew really didn't mean…"

Petula stopped cold, seeing the mask. She lurched back in horror.

"What in God's name?" Petula yelled out. The cards in her hands went flying. "That thing is ghastly! Why did you bring that terrible thing into this house?"

JJ pondered the implications as Petula backed away from the mask, holding her hands in front of her face.

JJ said, "That mask really works!"

All eyes turned to Cowboy who was writing on the board again. He wrote:

HANG IT UP PLEASE!

JJ and Josh nodded. Nurse Lutkenhouse respectfully moved the mask from Petula's sight around the side of the bed.

Petula stepped back up to the bed and read the words Cowboy had written. She figured she was the butt of some inside joke. "You Fletcher men," Petula said, as she shook her head, regaining her composure. "Always playing games. If all your nonsense isn't the why and wherefore of me going to my final reward, it won't be from lack of trying."

"Grandma," Josh said lovingly, "you know we wouldn't know what to do if you weren't around." Josh reached over and put his arm around her shoulder.

"Well," Petula conveyed proudly, "finally one of you Fletcher boys has come around to the truth."

4

The meeting room of *The Nashville Sun* was tinged with gray from years of no one taking the time to dust the place. Stale cigarette smoke saturated the air. The fluorescent lights above the small group hummed unsteadily.

Seated around an office table were Buster Ragsdale, *The Nashville Sun* owner; Alice Wexler, editor-in-chief; Ben Espinoza, head investigative reporter; head of legal, Rhonda Tollefson; and a timid, noticeably younger girl, Amelia Howard, a freelance photographer.

Buster was a calming presence in this otherwise tense group. He was a man in his seventies with the kind of good looks that summoned up images of a stalwart sheriff from an old TV Western.

Buster had been a printer's assistant at the age of seventeen for *The Knoxville Chronicle*. Shortly after that, he acquired a job with *The Tennessean* (known at that time as *The Nashville Tennessean*) where he became an editor in three years. After having a difference in opinion with the editorial staff, he left in 1982 and founded *The Nashville Sun*, a weekly newspaper. Although the readership of *The Nashville Sun* had seen growth every year, it never had been any kind of real competition for the hugely successful *Tennessean*. That had been okay with Buster. He liked his paper the way it was; small and easy to manage. It was the kind of paper that never had to abandon its moral integrity. And he had been able to keep most of his staff with him, all the way from the day the paper printed its first edition.

Amelia Howard, the odd-one-out in this group, sat quietly back from the table. She was young, but was already a noteworthy Nashville photographer who had won several awards for her photographs. Her strikingly beautiful images had gotten attention from many local Country Western singers. This attention was, indirectly, why she was here today.

"You can come closer, little lady," Alice said to Amelia. "We don't bite."

Ben countered, "I'd say that's being economical with the truth. We're about to ruin this girl's life."

Amelia pulled her chair up to the table. She knew where this was likely going, and she had already made up her mind about what she was going to do. But she respectfully waited.

Rhonda spelled it out: "There will be lawsuits. You will be summoned, and most likely you will be named in these suits. The media, in all of its forms, will ambush your quiet apartment. Your whole life will be subjected to their scrutiny, which is rarely fair or impartial. This is a powerful, well-loved family. Two of them, actually. You won't be popular in Tennessee. And that is understating it on all levels."

"I'm okay with all that," Amelia said. She had analyzed what she was about to say for days. "I know I am betraying a very dear friend. I'm not proud of that. I doubt I will ever feel less guilty about that part." She gained some confidence and leaned closer to the table. "But my guilt, or my personal popularity, are not what really matter to me. I believe a lot of people, who may be having trouble accepting who they are, could benefit from hearing about this. People I will never know. I'm doing it for them...And I don't hate many things, but I hate hypocrisy. If the governor knows about this, then he is a hypocrite. If he doesn't, then, I guess he'll have to prove he isn't. I have many friends who are gay. They don't have the same rights as

I do. That is, in part, because of our present governor. If you do choose to run this story, I believe we'll all get to find out what kind of man our governor really is."

"If you want to help people you should have gone to *The Tennessean*," Ben said. "They have a hell of a lot bigger circulation than our little dog and pony show here."

"I did," Amelia said. "I'm here. So I suppose that's all you need to know about what they told me."

Alice waved Ben off. "It was brave of you to come to us. To *anyone* with this kind of story. We figured you'd tried them first."

Rhonda nodded. "I checked this out thoroughly. It's all sound. The Fletchers will sue all of us, but they will lose. We have your tape here. I called the young man in question myself with the ruse that I was Amelia's assistant. It was his private number and he confirmed that he wanted to hire her as the photographer, and exactly what he wanted her to take pictures of. I feel bad for the boy. He's an innocent victim in this whole mess." She sighed. "And I've gathered more than enough other independent witnesses who will back up the rest of the story."

Ben added, "I have to say, Don Summerfield will be very grateful. We are going to push his whole Boy Scout debacle to page two."

Rhonda asked, "Do you really think this story will be that big?"

Ben nodded. "I do. These are two of the most recognized families in Tennessee. As a matter of fact, I hope Buster is prepared to triple our usual printing."

Looking at Buster, Alice said, "Buster, I am concerned for you, personally. They may never let you see Jewell, ever again. And I know how much you care about her."

Alice was referring to Jewell Whitecotton, Buster's close and – it could be argued – his best friend. He visited her at least twice a week. Jewell had no idea who he was most of the time (which was the "it could be argued" part). But Buster dropped by, with groceries and cooked her dinner. Or they'd watched movies he picked out for her (the old films that she loved and remembered from when she was younger). Some days he just sat and held her hand for hours. She often asked him to explain who he was again. "I am a dear old friend," he always replied. Even though it was sometimes heartbreaking for him, Buster returned every few days for another visit. He did this because he had been desperately in love with Jewell Fletcher Whitecotton most of his life.

He'd been in love all the way back when they were in high school together, before she left Nashville for Columbia, Missouri. She didn't know it then because he'd never been brave enough to tell her. Over the past few years, he had been brave enough, but when he returned a few days later, she appeared to not recall his confession of love for her. He learned to accept that as it was. Love was love after all.

This was the hardest decision Buster had ever made. With a word, even with all the work the people in this room had done, he could trash the whole story. And that would be the end of it. His team wouldn't be angry. It would be a completely valid reason to cut a story. The personal cost was simply going to be too large.

Alice said, "It's your newspaper, Buster. It doesn't matter one hill of beans what we think."

Buster nodded to her, grateful for her well-meaning gesture. Then, with no uncertainties or worry of consequences, he told them his decision.

No one was angry enough to speak out.
Egyptian Pyramid Inscription

FRONT PAGE NEWS

1

It was 12:45 A.M. at 4104 Hillsboro Pike in Nashville. For a week night it had been fairly active at this unassuming little nightspot. If you were from out of town, or didn't know about it, you might not even notice the music club or the unassuming blue canvas that covered the sidewalk. A small crowd, who *did* know, had congregated inside, seated at cozy tables. Some had gathered along the back walls where friendly waitresses brought them their drinks. Others had idled up to the welcoming bar.

Regulars here were music lovers and had come to hear singers premier their newborn songs, or maybe discover a fresh talent. During the show, one had to keep their talking low, or even better, just listen quietly, because at The Bluebird Café it was all about the music.

* * *

Inside the Bluebird Café patrons passed along walls where framed photographs of "The Greats", standard and contemporary Country Western stars, covered the walls from ceiling to floor. Josh Fletcher wound his way through the crowd until he could get a clear view of the snug, intimate stage. Dylan was seated on a single wooden chair strumming a guitar. He was accompanied by a piano player, Rusty

Olsen, a man with thick red hair and a beard that brought to mind a brawny lion.

As Dylan was playing the guitar, he was singing a Country Blues number that was soulful and sweet. The crowd was listening intently and tapping along. It was a new song Dylan wrote only three weeks ago, and he was trying it out on the seasoned Bluebird Café crowd. From the looks on their faces, it could well be on its way to becoming a big hit.

Dylan saw Josh, and gave him a devilish smile and wink. Josh was feeling truly happy to be home again with Dylan close at hand. As adventurous as his heart was, wanting to explore the whole world and absorb all the mosaic cultures it had to offer, it was becoming evident that when it came to Dylan, his heart was ready to throw all those dreams aside. It seemed that everything his young heart had been seeking out in the world was being supplanted by what existed entirely inside just a single man. As Josh watched Dylan singing on stage, he resigned with pleasure. To fight it would be nothing less than fool-hearted. There's just no denying one of the most fundamental facts about being human. Love changes everything.

Josh stepped over to the bar. A slender girl in a blue cowboy hat behind the bar asked, "What you having?"

"Guinness," Josh replied, with a friendly smile.

She nodded, and went to retrieve his request.

Josh noticed someone staring at him from the other end of the bar. He recognized the young man as one of Dylan's friends. Hispanic, head shaven, he was wearing a white dress shirt and loose tie. He remembered him being a pleasant guy, but he wasn't in a socializing frame of mind at the moment. He didn't want to be rude, so he gave the guy a friendly nod. Probably a mistake. He quickly turned away. The guy hopefully got the message he wasn't in the mood for conversation.

The bartender brought Josh his beer and he paid her, leaving a tip under the bowl of peanuts. The guy at the other end of the bar (who didn't get the message) walked up to Josh. He had a newspaper folded under his arm, and a rather grim expression on his face.

"Don't know if you remember me?"

"Sure. Glen, right?" Josh replied.

Glen nodded. Josh wasn't comfortable with the look this guy was giving him. He wished he'd not given him the friendly nod.

"You know I work for *The Nashville Sun*?" Glen asked.

"I think I remember that," Josh lied. He thought Glen was a musician, or at least in the music business in some way. That was because most of the people Dylan knew were in the business.

"I was wondering if I could talk to you." Glen pulled out a small recorder. Josh turned cold.

"It's one o'clock in the morning, you can talk all you want, but I'm not likely to hear much of what you're saying. Not with that on." Josh turned his shoulder to Glen and looked back to the stage. He hated the press.

"I'm guessing you have no idea?" Glen was now speaking in a consoling voice. Probably a ploy. It wasn't going to work.

"Is it too much to ask that I just enjoy the music?" Josh asked. "And hasn't your paper already gone to press anyway?"

"Yes, it has," Glen replied. "What the hell am I doing?" Glen turned off the tape recorder, and placed it back in his pocket. "The paper's already got their story. You don't need some jackass like me prying for more details. I had the misguided belief there might be something you'd want to talk about. But with your daddy being who he is and all, that was a pretty dumb-ass idea."

Josh ignored the guy, wishing he'd get the hint and leave.

Glen did not leave. He first established that no one but Josh was close enough to pay any attention, then he pulled out the newspaper from under his arm, and laid it flat on the bar.

Reluctantly, Josh looked over to the top of the bar. First he saw the recognizable *Nashville Sun* logo across the top of the paper, then his eyes drifted down to the large photographs of two very recognizable people. At first he was not entirely surprised. His daddy and Dylan's momma had graced the front page of not only *The Nashville Sun*, but *The Tennessean*, and many newspapers all across the country. In Dylan's momma's case, newspapers and tabloids all over the world had her face on the cover at one time or the other.

Josh read the headline, and his stomach clinched. He dropped his beer down on the bar, hard enough to splash some of the brown drink out onto the newspaper. The giant black letters of the newspaper headline could not really be what he first thought. *It can't be.* He turned around and grabbed the bar for support as he read the headline again. The words swirled like they were reflected in a swaying carnival mirror.

"This hasn't left the printer's building yet," Glen said, attempting to reassure Josh. He was becoming concerned Josh might pass out, or puke, right there on the bar. "But it will in about two hours. I wanted to let you guys know before anyone else got their morning copy. That's what I came here to do. I'm sorry I tried to get a personal scoop. It's not in me to do that to people, which is probably why I'm still a junior editor."

Josh turned to look at Glen, and pulled the newspaper from the bar.

"How did your paper get this story?" Josh asked.

Glen gave a head nod toward Dylan. "A photo chic, some friend of his." Glen shrugged. "Well she's not a friend, if you ask me."

Josh didn't need any more of this guy, even if he was doing them a favor. Josh rolled the newspaper into his fist, and pushed his way through the narrow crowd to the stage. His legs were heavy, like they were packed with lead.

Dylan looked over at Josh arriving at the edge of the stage, his face doused in beads of sweat. Josh's lips were shaking. Dylan felt a chill. He stopped strumming his guitar. Finally Josh managed to articulate words. They were kind of like words anyway.

"I...nee–neeeed...yuuyou."

2

A towering stone arch with a majestic cast iron ornamental gate blockaded the main entrance to Stardust Ranch. The gate was locked, and security equipment installed by Rhashan himself, monitored any unusual movements throughout the entire property. A high stone wall surrounded the perimeter and two other security gates at the East and South entries to the property were all securely closed.

The many hidden cameras placed throughout the ranch observed the nocturnal creatures who were up to their nightly routines. Coyotes ran yelping and howling (there was a tunnel under the stone wall that Rhashan had not been able to locate yet to keep the noisy pack-animals out). The various dogs who lived on the property endlessly barked at roughly fifteen minute intervals at any movement or sound. The cats pounced on unsuspecting mice, moles, and the occasional bat. Chickens slept safely in their coops. Rhashan's coyote and fox-proof enclosure had been a great success since last year's massacre when Kitty lost all twenty eight of her prize-winning Cochin China chickens to foxes. The horses and alpacas were all quiet in the tremendous barn standing near the property's natural creek (on maps identified as Hornbuckle Brook). Three other barns were on the property as well. The largest one was reserved for parties and special events. Kitty had the ranch designers use indigenous stones found on the estate to build the barns, as well as the entry gates and the high wall that surrounded the 160 acres.

The main house, a three story, rustic, Southern mansion, also built of stone, stood resplendently atop the highest point of the property surrounded by cherry trees and grand magnolias.

Someone entered a security code into the main entry key pad. The cast iron gate swung silently open.

* * *

In the upstairs hallway of the mansion there was movement. Two shadowy figures made their way down the corridor until they reached a solid oak door at the end. One of the figures opened the door. The intruders were met with a ferocious affront. A Maltese puppy, about the size of two snowballs, barked and spun in a white, furry tornado. This frenzied dance of defense was intended to inspire unparalleled fear in its victims.

It did not.

Kitty Stardust was completely unaware that her pet Maltese was attempting to protect her from intruders. She was sound asleep in her luxurious king sized canopy bed, wearing a sleeping mask and noise-eliminating earplugs.

Kitty had arrived home hours earlier from her charity event, the Critters-In-Crisis Run, which had left her exhausted. She had drank a sleep inducing and muscle pain relieving tea called *Relax and Dream Tea*, that Rhashan had purchased from a health food store. The tea worked. The aches and pains had dissolved. After she had her nightly guilty pleasure of a Goo Goo Cluster and a glass of whole milk, Kitty had fallen into a restful sleep.

"Momma," Dylan said. "Wake up." He turned on a lamp sitting on her nightstand and reached for Kitty's shoulder. He tapped lightly.

Kitty propelled straight up, still wearing her mask and earplugs. Rhashan had trained Kitty exactly what to do in urgent situations such as this. She reached under the edge of her mattress, knowing precisely where to grab. Out she pulled a Ruger LCP 380 pistol. She quickly snapped off the safety, and gripped both hands securely on the weapon. Her arms were rigid.

Dylan and Josh reeled back, and ducked down.

"This gun is loaded. I am a trained marksman. You've been warned." Kitty couldn't see or hear anything. She pointed the gun in every direction.

"MOMMA!" Dylan yelled.

Kitty twisted. She removed her earplugs. Her hands were expertly back on the gun in a half second. The little dog continued barking and spinning.

"Peggy Sue?" She listened carefully. "Run Peggy Sue. Go get help! I think someone is in the room." The puppy, not trained to do anything, just kept yelping.

"Jesus, Momma, would you put away that pistol before you kill us all!" Dylan yelled over the dog's frantic racket.

"Dylan?" Kitty removed her sleeping mask.

Kitty saw Dylan, and lowered the handgun. Peggy Sue jumped up on the bed into Kitty's arms, and stopped barking.

"Look who I brought with me," Dylan said, beaming, with his arm around Josh's shoulder. Kitty saw Josh. She was reduced to pure rapture, her face gushed into a big smile.

"Miss Kitty, could I trouble you for an autograph?" Josh smiled back.

"Hot damn, you better give me a hug."

Kitty, still brandishing her handgun, hugged Josh around his neck. She let him loose and looked at his face, then back to Dylan. Peggy Sue, feeling things were apparently safe now, went to curl at Kitty's feet and watch.

"Oh, I am so happy to see you boys," Kitty said.

"Put away the gun," Dylan said. "Then I'll hug you."

"Oh, yeah." Kitty pushed the safety back in position, and put the pistol on her bedside table. She looked back at Josh. "By Jiminy, I know for a fact I'm going to cry. Wrap those arms around me again."

Josh hugged Kitty again. Dylan joined in for a hug too.

"Sit down here, rest your buns, and tell me all about what has happened the past six months." Kitty thought quickly. "Aren't you home early?"

Josh nodded. He sat on the bed next to Kitty, while Dylan continued to stand. Josh said, "Grandpa Cowboy was in the hospital."

"Oh, I heard about that. Is he okay?" Kitty asked.

"He's back home. He has to have a wheelchair. He still drinks as much whiskey as he wants and smokes his cigars. So, he's doing alright."

Kitty nodded, then suddenly remembered something. She grabbed a picture from her night table. "Look what I did." Kitty showed them a framed picture of Josh, Dylan, Kasia, Mosi, and Kitty in Botswana. Next to Kitty in the photo was an African Warrior in full costume, a colorful display of feathers and face paint.

"I had your picture framed and every night I'd say a little prayer for you and your friends. How is Chief Zimbulu?" Kitty looked to Josh.

"He's fine," Josh said. "But he wouldn't give up on his plan to make you his wife. I explained to him that you being the Queen of

Country did not mean you were the queen of an actual country. But he didn't believe me. He was very upset you never came back."

"Oh, I hope he wasn't too disappointed. I did kind of lead Chief Zimbulu on. You know how I love to flirt."

Kitty saw that Josh and Dylan were concerned about something. "What's going on? You two look like a couple of polecats trapped in a bear trap."

Josh had the newspaper rolled up in his back pocket. He took it out. "*The Nashville Sun* got ahold of this story. I guess they feel like anything, or anyone, is fair game when it comes to Daddy," Josh said.

"Or you, Momma," Dylan added, then explained, "It's my damn fault. I confided in someone I knew from high school, a photographer I wanted to hire. I thought I could trust her. I guess you can't trust anybody. A guy I know came into The Bluebird and gave us this advance copy."

"You're involved," Josh said to Kitty.

Kitty shook her head. "Don't worry about what those half-cracked, hanky panky newspapers say," Kitty tried to assure them wistfully. "I only sue them if they print the lies on the back page instead of the front page where folks can see them."

"Well, we got the front page." Josh handed the newspaper to Kitty. She quickly read over the headline.

She pulled herself up in bed. "Is this true?" Kitty turned the newspaper out for them to see, as if they hadn't already read it several times. The headline that hovered over the adjacent photographs of Kitty and JJ Fletcher read:

SECRET WEDDING:
THE GOVERNOR'S AND KITTY'S
GAY SONS TO BE MARRIED

The rest of the story described Josh and Dylan having secret plans to marry each other the following Sunday. It also mentioned the fact that Governor JJ Fletcher signed into law a ban on same-sex marriage just two years previously. Kitty quickly glanced it over. But her mind was swirling and she couldn't even begin to focus.

"My baby boy is getting married," Kitty exclaimed, suddenly irate at Dylan. "And why am I, the mother of one of the grooms, reading about this news in some squirrelly newspaper?"

"That one is my fault," Josh explained. "I made Dylan wait until I got home from Africa. We thought it would be nice to tell you in person." Josh frowned. "This is not what I had in mind."

Kitty softened. "Well, okay then. But Dylan, you are my one and only child, and you know I have always told you what I wanted."

Dylan said, "I know, Momma. You never had your own big wedding, so Josh and I are planning on you overseeing the entire event."

"No one else could do it right," Josh said.

"That's damn right," Kitty agreed. She took Dylan's hand. "The day I married your daddy was not my finest hour, by any stretch of the imagination." Kitty suddenly welled up with tears ready to flow.

"I know Momma." Dylan had heard the story many times. "You were six months pregnant with me, and Daddy was so pig-eyed drunk he vomited on the feet of the Justice of the Peace. There's no need to get into all that right now. And please don't cry."

"That's right." Kitty blinked back the salt water in her eyes. "And your daddy knocked over the candles and set fire to the courthouse drapes. I never had a proper wedding."

Josh said, "Well, we aren't giving you a whole lot of time."

"That's my fault too," Dylan said. "My band's touring schedule kind of locks us into this coming weekend. We were planning on Sunday."

"I have an interview with that cute-as-a-button Jian Ghomeshi up in Toronto on Sunday. I'll need to reschedule that. He'll understand. And by that time I guess there'll be lots more to talk about." Kitty brightened up. Her mind had already begun to picture the wedding plans. "Don't you boys worry about a thing. I do my best work under pressure." Her voice was racing with excitement: "I won a song writing competition against Brad Paisley at the Nashville Fan Fair where I wrote 'My Tear Stained Pillow' in less than seven minutes. It went on to be number one here for sixteen weeks. In Japan it was number one for twenty two. Those Japanese folks just love my sad love songs."

"Momma," Dylan said. "There is one thing."

Kitty had a sudden realization. "You need me to write a song for the ceremony?"

"Momma!" Dylan shook his head.

"What is it, Darlin'?" Kitty asked.

Josh explained. "Daddy doesn't know."

"JJ doesn't know?" Kitty questioned, then added, "How much does he not know?"

Josh sighed. "Unfortunately, about me, a lot. He's so impossible to talk to. You practically have to schedule an appointment." Kitty nodded, as Josh continued, "Daddy has these narrow ideas of what it means to be a man. I've tried to tell him a few times, but once I was in the room with him I couldn't do it. I've never had the guts to even tell him I'm vegetarian."

"I understand completely," Kitty said. "I've dealt with your daddy more than a few times myself."

Dylan chimed in, "Which is why we're here. We want you to talk to him."

"Me?" Kitty was alarmed, and slightly confused.

"We thought you could break it to him gently," Dylan said. "Since you two have a past together, maybe he'd take it better coming from you."

"Oh Lordy, not from me. He won't take anything better coming from me?"

Dylan pushed in and sat on the bed next to Josh, taking his hand. Dylan looked expectantly into Kitty's eyes. "You're my momma, and you love me, and you understand how hard it must be for a parent to accept that their son, who instead of everything they ever dreamed of and hoped for, is gay."

Kitty started to tear up again. "You know I don't feel that way anymore. And you know I never really did?" She loved Dylan more than anything in the world. It shamed her to admit it now, but he was right. It was more than a small shock for her when he came to her on his sixteenth birthday with the news. She had told Dylan to go to his room and pray. Then she went to her room and cried.

After Dylan had come out, Kitty immediately read every book written on the subject and spoke to a few therapists, and she prayed a lot too. After her whirlwind self-education, she slightly overcompensated (as far as Dylan was concerned). She joined PFLAG and marched in Washington, D.C. In a particularly embarrassing period of time for Dylan, she wrote a song about the joy of being the mother of her gay son. After the song, which (thankfully, for Dylan) got almost no airplay, he made her promise to tone it down a little.

Kitty often imagined how her son must feel growing up in a world where perfect strangers said such hateful things about him. It made her angry and sad. Kitty did quit singing the admittedly corny song, but never stopped speaking out for gay rights whenever she could.

"So, will you do it, Momma?" Dylan asked.

"JJ Fletcher..." she said with great dismay in her voice. "There are only two reasons I would ever conceive of doing something like this, and I'm sitting here looking at both of them."

"Thank you." Josh was visibly relieved.

Kitty asked, "So where is your daddy right now?"

"Home," Josh replied. "At the governor's mansion. I talked to Byrdie. She has turned off all the phones and won't let anyone see him. She said he gets up for his morning swim at 5:00 A.M. I'll call her on her personal cell and tell her you're coming."

"Okay, boys. I can't go unarmed," Kitty said.

"No guns!" Dylan shot back emphatically, holding up his hands.

Kitty shook her head. "JJ is a typical straight man, and I know all of his weaknesses," she said with a confident nod. "No rational infantryman goes into hostile territory without proper fighting gear. I'm talking about my clothes closet and my makeup kit."

Josh and Dylan nodded. Anyone who knew Kitty Stardust knew one thing for certain; besides singing and songwriting - clothes, hair, and makeup were her other specialized fields of study.

A true friend stabs you in the front.
　　- Oscar Wilde

TROUBLED WATERS

1

The governor's mansion was covered in the misty darkness of early morning. Agent Noah Applegarth stood at the front door on watch for any unusual activities. Sometimes he swore he could see the silhouette of a pig just inside a shadow, or hiding around a corner, and his heart would skip a beat. Thankfully, it always turned out to be his imagination.

Byrdie had spoken to Noah a few minutes earlier. She had asked him to turn everyone away from the governor's mansion, except one person. Noah worried briefly that he could lose his job. He wasn't supposed to take orders from a personal assistant. But he liked Byrdie, and she promised him she would take the fall if anything went badly. He was a big fan of Kitty Stardust anyway. He was excited to have the chance to get to meet her.

* * *

In the back section of the governor's mansion, an enclosed area housed a heated swimming pool. JJ Fletcher was doing his morning laps at a brisk pace, the glimmering blue water illuminating his fluid, graceful strokes from below.

He saw a flash of red through his swim goggles and stopped mid-lap. JJ lifted up the goggles and cleared the water from his eyes. He saw a pair of red, high-heel cowboy boots strutting toward him from the den doorway. He rubbed his eyes again, and pulled himself to the side of the pool to get a better look.

Kitty's outfit was red-hot. She knew how to dress to make most anyone go weak in his knees, but she had more insight into JJ Fletcher than any other person. She knew exactly what to wear to grab his attention, and hopefully, as she had promised the boys, lull him into a quick surrender. There was a very good chance the plan would work flawlessly. She was a delicious, sparkling temptress and, as anticipated, JJ Fletcher was swallowing the bait, hook, line and sinker.

The vigorous smile on JJ's face was not returned. Kitty inexplicably had a look of pre-determined contempt on her otherwise beguiling face. She was clinching tightly to a newspaper in her hand, and appeared to be consumed with some purpose. None of that registered deeply with JJ. He felt like Lady Luck had just walked into his pool-house.

"Well bless my eternal soul," JJ said.

"Don't worry, your cute Secret Service agent, with the puppy dog eyes, already frisked me for a gun."

"Why would I be worried?" JJ asked, with a sportive grin. "I might be a little jealous, though."

Kitty glared down at him in the water. Her grip on the newspaper grew tighter.

Byrdie was standing at the den window that looked out over the pool watching Kitty and JJ. She made the sign of the cross. Her Italian father was a devout Catholic and she had learned to do this in times of impending disaster.

JJ noticed Byrdie. *She's here awfully early,* he thought. *That probably means I'm going to have a busy day.*

JJ stepped out of the pool and grabbed a towel. Kitty could not help but steal a look. She noted a little aging in his face. Likely, too much sun. But the body still seemed to be in more than satisfactory condition. A quick second glance made her sigh. Old feelings whipped through her mind and body. New feelings were making themselves known as well. And those bright yellow Speedo racing briefs JJ was wearing left little to the imagination. The suffocating feelings suddenly made her rife with fear and her impulse was to turn and run. But she didn't. She had made a promise after all.

Kitty said, "You may be getting the wrong idea of why I'm here." She forced her glance away, musing it over. "And in all likelihood, I probably didn't think this all the way through myself." She looked back at JJ. "I have come here today on someone else's behalf."

"Okay. Sounds intriguing. Can I have Byrdie get you something? She makes a great chai tea that the staff can't get enough of."

"I'm not going to be that long," Kitty said, a little frosty.

JJ was disappointed at the chilly tone, but he disguised his feelings with a confident toss of his towel. He plopped down in a pool chair, his legs dropped open, and he leaned back with the bravado of a knight who had just slain a dragon.

Kitty, feeling a little light headed, looked around to find a chair for herself, but then reconsidered. She wanted to make this quick. That was the plan. She needed to stick to the plan. Damn her heart though, it was racing. And her mind was dashing along at a ridiculous pace too. She couldn't stop herself from looking at JJ. She could remember him slipping his arm around her waist; the soothing, warm feeling of his husky, bare chest next to hers; her fingers running through his silky blond hair; his lips unyielding, firm, running from her mouth, down her neck. Down and down. His hands reaching, pulling her closer, and closer and clo—

STOP! Lord help you, stop! She shook it off. She thought of slapping her own face or jumping into the pool to cool herself down. She looked up, then closed her eyes and inhaled deeply. After a third breath she was feeling more under control.

"I'm glad to hear your daddy is doing better," Kitty said, doubtlessly to clear her head and buy some time.

"Cantankerous as ever," JJ replied, looking her over curiously. He could tell she was struggling with something, *and he liked it.* "I'm just dying to know what the hell you are doing here. It's been a long time. Have a seat."

Kitty shook her head. "I promised Josh and Dylan I would do this, but let's be clear from the start how I feel coming and talking to you today. Honestly, I'd rather be riding a wild bull with a porcupine tied to my ass." She didn't smile.

"H'mm." JJ took that in. "So you've seen Josh? Hasn't he turned out to be one hell of a great young man? Both of our boys have."

"Yes, they have," Kitty replied. She looked at the newspaper in her hand. "Damn, there's no easy way to say this. I came here to tell you that Josh is getting married this coming Sunday."

"Married?"

"Married."

"Josh, my son?"

"Yes, Josh, your son."

"As far as I know he doesn't even have a steady girlfriend. And why on earth would he send you, of all people, to tell me he was getting married?"

JJ's slightly smug tone at the end of that comment didn't sit well with Kitty.

"You know, I didn't realize how angry I still am, but I underestimated myself," Kitty said, having to steady herself. "Our past is the past. It's dead and gone. I'm here for Josh. So I need for you to listen."

"You know, Kitty, if it will make you feel more at ease, I am feeling exactly the same way. I've missed you too."

"I didn't say I missed you." Kitty's temper began to flare, but then she deliberately calmed her voice. "I've told you that your son is getting married. And well...he's getting married to my son, Dylan. Do the math. That means he's gay," Kitty said, realizing the words came out more abrupt than she intended. "Well, they're both gay. Which is not a problem for me, and given some time I'm sure you will warm up to it too. There, I've said it. That wasn't so hard. The wedding is this coming Sunday at four, but of course you can come early. Bring a guest. Now you can get back in the pool and finish your laps." Kitty quickly turned and began to walk briskly toward the den door, then suddenly remembered something. "Oh, and it's at Stardust Ranch." Kitty didn't anticipate what she saw next as she turned back. JJ's face was contorted into a blur of confusion. Some angry exasperation was in there too. It disarmed her a bit, but she didn't want to hear what he had to say, so she spoke very quickly. "They've asked that in lieu of gifts, donations be made to my Critters-In-Crisis charity. I'm willing to pay for the whole event, but if you want to pitch in that would be a very nice gesture. See you Sunday." She practically tripped over her boots as she scurried away from the pool.

"Hey, not so fast!" JJ sat up in the pool chair. "Turn back around and repeat what you just said!"

Kitty stopped.

"Kitty!" JJ called out to her. He sounded contentious, and distressingly bewildered.

She tried to justify continuing on through the door. She knew that Josh and Dylan had much more in mind when they asked her to come and talk to JJ. She had only confused him, and probably would be leaving him extremely upset. She had to at least try. She turned back to face him. "Josh and Dylan are getting married. Marriage has never been an easy concept for you, JJ, but luckily for my son, your son Josh doesn't have the same problem with the idea as you."

"So, this is about us?" JJ nodded, self-satisfied.

Kitty let him indulge in his pretentiousness for a moment. "I'm sorry I alluded to the past. My mistake." Kitty stepped closer to JJ. She clarified, "You just need to know that Josh and Dylan are in love with each other. They thought it would be nice to have some family and friends come together for a private little ceremony. That's all." She nodded in a fruitless attempt to get him to say he understood.

"They thought what?"

"All they want is what anybody else who is madly in love wants, JJ. They want an old fashioned wedding to show off what they've got for each other. Contrary to what people might say around here, it's not a new concept."

"Is this a joke?" JJ looked around. "Channel 2 has that hidden camera show on me again, don't they? Last time the camera was hidden in a potted plant."

Kitty shook her head. "It's not a joke, JJ. You've been kept in the dark..." Kitty pulled up a chair and sat near him, close enough to smell the light sweat and drying pool water emanating from his body. "...and for good reason, I suppose. Although, if you could have shifted your focus off fund raising dinners and kissing all the babies in Tennessee for one second, you might have noticed that your son and my son have been wearing matching rings on their fingers for more than three years now."

JJ looked lost in the wilderness. He clearly had never noticed.

Kitty continued, "Not to mention they have each other's names tattooed on their butt cheeks."

"My son is not..." JJ stumbled over his words. "I don't even know what you're saying. It's so ludicrous I can't even say it."

"Gay?"

"Yes! He is not that!"

"That?"

"That," JJ repeated. This time he had a sneering look on his face like the word had a repellent taste to it.

Kitty stood up. "*That* is my son you're speaking of as well." Her eyes glared, black as ink. "And you know what. I don't need your imbecilic approval, and neither does my son!"

"Well, the only person I'm talking about right now is *my* son. And Josh is not... whatever." This whole conversation was making him angry now too.

"Alright, Josh's and Dylan's wedding is this Sunday, as I mentioned, at Stardust Ranch, come and decide for yourself."

"Don't go planning any weddings. There's not going to be any wedding. I'm his father, not to mention the governor of this state. Nobody's getting married unless I say so."

"Really?" Kitty shrugged incredulously. "Well, there's going to be spectacular food, lots of beautiful flowers, a reverend, a harp player, a champagne fountain, a magical display of candlelight, a lovely exchange of vows and gold rings, followed by an awe-inspiring release of white doves. That sounds like a cotton picking wedding to me!"

Kitty strutted off. JJ jumped up from the pool chair and followed her.

"What reverend? You're not making any sense. My son would never get involved with some harebrained scheme like the one you're describing."

"You're an idiot!" Kitty said. "And I'm an idiot for thinking you'd be any other way." She turned to JJ. "You must have known Dylan was gay. Didn't you hear my song, 'This Momma's Proud'? It was on the radio."

JJ searched his mind. "I must have missed it."

Kitty replied, "Well I sang and released a record of it, and I am proud. They just didn't play the song very much locally, apparently." She sighed.

Kitty shrugged. Then she walked on, as JJ paced her.

"Wait Kitty," JJ said. "Just stop with all the crazy stories, and tell me what you really came here to tell me."

JJ reached out to take her hand. She stopped, and pulled away.

"You think I came here to tell you anything other than what I've already just said?" Kitty asked.

"You still have feelings for me, and I still have feelings for you." JJ smiled.

"JJ, you are not listening. This is not about us."

"If you wanted to see me, all you needed to do is call me."

Kitty considered punching him, but then – once more – she recalled her promise to Josh and Dylan. So she took in a deep breath, ignored JJ's comment, and tried again. "JJ, your son is a grown man, but at the same time he is very frightened, and if he has ever needed a father, then that time is right now. Your son, who hasn't changed, who will always be your son, is gay. Please, don't break his heart."

"Why do you keep saying that?"

"I keep saying it because I think if I keep saying it, eventually you might actually hear it."

"Kitty, do you have any idea how sexy you are?" He reached for her again.

Kitty stepped back.

"I'm just trying to take your hand," he said.

"Well don't," Kitty said sharply.

"Okay, I'll just step a little closer. I won't touch you." JJ stepped up near her, and she turned her face away.

"Why are you doing this?" she asked. "I need to go." She tried to take another step away, but her feet wouldn't move.

JJ closed his eyes. A spicy, exotic bouquet of jasmine, vanilla and honey wafted over him from Kitty.

She still wears the same perfume.

Kitty could feel JJ beside her. She was afraid to look directly at him. His heavy workout had left a powerful musky, sweaty scent under the aroma of the clean-water from his morning's swim. The heat from JJ's body was close and warm. Too close. She began to feel woozy and vulnerable. Her pulse was increasing. She closed her eyes. She could feel his breath - *smell it* - balmy, comforting, with a roasted, thick, familiar aroma.

He still smokes Lucky Strikes.

JJ placed his hand on Kitty's thigh. Kitty could feel his breath on her neck. He whispered, "I still love you Ruth-Adele Holloway."

Suddenly, as if awakened from a bad dream, Kitty opened her eyes and turned around to face him, her strength regained.

JJ opened his eyes. He saw a face boiling with rage. He pulled back involuntarily, baffled by what he was seeing. "What's going on?" JJ said, starting to become frightened.

Kitty stepped toward JJ in determined, unrestrained steps. He matched her steps in reverse, sensing the growing fury in her eyes. She'd become a seething powerhouse. Kitty said, "I honestly thought on the drive over here that the love of your son would surely be stronger than your unbridled, self-absorbed stupidity. But nothing has changed."

JJ stepped back again, this time he plopped down in a chair next to the edge of the pool. He was genuinely frightened as he straddled the chair.

Kitty continued, "I had forgotten what a low down, snake bellied, bug farting, wart on a hog's ass you really are." Kitty jammed her cowboy boot directly between JJ's legs. The metal chair stopped her foot from making contact with him. His spread legs left his most susceptible parts open-to-attack. What had been a burgeoning source of pride seconds before, was now laid bare, protected only by a thin layer of Lycra. He swallowed hard.

"Don't ever say those words to me again," she said. Then, with her boot, she heaved the chair with all her might. JJ catapulted backwards until he and the chair splashed into the pool.

Kitty didn't bother to watch. She took off toward the den, as JJ came thrashing to the surface.

JJ yelled, "Byrdie! Byrdie!"

Byrdie, who had been watching the embroilment unfold from safe inside the house, stepped out from the den. She passed Kitty with a quick look of concern, then she stepped up poolside.

"Yes, Governor?" Byrdie said, in a futile attempt to sound as if everything was just a matter-of-course.

"Byrdie, I want you to show Ms. Stardust the way out."

"I know my way out," Kitty yelled back.

Byrdie nodded and followed Kitty back toward the den doorway. Then Kitty suddenly stopped.

"The front door is this way," Byrdie said, hoping to keep Kitty moving along in the opposite direction of JJ. She was afraid any more interaction between them could be lethal.

Kitty ignored Byrdie, and stepped back to the swimming pool's edge. "You will not do to those boys what you did to us. If you do, or say, anything to spoil their wedding day, or their relationship, I will be back here. And then you'll have a lot more to contend with than my boot." Kitty leaned down closer to JJ. "I am carrying a gun right now. Your cute little Secret Service agent with the puppy dog eyes just couldn't find it."

"I would have Byrdie call the police and have you arrested on the spot, but I know it would just make the headlines. The last thing I need right now is to be in the headlines with a demented, sociopathic woman like you have obviously become!"

"Too late," Kitty said, suddenly remembering the newspaper clinched in her hand. She tossed the paper in the pool. It flopped down on top of the water and floated directly in front of JJ's eyes, front page and headlines displayed for him to see.

JJ read the newspaper in befuddled horror. *The Nashville Sun* headline glared back at him like a blinding, terrifying neon sign.

Kitty said, "I'm seeing that Byrdie clears your schedule for the wedding. The wedding that you're reading about now in this morning's copy of *The Nashville Sun*. Josh said he wanted his father to be there and to give him away. He has his heart completely set on it. I dressed like this to get your attention only because I thought it might help Josh. That was a mistake on my part. I hope I haven't screwed everything up for him. But after you've had some time to think about what I've told you, I hope you'll find it in your heart to give Josh what he's hoping for."

Kitty wiped her hands with finality, turned and marched back into the main house. Byrdie quickly followed after her.

* * *

Kitty stepped out the front door of the governor's mansion, fist clenched, growling under her breath. Byrdie glanced out quickly, then closed the door. The sound of the locks were clearly audible.

Noah saw Kitty, and approached her shyly. "I'm sorry to bother you, but my girlfriend would kill me if I didn't get your autograph."

Kitty, pure professional, quickly turned on her public smile. Noah searched and could only produce a pair of handcuffs and a permanent marker. He handed them to Kitty. "Can you make it out to Sally? We know every one of your records by heart, and Sally's read all your books."

Kitty signed the handcuffs. She handed them back. "There you go, Sweetie."

Noah stared at her signature, abuzz with excitement, as Kitty stomped off down the drive where her car was parked and waiting.

2

Inside the governor's mansion Byrdie carefully skipped around the puddles of water to get to the bottom of the grand marble staircase in the foyer – and braced herself.

"Byrdie!" JJ yelled down. He was near the top of the staircase, his soggy wet hair was dripping pool water onto the keypad of his cordless phone. He kept pounding the buttons in futility. In his other hand he gripped the soaking-wet newspaper.

"Damn pool water has fouled up my phone," he said to himself, then yelled again, "Byrdie!"

Byrdie continued to look up. "Yes?"

She was deeply worried he was going to confront her about why the phone was turned off. She had tried several times to turn it back on, but never got out of his line of sight. And now she was concerned that JJ was going to slip on the freshly polished marble staircase steps he was dripping water onto. He had already taken a harrowing dive just moments earlier when he tripped over a lounge chair as he made his way out of the swimming pool. He wasn't badly hurt. Just a cut on the shoulder and a nasty scrape on his knee from the looks of it.

JJ yelled down, "The pool water has shorted out this phone!"

Thank the Dear Lord and Buddha above. He thinks it's the pool water.

"I'll get you another phone."

"I'm trying to get Elliot," JJ said, and continued climbing the stairs.

"Elliot already called."

"He knows?" JJ stopped climbing.

"A friend of Elliot's faxed him over a copy of the newspaper story before it gets officially released later this morning." Byrdie cringed as she waited for JJ's response. "Elliot said he's going to stop the paper from going out, and for you not to worry."

JJ felt a sudden flush of oven–like heat pass over his body. It took a moment for him to realize why. JJ imagined Elliot reading the morning's headlines. Then, the short leap to imagining how Elliot would be reacting to the story. That led to an even shorter leap to imagining all the people who got *The Nashville Sun*.

Not to worry?

What if it does get out? Thousands of people would read it. It would spread like wildfire. Through other media too. The numbers of people who were going to read and hear this story would be impossible to even imagine. This fever-hot rush radiating to all his extremities was something not familiar to JJ, and it was only fleeting – but there it was.

JJ felt *shame*.

I feel shame *for my own son.* The thought made him queasy.

He quickly reassured himself —

It isn't true, Josh isn't gay. There was no reason to be ashamed about anything.

"Are you okay?" Byrdie asked.

"Fine." He didn't sound fine. His voice was shaking.

It would be cleared up soon enough. Whoever was responsible will be appropriately punished. They will be befittingly prosecuted and their pictures will be on the front page.

JJ looked down the stairs to Byrdie. She was waiting patiently. He struggled to speak, and stopped a few times before he pinpointed what he wanted to say. "Buster Ragsdale is a dear friend. Hell, he's practically family. Why on earth would he do this to me?"

"I don't know," Byrdie answered honestly.

3

Frankie Fairway and Banjo Flo were in the back seat of a taxi from Waco's Heart of Texas Cab and Shuttle. They were drunk, beaten, and surprisingly content. The typical rancid odor rising from the back seat of the cab was of no matter to these two because the smell of dried blood, pungent beer, and cigarette smoke saturating their clothes sufficiently dominated the space around them. And they were essentially out cold. The alarming level of alcohol that was flowing through their circulatory systems made their cuts and bruises feel miles away. If their blood had been tested in an emergency room setting, unnerved staff would be frantically treating them both for alcohol poisoning. The taxi driver, a strikingly handsome man from Pakistan, looked at his passengers with only a passing concern for their health. It was Texas. He had seen a lot worse.

Flo had given the driver an ample wad of cash, more than enough to fulfill the instructions she gave to him – "Just drive and don't ask questions." When she noticed his magnificent dark eyes, and his creamy jet-black hair, she added, "Make the drive smooth and I might just give you the kiss of your lifetime."

The driver, a recent refuge to the United States, didn't recognize the repellent, wretched looking pair in the back seat as extremely famous Country Western icons. He just knew he was driving them to the Hilton in Fort Worth and that they paid – in cash – at least ten times what the fare would be. To help pass the time he turned up his classical sitar music on his cab's MP3 player.

It had all begun earlier at a bar in Waco, Texas called The Purple Buzzard Saloon. The barn-wood walls, peanut shell covered floor and hand-carved mahogany bar of this renowned ramshackle tavern was marinated with the pungent smell of beer, whiskey, tequila, wine and cigarette smoke, slathered over with multiple layers of wood lacquer. A sign over the cash register behind the bar read:

WHAT DOES NOT DESTROY ME
MAKES ME THIRST FOR A STRONGER DRINK

As she did every night at just before the midnight hour, the bar maid had called out, "Put your money down! Chicken Shit Bingo commences in five minutes! Absolutely no bingo cards issued once Ginger hits the table!"

Chicken Shit Bingo drew customers from miles around. Twenty dollars got you a bingo card and one chance to win the legendarily large pool of money. Ginger, a Rhode Island Red hen, would be released onto a pool table that had been fashioned into a giant-sized bingo card, with fencing around the perimeter. Ginger made her deposits on the four-by-eight foot bingo card, and numbers would be called out to eager, increasingly more intoxicated, game players based on Ginger's excremental droppings. Two capable, and always captivating, sexy women in short skirts and cowgirl boots were stationed on either end of the table, to prevent anyone from influencing Ginger's excreta activities. There would be no cheating in Chicken Shit Bingo.

Frankie's band had played earlier in the evening at Jake's Back Room in Lubbock, Texas to a standing room only crowd. Afterward, the band decided to go to their favorite night spot in Waco, The Purple Buzzard Saloon. Whenever the band was in this part of Texas, they'd stop by for the world famous slaw dogs, fried pickles, and a chance to win the much-touted Chicken Shit Bingo pool.

After ample amounts of greasy food had been consumed, Frankie and Banjo Flo were abandoned by their other band mates. They had taken the tour bus to the Hilton Hotel in Fort Worth where they all had reservations for the night. George had come across an aggressively horny fan who was joining him for the night. Donnie had a sinus headache and would soon be deep into a Theraflu induced sleep. Little Preacher and his wife were in the hotel bed eating Ben and Jerry's, watching a BBC marathon of *Doctor Who* (the episodes with David Tennant, who they both agreed was the best Doctor).

Frankie Fairway and Banjo Flo had been writing songs and playing in various bands together since they met in Nashville in 1979 at a Jerry Lee Lewis song writing workshop. Banjo Flo was born into the business, the daughter of blues singer and pianist Deloris King who started her career at sixteen playing gigs with Professor Longhair in New Orleans in the fifties. Banjo Flo, a singer herself, and a mean banjo picker, moved to Nashville and had made it big as a solo artist in the late eighties with two number one hits, "Afflicted" and "Too Crushed to Cry". Frankie Fairway had written hit songs for Alan Jackson, Reba McEntire, and even The Red Hot Chili Peppers, among many other big names. He had many Country chart topping hits in the eighties himself, including a Grammy winning number one, "Devil's Got my Number, So I'm Screening All My Calls" and the international smash – and college party favorite – "I'd Watch Your Porn".

TENNESSEE WILDFLOWERS

He became a household name in 1991 when he married Kitty Stardust. The two became celebrated Nashville sweethearts and tabloid favorites. The tabloids noted – but were surprisingly kind in their reporting – that Kitty was visibly pregnant at the time of their marriage. Neither Frankie nor Kitty had really fallen in love, at least in the romantic category of love. They divorced in 2008. It was amicable. Sixteen years seemed more than enough for them both. They agreed the best thing that they had done together was produce their amazingly talented, fine-looking son, Dylan.

Frankie had gone into rehab clinics countless times during his marriage to Kitty. But for him, it never took. He finally reached the conclusion he had the kind of psyche that thrived best in an environment of a loud Country-style rock and roll, random reckless sex, and a perpetual intake of recreational drugs and alcohol. He famously pronounced his assessment of his battle with his personal demons at the 1994 CMA awards: "My problem with addiction is that it's the solution."

Frankie had married twice since Kitty, but those marriages did not conclude as harmoniously. His second wife took his two houses and most of his money. His third shot him in the stomach with a Smith and Wesson .38 Special. He survived both. But he vowed thereafter to stay a bachelor for the rest of his life.

As it was well reported in the media at the time, Frankie sued for divorce from a fourth wife a few years after his third, but when his attorney attempted to file the papers, he discovered that Frankie had not been joined in holy matrimony a fourth time. Frankie's doctor confirmed that the woman was only a Moroccan-hash generated hallucination. This imaginary wife had manifested to Frankie due to six months of uncurtailed partying in Northwestern Africa. Frankie was elated with the doctor's prognosis (The hallucinated wife had been really mean to him). It was reported correctly in *High Times* Magazine that Frankie celebrated his lawyer's and doctor's good news with another pleasure-seeking trip to Morocco.

Back at The Purple Buzzard Saloon it was a slow night for Ginger. She had selected quite a lot of numbers, but still not enough to ascertain a bingo winner. Frankie and Flo were seated at the bar well into an important conversation and a second bottle of Don Julio 70. They had purchased the two bottles from the bartender to save time.

Frankie had long, silky brown hair kept in a ponytail, cagey brown eyes, and a brutally handsome face. He was tall, with a scraggy-slim body hugged into tight blue jeans, and he almost always had a bedeviling smile on his face. "Beddable" was how the "Frankie Freaks" - the devoted girls who followed him to every single concert - described him. These girls would usually be speaking from experience.

Banjo Flo, who was sporting an ink-black Pat Benatar hairstyle and a leather miniskirt, was married to Red Conway, a record producer. Their marriage was strong, even though they often were away from each other when she was on the road. Red didn't worry about Flo too much. He'd say, "She's a tiny thing, but tough as boot leather." Anyone who had ever crossed Flo discovered Red's assessment was right-on-the-money.

Frankie asked Flo, "If it sounds like a compliment, but it don't feel like a compliment, then what is it?"

Flo thought it over. "Give me an example."

Flo poured them both another shot. She had taken over the bingo cards for her band mates and her fingers were saturated with neon blue ink from the leaky bingo marker.

"Those women earlier. Remember that blonde one with tits twice the size of ostrich eggs, in the pink jumpsuit?" Frankie asked. Flo nodded. He continued, "She said that she pictures me in her mind when she fucks her husband…but then she went on and said her husband can sing a hell of a lot better than I do. How do I take that?"

"Oh, that's a 'complisult'," Flo answered confidently. "It sounds like a compliment, you know, when they say it out loud, but in actuality it's an insult. It's like when Red says to me, 'I love you in that dress, Honey. It makes you look skinny'. It sounds like he's made a good-natured compliment about my dress, but what he's really saying is that, absent the dress, I'm normally walking around looking like some kind of blubbery, fat-ass, cow. I call that a 'complisult'."

"Hey, aren't you Trace Atkins?" This question was coming from a man who was stationed at the bar behind Frankie. He was generously proportioned, his unwashed hair tied up in a grimy bandanna, wearing a Harley Davidson T-shirt with the sleeves ripped off.

"No, I am not Trace Atkins," Frankie answered. He didn't turn away from Flo.

"'Honky Tonk Badonkadonk' sucked," the muscle thug said while flexing his pit bull tattoo. He downed an entire bottle of Miller High Life to give weight to his personal critique of the Country Western hit single.

"That song was by Trace Atkins, and we've established I am not him." Frankie took a quick glance at the man at the bar behind him. "But Trace is a friend of mine, and so any further commentary you can keep to yourself."

"I divorced my wife because all she wanted to do was listen to that 'my dog died, my muddy truck has big wheels, I sing about drinking booze but I don't really know how, and I'm a big-ass cry baby' Country shit!"

Frankie turned full body around to the man, who was grabbing the last Marlboro from a pack into his lips. His jowly face swaggered sinisterly back at Frankie. The man crunched the empty Marlboro package into his fist. The cigarette pack bizarrely disappeared, like a magic trick, into the man's implausibly large hand.

After realizing the man was twice as big as he was, in every conceivable way, a sober, more judicious Frankie might have concluded it was best to say something non-confrontational, or nothing at all. What Frankie did say was: "You know, you've got a nose to breathe through, so there's really no good reason for you to keep opening your mouth."

"What did you just say to me?" The buffed biker flexed the pit bull on his leathery arm to look like the dog's face was getting all fired up. Just like he was.

Flo took it from there: "What I believe my friend, Frankie, was trying to say is, 'What are you going to do with your face when that baboon comes around here again and wants his ass back?'"

A prolonged, perplexed look blazed across the colossal tattooed man's face. Then he punched Frankie right in the kisser, with the hand that held the cigarette package hidden inside. Frankie regained his constitution fairly quickly. He had a bloody lip and a few stars were circling in the periphery of his vision. Frankie steadied himself on the bar, then fired back and hit the Harley guy in his very square jaw. This hit had very little effect, although the wallop did break the man's Marlboro in half. A woman in a black leather tasseled top, possibly the buffed-up troublemaker's girlfriend, hit Flo in the stomach with her fist. She took the blow, then with a piercing right punch, Flo knocked the girl to the floor. Frankie swung for the muscled brute again. This time he missed and smashed his fist into the pickled egg jar, sending a sea of eggs across the bar.

Another bar patron, maybe a Frankie Fairway fan (or perhaps a Trace Atkins fan), decided to join in and smashed a bar-chair over the Harley thug's head, dropping him to his knees. Someone threw a glass bottle of Keystone Light hitting Flo in the back of the head. Flo turned around, and because she couldn't determine who threw the bottle, face punched each of the two women standing there.

A frat boy in a Texas A&M sweatshirt, without any clear motivation, threw his roommate headfirst into the jukebox, abruptly cutting off Big and Rich's "Save a Horse (Ride a Cowboy)". Soon, most everyone in the bar was hitting someone else with either their fist, a pool cue, a barstool, a pitcher, or anything at hand not nailed down.

The barmaid quickly grabbed Ginger and whisked the hen to safety. The bartender and doorman began to grab people, and hurl them out the front door. Bingo cards were flying to and fro.

This kind of evening was not unfamiliar to Frankie or Flo. Flo knew to snag her purse (and Frankie) before they were grabbed and thrown out as well. This was not just because her wallet was in her purse, but her cell phone. It was imperative to call a taxi before the police arrived on the scene. One night locked up in a jailhouse drooling on a foul-smelling floor mat is a mistake. To ever do it again was just plain stupidity. She Googled local taxi services, and had a cab on its way in less than five minutes. Well before anyone in The

Purple Buzzard Saloon even thought to call 9-1-1. Frankie and Banjo Flo had just enough time to roll a joint and smoke it before the taxi cab pulled up to collect them.

Now, inside the taxi, Frankie and Banjo Flo sat dozing off, in and out of a dizzy, swirling peaceful daze. The Pakistani man was a very good driver. The ride was extraordinarily smooth. A kiss could be in store for him.

What sounded like loud angry crickets chirping pierced the calm inside the cab.

"What the hell is that?" Frankie yelled out, completely lost to where he was.

"It's your phone, you harebrained fishdigger!" Flo replied. Getting woken up so abruptly made her a little cranky.

Frankie searched his leather jacket pocket and pulled out his phone. He wasn't comfortable with modern technology sober, much less in his present shape. It took a minute, but he finally focused in on the screen. "Hey, it's Dylan." Frankie punched some buttons and put the phone to his ear. "Hey, Son. How the hell are you?"

* * *

Dylan and Josh were sitting at the kitchen table in Kitty's home. Dylan had made coffee with Bongo Java beans in Kitty's Chemex coffee carafe. Kitty still hadn't returned from her meeting with JJ. The fact that Kitty had not called them back meant that she probably needed to break the news in person. They agreed that likely meant it went badly. But they were still holding onto hope.

Dylan said into his cell, "Remember Daddy, when I said to free up the weekend after Thanksgiving on your schedule?"

Frankie said, "Oh Jesus I missed something again didn't I?"

Dylan replied, "No, you didn't miss anything. I couldn't tell you what the event was yet? Well, now I want to tell you."

"Do you need bail, Son?" Frankie asked.

"No." Dylan was beginning to sense his call was badly timed.

"Do you need a kidney? I think I still have a good one."

Josh drank his coffee. He was nervous, and only half able to listen to Dylan talking to his daddy on the phone.

"No, Daddy," Dylan said. "Where are you?"

Frankie realized he had no idea. He looked to Flo for help. "Flo, my son wants to know where we are."

Flo searched around the small dark space they occupied for a clue. "It's too small to be the tour bus."

"It could be a train," Frankie said. "I bet-ya it's an airplane. It's very dark, Son."

Dylan asked, "Where were you the last time you remember anything?"

"It could be a boat," Flo said, trying to find a reliable point of reference.

Frankie glanced out the window of the cab. "I just saw an armadillo."

The cab driver turned on the light over the back seat to check on his passengers. They looked hopelessly bewildered, but harmless. He decided to leave the light on just in case.

Frankie said, "Maybe that armadillo is a clue?"

"Forget it." Dylan realized his father was drunker and likely more stoned than he had predicted. "Daddy, I'm getting married. That's what I called to tell you."

"Well, hell, that is big news, Son." Frankie quickly added, with a hushed tone, "Does Josh know?"

"Yes, Daddy. Josh is who I'm marrying. He's right here with me."

Frankie was soothed. "Oh, thank God. I thought you had gotten into some kind of pickle with a woman." Frankie opened one bleary eye, wide. "Under all those curves and perfumes, and Victoria's Secret silky panties, women are homicidal demons. An untrained eye simply cannot see it." Frankie became drunkenly emotional. "I love you, Son. You're my little baby boy, and now you're getting married. You know what I always say about love?"

Dylan replied, "Love is a battlefield? Love is toxic? Love is a road littered with broken hearts?"

"Those are just songs I sing. No. The Frankie Fairway doctrine on love is, love should free your body, your soul, and your mind. If it doesn't set you free, it's not love."

"That's a nice thing to say, Daddy. I think I'm okay there."

"Let me talk to Josh."

Dylan gave the phone to Josh, with his hand over the receiver. "He wants to talk to you. He's looped."

Josh nodded. "Hello, Mr. Fairway."

Frankie replied, "Josh, you are a sweet, sweet boy. Does Dylan treat you right? I raised him to be a gentleman. Did he get you a nice ring?"

"Yes, Mr. Fairway. I have a very nice ring. You did a perfect job."

"I remember you came to Dylan's eighth birthday party. Do you remember that?"

"Yes, I do."

Frankie said, "Dylan took out his guitar. That guitar was almost as big as he was. And he sang that song to you. 'You Are My Sunshine'. It was the sweetest thing I ever saw in my life."

Josh put his hand over the receiver. "He's telling me about when you sang to me at your birthday party, when we were kids."

"He loves that story," Dylan said.

Josh smiled. "I love it too."

"I knew you two were going to be good friends. And now you're getting married. You know, Josh, I love you, too. Like you were my own boy. Do you want a house? I have one in the Bahamas that my wives never found out about. It will be my wedding gift. Let's just keep it between you and me though. I find it best to not get outsiders like the IRS, lawyers, or my old record labels involved."

"We don't really need a house, but thank you. We're going to stay right here in Tennessee anyway."

Kitty entered the kitchen noiselessly. Her face was drained of color, and her eyes looked disconnected from reality.

"Momma?" Dylan said.

Josh looked up. Dylan and he both looked at Kitty's eyes for clues. What they saw gave them a mutual chill.

"Mr. Fairway, I have to go," Josh said. He kept attempting to hang up. "I love you too…I really, really love you, too…Dylan loves you…I know you love—"

Dylan grabbed the phone. "I'll call Daddy back tomorrow." He hung it up.

Josh and Dylan looked to Kitty hoping she would convey something. She was just a ghost of a person, her feet barely moored to the floor.

"Sit down Momma, and tell us what happened."

"My beautiful, beautiful boys," Kitty said, looking back and forth between Dylan and Josh. "My handsome, handsome boys." Her words sounded spacey. They provided no information, or comfort.

"Momma!" Dylan said. Her demeanor was starting to freak him out. "What the hell happened to you?"

"Mayhem," Kitty finally said. She looked askance, like she was starting to remember something. "It's mostly just a hazy blur," she explained.

Josh reached across the table and took Dylan's hand. They both felt deathly ill.

"JJ Fletcher," Kitty said. Her eyes were cocked slightly, and filled with revulsion. Kitty completed her thought in a bone-chilling tone: "I remember mayhem."

* * *

In the cab, Frankie stared mystified at his silent cell phone.

Flo had taken a crumpled piece of paper from her pocket and was looking it over with more or less the same state of puzzlement.

Flo shook her head. "Will someone please knock me in the head with a bag of rocks?"

"They can communicate with a damn rover on the planet Mars, but I can't get a decent connection here on Earth," Frankie said, confounded by the device. He put the phone back to his ear. "Hello Son? Josh? Are you there? Hello? Anybody?"

Flo stared at the card she had paid twenty dollars for a few hours earlier (it seemed like an eternity to her now).

Flo declared, "I had a goddamned bingo."

> *It is not necessary to understand things in order to argue about them.*
> — Pierre Beaumarchais

MEMORIES LAST FOREVER

1

The waterspouts in the shower of the governor's mansion (mounted on the side as well as the showerhead above) were spraying on JJ at full blast. It was as if he were standing naked in a blistering hot monsoon. Everything around him had become obliterated by the steam and scorching water – the desired effect. His skin was scalded a scarlet red. Time had become distorted and gnarled in JJ's mind by the morning's uninvited guest, and her uninvited – unthinkable, unbelievable, unacceptable – news. He had put shaving cream on, but had neglected to shave it from his face. He thought he heard Byrdie call out for him a few times. He ignored her.

I wonder how long I've been in here?

He had, in fact, been inside the shower for just under an hour. He saw no good reason to leave. He knew once the shower ended he would have to talk to Elliot. Then after Elliot, he'd have to explain everything to the media. And then there was President McKenzie's people. He'd likely have to talk directly to Bob McKenzie, at some point. That conversation promised to be unpleasant. He needed to understand things himself before he explained them to anyone else. Therein was the problem. He didn't understand any of it. Every time he pushed the newspaper headline out of his head, it would come racing back. Every time he pushed Kitty Stardust's image from his mind, it came racing back as well. Each time with less and less clothing.

Those lips, those breasts, that ass. Ruth-Adele Holloway you have a body like no one I have ever met.

Kitty's sexuality had always made JJ crazy. When he had been married he had been able to forget his high school crush on Ruth-Adele Holloway. His beautiful wife fulfilled his needs unreservedly. But after his wife died, his feelings for Kitty Stardust came seeping back - devilishly erotic feelings. It was impossible to escape her. She was on TV, the radio, the Internet, magazines, book covers, the sides of busses and billboards. JJ didn't stand a chance.

One time, when he was dating a nice young lady named Linda Turner for a few months, JJ had cried the name Ruth-Adele, right out loud, while they were having sex. It had sounded nothing like the name Linda Turner. JJ had seen Kitty on Good Morning Nashville earlier, and he didn't even realize what he'd done until *Linda* slapped him across the face. After that, he was careful to never speak at all during sex.

JJ knew most of the details, now, of how his teenage romance with Ruth-Adele had ended. His mother, Petula, and Ruth-Adele's mother, Estella-Jeanne, had conspired together to break them up. Petula's motivation was her belief that the Holloway's were poor, white trash, and not good enough for her only son. Estella-Jeanne's motivation was simply for the money. Petula had paid several large monetary installments to Estella-Jeanne - a desperately poor widow at the time - to make certain the plan was maintained for the length of time necessary. JJ had been pulled from high school and sent to a military school. All contact had been successfully cut off, and both Ruth-Adele and he were fed constant lies about the other.

When JJ found out what his mother had done, he swore he would never forgive her. He had kept that promise. And as far as he knew, Kitty Stardust had never forgiven her mother either.

JJ and Kitty had gotten together for their second go at a relationship just over six years ago. At that time JJ believed their old romance would have a fresh start. It did for a few months. But again, it had ended abruptly. This time he did not know why. Kitty had refused to speak to him after that. If his mother had anything to do with it, JJ had not been able to get her to admit to anything. He was left in the dark, and no one seemed willing or capable of shedding any light on the subject for him. This morning's confrontation certainly offered very little to clear it up.

The fog-free mirror was getting drenched. JJ wiped a circle away with his hand. He noticed a few gray hairs. He wasn't surprised. He felt old and worse for the wear at the moment.

JJ turned the shower off, and stepped out into the bathroom tile floor. He didn't bother grabbing a towel, just stood and let the water puddle around his feet. He looked at a ceramic duck on the bathroom shelf. He wasn't sure where it came from. It was a mallard duck that had cologne inside. He didn't like the smell of it. It was a gift he'd gotten from someone who obviously didn't know that he only ever wore Stetson.

JJ recalled the last time Kitty and he had ever spoken to each other. It was just over six years ago. They were at The Peabody Hotel, in Memphis Tennessee.

JJ had gotten a small suite at the world famous hotel, under an assumed name. Kitty had snuck in later in a disguise. JJ and Kitty had been meeting in motel and hotel rooms, using the same secret ruse, for just over three months.

When the affair started, Frankie and Kitty had been separated. JJ's wife had passed away ten years earlier. The relationship they were having was nothing to be ashamed of. But because Kitty was still legally married, and JJ was a state senator at the time, they kept their meetings a secret.

The affair had begun because of an accidental meeting. JJ and Kitty had both been scheduled to appear at Nashville's Country Music Hall of Fame. An award was being given to Garth Brooks, a mutual friend. Garth, not knowing JJ and Kitty had a past, introduced them to each other: "Senator Fletcher, this is Kitty Stardust," Garth said. "Of course you two probably have heard of each other. If you haven't heard of each other, I'm going to have to see your Tennessee passports." Garth immediately felt a weird vibe. Neither of the two people he had introduced to one another offered up even a friendly smile.

Kitty broke the uncomfortable silence. "Actually Garth, Senator Fletcher and I attended the same high school. It's probably something he wouldn't remember." JJ just stared at Kitty's face (breasts, face, breasts, face). "It was a long, long time ago," Kitty finished.

Garth was relieved when he was suddenly called away to the stage by his assistant. Garth said, "You two obviously have a lot of catching up to do. Or whatever." Then he scooted away.

After the ceremony, JJ followed Kitty to her limousine. He left her with his private cell phone number. Neither said much as they stood by the limo, the driver patiently waiting. Even though they both knew it was their conspiring mothers who did all the damage, it still brought up confusing and painful memories to again be so close to one another. Both had strong feelings, but those feelings were kept quiet. Expressing them, in any way, felt far too dangerous. But there they were, the embers getting a big fresh supply of oxygen. A fire could so easily ignite.

Kitty had considered throwing the phone number away, but instead put the piece of paper in her purse. She was at a place in her life where she was in need of something, *anything*, new.

Or, in this case, something from the past.

When Frankie called her from the road, later, it made her glad she had kept the phone number. Frankie was at a party in Las Vegas having his usual good time with the standard mix: friends, the usual Frankie Freaks, fans who managed to get back stage, other bands, and their groupies, prostitutes, drug dealers, and the like. The sound of Frankie's incomprehensible drunken monologue made her feel intolerably lonely. After she hung up, she fixed herself a strong drink. It took two more of the vodka stingers before she mustered up the courage. Kitty took the piece of paper with JJ's phone number on it from her purse and punched in the numbers.

They quickly cut through the small talk. They decided to meet secretly at a La Quinta Inn on the far edge of Nashville. Far enough away where they were certain they wouldn't run into anyone they knew.

They checked into the La Quinta Inn room separately, using fake names. Once the motel room door was closed, they barely got the word, "Hello," out of their mouths. The combustible inferno they had experienced together in high school resumed instantly and effortlessly. The sex that night in the tiny room of the La Quinta Inn had been merciless; a ferocious, beastly, mindless abandon both had forgotten was possible.

The next morning they agreed that they would meet again at the next possible opportunity. They saw no reason to stop. The sex train had left the station and was rushing full steam ahead. Whenever they could, they made arrangements to continue the affair. Extremely busy people who travel all the time can fairly easily fall off the radar for a few hours. No one, even their assistants responsible for nearly every scheduled move, ever caught on.

In The Peabody Hotel room, Kitty laid face-to-face with JJ on the bed. They were both naked. Her hair was in sexual disarray. JJ's hand was gently nestling one of Kitty's breasts.

Her heavenly, voluptuous, touchable, kissable breasts.

"Frankie signed the papers," Kitty said.

"Really?" JJ was genuinely surprised. "You mean divorce?"

Kitty nodded. "Frankie is a good friend. Probably my best friend." She held up her left hand. An un-tanned ring around her finger indicated where her wedding band had been. "I'll always love him. He just never wanted the party to end."

"Can't blame a man for trying."

"Of course, all that howling at the moon did come with its consequences. Frankie gave me a few STD scares over the years."

JJ drew his hand away.

"Don't worry. I'm fine. After the last one, I cut him off. That was over three years ago."

JJ relaxed, and put his hand back on her breast, stroking it. He reached in closer, nuzzling them both. He kissed up to her nipple, relishing the honey-sweetness, and the feel of it in his mouth, a lingering moment. He fell back on the pillow in bliss. "I'm glad you got the divorce. Frankie is a likable guy, but you deserve better," he said.

"Like you?"

"I've always been told I'm better." JJ smiled.

Kitty grinned. "You are pretty damn good."

JJ nodded. "I am, aren't I? I try to imagine there may be others out there, like me. Possibly even better. But I think I'm just being modest."

Kitty grabbed a pillow and swatted him. "You said you had some news."

"It's official. I'm making a run for the governor's office."

"Governor?" Kitty said. "Really?" She felt a small pang of anger. She wasn't sure why exactly. It just seemed like he should have mentioned something about it to her before now.

"I had a little team working on testing the waters, and it looks like a good time for me to jump in. Daddy's been out for seven years, and Jeffery Reynoso has decided to not run again. Anyway it's the perfect time if I'm ever going to do it."

Kitty ran her hand over the soft hair on JJ's solid chest, then let her fingers drift down to his smooth firm stomach. JJ closed his eyes, and let the warm feeling flood over him. "Why am I only hearing about this now?" Kitty asked.

JJ noticed the hint of anger in her question, but he was starting to get excited. "I promise, you're the first person I have told outside the team. I wasn't trying to keep you in the dark."

"Okay. I just hate secrets." Kitty decided she was being silly. She said, "Your family does love politics."

"I guess, like organized crime is for the mafia, it's the Fletcher family business," JJ said. He still held his eyes closed. "So you're a free woman?"

Kitty let her hand draw further down his abs. JJ kept up a vigorous workout routine which gave him a body he was proud of. Especially the past few months, with Kitty deriving so much pleasure from it. Kitty moved her hand over his well-muscled abdomen, reaching around and pulling herself closer to him. His seductive, husky body was a potent drug. She wrapped her legs through his, enveloping him as much as she could. Kitty ran her fingers through JJ's hair. Then she tenderly pulled his head closer to kiss his lips. Their tongues intertwined, and played. She nuzzled his coarse face, basking in the musky, manly fragrance.

"I wouldn't say free. I'm married to my career," Kitty said softly.

JJ opened his eyes, just a sliver. "I'm serious. You're available, and I am too. Finally."

"You want to date me?" Kitty asked.

"Why not?"

Kitty thought it over. She relaxed lightly back on the bed and pillows. There were good reasons to hesitate – old reasons. "I remember Momma getting that wall to wall carpeting and asking myself, *'Where did she suddenly get all this money?'* It was really nice too, Berber. After Daddy died, we were so poor we were lucky to get shoes once a year. And suddenly we're getting Berber carpeting."

"It was shitty what my momma did. I'm so sorry about all that. But that was a long time ago."

"I was embarrassed about my family back then. I can't completely blame your mother for watching out for her only son."

JJ had been told the teenage Ruth-Adele was engaged to marry a boy from Armadillo. Petula had added, to the concocted story, she heard there were "lots of *other* boys!" Kitty had been told JJ had gotten another girl pregnant. Both mothers prevented their children from contacting each other (not that they tried much after both being so desperately crushed). So the lies became the story they both believed. It wasn't until many years later that they both found out everything they had been told was completely fabricated. By then, it was too late. Just as their mothers had hoped.

"I don't recall you having anything to be embarrassed about," JJ said.

"Oh really?" Kitty asked.

"No, you didn't seem that different to me."

Kitty shook her head. "I was different. Believe me. When I was twelve, my momma made me help her dip sparrows into peroxide and yellow food dye, and then we'd sell them at roadside stands as canaries."

"You can dip birds in peroxide?" JJ asked.

"They didn't all survive," Kitty replied, disparagingly. "You have no idea how humiliating it was to be so poor, coming to school, praying to God no one had parents who bought a fake canary from my momma."

"You're right. I can't," JJ said. "I just saw you as the sexiest, most interesting girl I'd ever met."

"In the end, it was some of your momma's pay-off money that got me my first recording contract. So I have her to thank for that."

"Don't thank her so fast. She sent me to a private military school in Virginia where I didn't know a single person. That first year I got mono. And I got the nickname Bucephelus. I am not so grateful to Momma."

"I have an idea," Kitty said. "I can go downstairs to the restaurant. I'll wait for you to join me. We let a few people see us together. Then we can start making this public. Besides I'm hungry."

JJ smiled. "I would love to be able to kiss you in public. You're right. It will be our first real date since high school."

Kitty pulled herself on top of JJ, moved both her hands down his powerfully-muscled back. She let her fingers reach down until they were both clutching him tightly. JJ responded by eagerly wrapping his hands around her smooth, slender back, pulling her closer. The palpable, throbbing response from JJ was rapid. Kitty arched back up as he made his way inside. JJ's body instinctively began thrusting harmoniously with Kitty's. She took his head into her hands, grabbed his thick, sweating hair, and placed his eager face between her breasts. He devoured them. Sexual fervor released from deep within her. It undulated and quivered all the way through her body. "Give me another twenty minutes," she gasped. She reached down, pulled him back up to her mouth, and kissed him hard. The skin on their bodies was hot and dripping sweat. She exhaled, a deep throaty moan, and bent close to JJ's ear. She whispered, "Then let's go have our date."

* * *

After their mind-blowing sex, Kitty had gone down to the restaurant, as planned. JJ had gone to meet her, as planned. But before JJ left the room he had gotten a cell phone call.

That was not a part of the plan.

If he had not answered the phone that day, everything might have been different.

But he did answer. And when he did, he made a terrible, life-changing, mistake. He should have had more sense. But JJ was a true Southern boy. It's very hard for a Southern boy to not confide in his momma.

* * *

JJ stood naked in the balmy hot bathroom looking at the ceramic mallard duck. He was looking *through* it into some nether-worldly abyss. By the end of that day six years ago Kitty had never spoken to him again. Something must have gone wrong. He knew that. He wasn't stupid. *Imbecilic, was the word she'd used. How does she even know words like that?* He had tried many times to contact her, but he had never been successful. He'd even gone so far as to accuse Petula of meddling once more. But his mother denied it entirely. He imagined one day he'd see Kitty again, and she could explain. Of course this morning at his pool he didn't exactly have the chance to get all his questions answered. Clearly she had a lot of rage bottled up and had decided this morning would be a good time to pop the cork off that bottle and release some of it.

Yes, JJ thought, *something had gone horribly wrong.*

2

Kitty sat at the table with Dylan and Josh. She had relaxed, a little. She managed to recall most of the details about her morning encounter with JJ. Dylan had asked her to repeat three times the part where she had kicked the pool chair and flung JJ into the swimming pool. The first telling, they were all in a kind of sustained shock that she had actually done it. The second telling, they all laughed until tears fell from their eyes. The third telling, sobered them up. They knew that things were going to get bad. Kicking the governor of Tennessee into his swimming pool could not possibly lead to anything good. The three of them agreed that the morning's poolside event had resulted in an outcome that they all had hoped was going to be the opposite. The disastrous situation they were in had taken a mind boggling turn for the worse.

Dylan looked at Josh's face. He didn't like what he saw there. Josh was terrified. Dylan loved Josh so thoroughly it caused him unbearable anguish at times. He knew Josh was extremely smart, spiritually sound, and physically strong. But Josh had a vulnerability about him too. Dylan had imagined that this vulnerability was there because Josh had lost his mother at such a young age. A good guess any psychologist would likely agree with. It was always an unspoken observation. Dylan wanted Josh to never know he saw anything but the strongest and best in him.

One time, at a Wal-Mart, a guy in a Range Rover cut Josh off and stole their parking space. Josh was letting an elderly woman pass in front of them in her walker, and the man in the truck took advantage of the situation, snatching the parking space. While Josh was in the store, Dylan had snuck out and slashed the tires on the Range Rover with his pocket knife. He never told Josh, and he knew it was an over-reaction. But when it came to Josh (no matter how unreservedly rash and immature it was), there simply was nothing he wouldn't do.

"I should have talked to him myself," Josh said.

Kitty sighed. "I swear boys, I tried to keep my cool. From his point of view, it was probably kind of an ambush. But he wouldn't listen to me." She sighed. "I made a bad situation worse, didn't I?"

"You did what we asked you to do," Josh replied. "It's Daddy, not you. I should have known he'd react like he did."

Dylan said, "He can go take a flying fuck at a rolling doughnut, he's not invited to the wedding. Problem solved. We're making way too much out of this. It's his loss."

"I think Josh would like to have his father give him his blessing." Kitty said. "That shouldn't be asking too much, in my opinion."

"Maybe it is?" Josh said. "Maybe it is asking too much?"

Kitty took Josh's hand. "I feel so bad for you, Josh. But you know we'll always be your family."

Josh nodded, appreciatively.

Olga, one of Kitty's housekeepers, entered the kitchen, in a huff, holding a fresh cut bunch of roses. Olga was a Russian immigrant who had been on the staff for over eight years. Her blonde hair was rolled up tightly into a bun and her gray dress was homemade. Kitty paid her more than enough to buy new clothes. She even offered to go shopping with the woman herself. But Olga always insisted on making her own. She was from a rural part of her home country, and very proud of her Russian heritage. For her, buying new clothes was an absurd American custom, and yet another good example of Americans wasting their hard earned money.

"What is it, Olga? You look upset." Kitty said.

"I go to collect the flowers for house by back gate from Fernando, like Olga do every day. Roses grow very big because Fernando know how to give them best love." Olga had an obvious crush on the man who delivered Kitty's flowers. The Primeval Florists Shop was Kitty's favorite, because Fernando did have the best flowers. Kitty loved to have her home filled with flowers, so she had Fernando deliver fresh ones every morning. Fernando was a robust, charming, Argentinian man, with thick black hair and an equally hefty black handlebar mustache. He had burly, hairy arms with biceps and a chest that stretched his white T-shirts to their maximum capacity. Kitty wondered if it wasn't just flowers that were being delivered from the back of that flower truck. It often took Olga an unwarranted amount of time in the mornings to go collect the six to seven bundles of flowers. One time, about six months ago, Kitty actually saw the truck - with the back closed up, and no Olga or Fernando in site - rocking in a rhythmic steady up and down motion that couldn't honestly be attributed to rearranging flower assortments for future deliveries. Kitty had thought it was kind of romantic, with that big delivery truck full of beautiful flowers inside it and all.

Olga pointed to the large blooms in her arms proudly. "I never see roses this big in Russia. I waved good-bye to Fernando. But as Fernando drive away in his truck my heart stop. Some crazy lady is right on other side of gate. I lock it up right away. She yell at me. She throw wad of money through gate. A big roll of money. Crazy lady. She say, 'My name is Rebecca C. Hooper and I need to talk to Kitty Stardust'. I say I do not care if she The Virgin Mary, nobody talk to Kitty Stardust. She resting her voice. Crazy lady. I keep the money."

"Is she still out there?" Kitty asked.

Signs of deep concern began to flush over Josh and Dylan's faces.

"Crazy lady has lots of friends. They have big vans with those electrical, metal devices on top. What is the English word?"

"Antennas?" Dylan asked.

Olga nodded. "They drive on grass. Run over new Dogwood trees in back. In Russia we shoot such irresponsible people." Olga shrugged.

Kitty looked at Josh and Dylan with distress. "We need to get you boys someplace safe," Kitty said.

Josh said, "I need to talk to Daddy first."

"Are you sure you want to do that?" she asked. "He is your daddy after all. And because of me, he's in a pretty rotten mood right now." She thought her words over. "Okay, rotten is not even close to describing the mood he was in when I left. You may want to wait."

"I have to," Josh said. "I know it sounds crazy, but I want him to be at my wedding. I know he loves me. I'm not different today than I was yesterday. I'm still his son. And if he says I'm not anymore, I need to know that too."

"Okay. You talk to him. It probably can't get any worse. But Rhashan is going with you, just in case. Then, when you're done with that, you both need to get far away. Josh, I want you and Dylan to enjoy your wedding day. You aren't going to be able to do that if you're here dealing with all this right up until the day it happens. I know the perfect place. No one will ever find you there. You can relax. And when you come back, I'll have the perfect wedding waiting for you."

"Where might that be, Momma?" Dylan asked.

"Someplace safe," Kitty replied. "Someplace far away and safe."

3

Kitty had wanted to fall sleep quickly, so she had eaten two Goo Goo Clusters and drank a big mug of Rhashan's Relax and Dream Tea with a dash of milk. This routine was all she usually needed to make her sleepy when she was feeling a little stressed. She also had taken a long shower to help relax her muscles. But she still felt agitated, so she had taken a bottle of Nyquil from the medicine cabinet and took two lingering gulps. The light-blocking shades on her bedroom windows were pulled down. She laid down in bed, and placed her lavender scented sleeping mask over her eyes. Peggy Sue curled up at her feet. She tried to count sheep, but all she could see was JJ Fletcher's face – his smug, willfully-stupid face – and she wanted to punch it with her fist.

I still love you Ruth-Adele Holloway.

She rolled on her side, then her back, then her side again.

That is my son you're speaking of.

She moaned and took off her mask, and then opened her bedside table drawer where she kept her prescription sleeping pills. She rarely ever took even a half of one because she didn't like taking pharmaceuticals. She took out two, and swallowed them with a glass of water from her nightstand. Within roughly ten minutes her thoughts began becoming disconnected and nonsensical. She laid on her back unable to lift her gelatin-like hand up to scratch an itch on her nose. She worried, for a wisplike moment, she had taken too many sleeping aids. The voice of Grace Slick was adrift, jumbled, in her brain: "...one pill makes something, something...ask Alexis...she's ten feet...no, Alice...somebody...", then it floated away into nothingness. She tried to recall – with momentary concern – what she'd read that Heath Ledger had taken the night he died, but that train of thought was soon just gobbledygook. But she did feel less angry, so at least that goal had been achieved.

At last she laid still, submerged under Italian velvety sheets and a thick Batiste goose-down comforter on her king size bed, adrift at sea. She was extremely relaxed, but her mind still was churning away with memories – recent ones and old ones.

She had called Rhashan and asked him to watch over Josh and Dylan. They needed security more than she did now. Dylan had gotten several death threats on Twitter. The threats, even though they were probably just cowards shooting off their mouths, still made Kitty worried, for both the boys. Dylan and Josh had insisted she go to bed. They had their own thorny problem to take care of. Josh was planning to make arrangements to speak to JJ himself. The last thing now that anyone wanted was for JJ Fletcher and Kitty Stardust to come within shouting distance – or more to the point, shooting distance – of each other. Kitty needed to get some sleep, so she took the boy's advice.

She was scheduled to do a show later that night at The Station Inn, a small concert venue on 12th Avenue where she often sang as a guest with the bluegrass band *Every Mother's Son*. She considered canceling, but then reconsidered. Canceling might give the impression she wasn't supportive, and proud, of Dylan and Josh. She would be there, oh yes she would, expounding exuberantly about how happy she was her son and the governor's son were going to have the wedding of the century right at her very own home in Nashville. Kitty knew some of her fans might not like it, but for Kitty, now that *The Nashville Sun* had thrown all the cards out on the table (and she'd thrown down the gauntlet with JJ Fletcher), this issue had become her most personal crusade ever.

One of her Country Western peers – someone she called a friend, and had as a guest in her home for dinner on occasion – had sent her a text message:

TELL YOUR SON TO GET BACK INTO HIS PERVERTED CLOSET OR I WILL PERSONALLY SEE TO IT YOU NEVER RECORD ANOTHER SONG IN NASHVILLE AGAIN

Rhashan had advised her not to get into a jousting – texting, tweeting, Facebook or any social media – match with anyone. "Those things are certain to show up on the Internet forever," Rhashan cautioned. Kitty had texted back anyway:

BRING IT ON CHUMP BRING IT ON

Kitty attached the video for her song "This Momma's Proud" to her text message. It was becoming woefully clear that not many people had ever heard or seen the video of her gay-parent tribute, or apparently had any idea she had a gay son.

She thought, *Well, those days are gone now.*

Peggy Sue watched her master's face. The little dog knew Kitty was upset. She moved up from Kitty's feet, and snuggled up closer, licking her hand and whimpering.

"I'm okay, Peggy Sue. Go to sleep," Kitty said, her words slurred with a thick, heavy tongue.

They both knew she was not okay.

The previous morning's encounter with JJ Fletcher had left her in all kinds of emotional pain and turmoil. Seeing JJ in those Speedos didn't help matters – *WHY DID HE HAVE TO BE WEARING THOSE SPEEDOS?*

Her mind was flooded with memories – ones that should have been weak or faded, or even obsolete by now. She had no idea she could react the way she did, or feel the feelings she had.

She recalled a memory from a long time ago, the summer before her father had died. Kitty was five years old, and one of the family's many hunting dogs had come onto the porch. The dog was foaming at the mouth, his eyes had blurred into madness. He was shivering and staggering with a fever. She had thought the dog (a pet she had raised from a puppy) was going to kill her. Her father pushed her back into the house. Then she heard the gunshot. It was so loud it pulsated through the floorboards of the house. The look she had seen in that pet hound's eyes, so many summers ago, reminded her of what she had become at the governor's mansion that morning.

Rabid.

How had it come to this?

The last time she had ever spoken to JJ Fletcher had been over six years ago. It was the day after Frankie and she had signed their divorce papers.

Six years ago.

Kitty had tried to forget. But six years was clearly not long enough of a time period to erase the memories, or more to the point, the emotions.

The affair with JJ had been going on for over three months. She hadn't told Frankie about it either. The guilt was not easy to just ignore. She honestly had no understanding how Frankie could effortlessly have so many sexual encounters, and feel no overt shame whatsoever. Frankie never lied to Kitty about any of his other women. That was a mixed blessing. On the contrary, he had told her as many details as she was able to endure. Kitty knew that she simply wasn't cut from the same free-love cloth as Frankie.

Rather than keep lying to her husband, she filed for divorce. It seemed like a fair and acceptable compromise to her. It had alleviated most of the feelings of guilt, and to be honest, she knew it should have happened years before.

Frankie assumed it was all his fault, and complied with no argument. When they finally met in the lawyer's office, Frankie kissed her and said, "Finally, you're taking care of yourself, Sweet Darlin'. That makes me happy. I'll sign those papers, but you keep in mind, I'll always be your best friend. Always."

Kitty knew he was speaking directly from his heart, and she knew it was true.

Neither JJ nor she had told anyone about their affair, and she wasn't about to start now in a lawyer's office with Frankie. Instead Kitty reached over and kissed Frankie more intensely than she had in years. "I love you, Frankie Fairway," Kitty said to him. "I think this divorce is what this marriage has been needing for a long time."

Frankie nodded. "I agree. Do you want to go back to the bus and get stoned with me?"

He never will change. Kitty thought. *What a wonderful, beautiful, almost irresistible, mess.*

Frankie went on, "I have a hybrid strain I picked up in Stockholm. It's called Russian Concussion. Take my word for it, it will break down your doors and kick your ass into another dimension. You won't remember what your fingers and toes are used for, and you won't care. Swedes know their weed."

Kitty smiled at him. "It sounds tempting," she said, distorting the truth. Kitty almost never smoked marijuana, certainly not some genetically modified cannabis Frankie likely picked up from a Swedish prostitute. She added, to make him feel okay - she always wanted him to feel okay - "Can you give me a rain check on that?"

"Sure thing, Babe," he said with a wink. "A rain check it is."

The next morning after the divorce signing from Frankie, Kitty had arranged to meet JJ. It had been three months of fairly non-stop sex, and the feelings were still very fresh and hot. They both couldn't wait to be ripping each other's clothes off again. It didn't take a lot of talk to convince him - "It's me. Do you want to get lucky, again?"

"Where and when?" JJ responded enthusiastically.

That day had started out as one of the best days of her life.

Kitty had a scheduled event in Memphis, at Graceland, in the morning. It was the anniversary of The King's death. JJ was supposed to meet her later that afternoon at The Peabody Hotel, but he had stopped by the event, hours early, to surprise her. They were attempting to keep their meetings a clandestine affair, but there he was, in the back of the room staring at her like some kind of sex-crazed stalker.

While the thoughtful crowd was listening to Lisa Marie give a touching, emotional tribute to her father, JJ and Kitty had snuck into a linen closet, and had quick, voracious, *whispering*, dirty-talking sex.

Kitty and JJ met later that day (as the original plan had been to do) at a suite in The Peabody Hotel. She remembered them talking about her divorce from Frankie, JJ's plan to run for governor, and their mutual interest in making their relationship public. They also had more spectacular sex, as she recalled.

But the most prevailing memory from that morning, for Kitty, was that she had believed she was more in love than she had ever been in her life. It was the perfect storm of lust, intimacy, and the deepest needs of two people being fulfilled completely – needs that hadn't even been evident until they were suddenly satisfied.

Kitty walked out of the suite in the Peabody Hotel, and quietly closed the door. She was in a white pencil skirt, matching blouse and turquoise ostrich print boots; and she realized her brassiere was showing. She sighed, and buttoned up one more button. She looked both ways, making certain the hallway was completely clear. It was. JJ was to follow her down to the ground floor in a few minutes.

She stood there in the hallway a moment, alone. She was feeling as giddy as a little girl. An old Country hit by Donna Fargo popped into her head: "The Happiest Girl in the Whole USA". She practically floated down the hallway humming the song in her head. A pop Country hit that embodied the sugary daydreams of a doe-eyed Disney animated character was not Kitty's usual style – but today, for Kitty Stardust, it was like the perfect fitting glass slipper.

The elevator delivered Kitty to the ground level and – as if the universe wanted to sustain her blissful mood – she walked out to witness the world famous Peabody Mallard Ducks clopping down the red carpet. The Duck Master, donning a top hat, was encouraging the ducks to march along with his duck-herding cane, as children were stepping up to watch. Their faces were lighting up with youthful delight.

Kitty loved seeing the ducks. Whenever she was in Memphis she tried to come to The Peabody to see them. Her mother had brought her there when she was little. They were always too poor to stay in one of the rooms or eat in one of the restaurants. But the mallard ducks were free entertainment, and free was most often the only kind of entertainment they had when Kitty was growing up.

Kitty went to the restaurant, and secured a table for two for brunch. She ordered a mimosa, signed a few autographs, and told the waiter she was expecting a guest. She would order when he arrived.

JJ was taking a lot longer than she expected. There was a piano player sitting at a Steinway Grand who, when he recognized the celebrity seated at one of their tables, played one of her hit songs, "I'm Single Again, So Make Mine a Double". Five years ago it was number one for sixteen weeks, and had stayed on the charts for nearly a year. It had also been a big crossover that won her two Grammys. The piano player did a fairly good interpretation. Kitty nodded hello to him. She read some of her e-mails from her fansite. She then called Dylan, and left a message: "It's your momma. Just wanted to hear your voice. I swear I am so sorry for what I said. Please call me back. I love you, Darlin'". She had a second mimosa. She asked the waiter for some strawberries because she was starving, and had a third mimosa. She had a pleasant conversation with the waiter, a real sweetheart from Hawaii – a boxing champion with two darling daughters (he showed her his cell phone pictures of them). By the time JJ arrived, dressed in his suit and tie, she was practically drunk. He now appeared strangely anxious. He hadn't been that way when she left him in the room; quite the opposite.

She would think back later and realize he also looked confused. The fact that JJ had anything to be confused about at that moment would be one of the major factors she considered when, later that very day, she made her personal, unconditional vow to banish JJ Fletcher from her life until the end of time.

"Is everything okay?" she asked JJ.

"Sorry I'm late. My new campaign manager called. We had to get some things ironed out. His name is Elliot Pendleton. He's a little sloppy looking, but I think he's going to be good."

"Where's he from?" Kitty asked.

"New York," JJ said. "He's fresh off Senator Jerry Cook's campaign." JJ sat down across from Kitty at the small table.

Kitty said, "Well I hope he knows Tennessee politics is altogether different than New York politics."

"He'll need to be brought up to speed," JJ agreed. "He didn't know rodeos and county fairs were major political events here."

Kitty smiled. "Don't forget church houses on Sunday morning, and Wednesday night at the bingo halls."

"Maybe I should have you be my campaign manager?" His broad smile turned serious. He said, "I want you to know I'm sorry I didn't say anything to you about throwing my hat into the ring. I didn't want to get you excited until we needed to be excited. I hope you're not too mad at me."

"That's okay. I'm not worried," Kitty said. "I know you're going to win. And I'll be right behind you the whole way. I don't know a lot about politics, but I'll do whatever I can."

JJ looked at his cell phone. A wisp of a grimace swept across his face as he looked at it. Without responding, he put the phone down on the table.

Kitty noticed his nervousness again. He unbuttoned the top of his shirt as if he was hot, but it wasn't remotely warm in the room. She let it go. "I bet your daddy is excited to have his son stepping into his old shoes? He was a very popular governor," she said. "That should help."

"Yeah, he's excited. I guess it was inevitable."

The waiter stepped up to their table and asked, "Are you ready to order? Or would you like a drink first?"

JJ smiled at the young man. "Sorry, but I'm not going to be able to stay." JJ flashed a look over to Kitty. "Elliot wants to meet with me in Nashville and I have to catch a flight."

"You're *flying* back to Nashville from Memphis? You're kidding?"

"Elliot sent a little jet over for me. We're going to use it on the campaign. He's not wasting any time."

"Or money, it sounds like," Kitty said. "So you're not eating brunch with me?"

JJ shook his head.

The waiter nodded, and said, "I'll check back."

"You have to eat, JJ," Kitty said. "Call him back and tell him to hold his jet. I would love to talk to you about this run for the governor's office. You're going to need a campaign theme song and I have some ideas."

JJ said, "I was just discussing with Elliot how a run for such a high-profile office is going to uproot my life. And when I thought about it, I had to wonder. I don't know if you want to get dragged into an ugly political campaign too."

Kitty shook her head. "I can handle a little mudslinging, if that's what you mean. We Holloway women are tough."

"You just got divorced from someone who, although he's a little kooky, is very beloved here in Tennessee. Frankie and you were kind of Nashville's sweethearts. Your fans might not like it if you suddenly were dating a Fletcher. A lot of people don't agree with my family's politics."

"I don't care what people think."

"The people who run your record label might care."

Kitty started to dispute JJ, but then she stopped. She didn't have many issues with her record label, but sometimes they were more conservative with her career than she believed they needed to be.

JJ continued, "If you want to be a part of this crazy campaign, you know I'd love to have you right at my side."

"I think my fans are pretty loyal. They'll follow me wherever I go," she said. "And you can't please everybody."

"Good," JJ said.

"And when people find out I'm divorced from Frankie, they'll probably think I finally got some damn sense."

"And Dylan? He'll be okay?" JJ watched Kitty closely.

She started to answer, then she caught herself. She had not considered Dylan.

JJ continued, "Josh is sixteen now. He believes I never date anyone. I think he feels I need to stay single for the rest of my life. Teenagers have a strange way of looking at things."

"Maybe you're right. Dylan doesn't even know Frankie and I are divorced yet." Kitty took another sip of her mimosa. She thought of something else that never occurred to her before. She then downed the rest of the drink, and motioned to the waiter for another one.

"What is it?" JJ asked.

"Maybe we should wait," Kitty responded.

Kitty looked at JJ, and noticed it again. JJ was biting the edge of his cheek. And now she was nervous too. He reached across the table, and took Kitty's hand. "I don't know if I want to wait."

Kitty looked into JJ's eyes. They were pleading, and she thought they seemed a little sad. They had a puppy dog quality that Kitty always found downright irresistible.

Kitty almost blurted out her secret to JJ. She had drank too much to be as discerning as she would normally be. But before she spoke, an instinct kicked in. It was a mother's protective instinct.

Her sixteen-year-old son, Dylan, had made a personal revelation to her only two weeks before. To her utter shock, he had told her he was gay. Kitty had never seen Dylan so resolute and emotionally bare. She had not handled it well at all. She had blurted out that she didn't understand. She told her son – right to his frightened face - he had to be wrong. Such a life changing decision at his age could not even be possible. She had even told him to go to his room, like he was a child. In short, for Kitty, she had lost it. He had been crushed. Instead of his room, he had run out the front door. She hadn't seen or heard from him since. It made her worry in ways she had never known were possible. In truth it actually frightened her more than she had ever been for Dylan. She had convinced herself he was just being a rebellious teen, and all would be resolved soon enough.

But what if I'm wrong? She thought.

The waiter brought her the new mimosa, and placed it on the table.

She honestly had no idea whatsoever how JJ Fletcher would react to her having a gay son. It was a subject they never discussed. Never had a need to until now. She loved JJ, but she knew he wasn't the least bit progressive. He still drove a Hummer with a bumper sticker that read:

MY HUMMER ATE YOUR PRIUS FOR BREAKFAST

"I think we should wait," Kitty said.

JJ held more tightly to her hand. He asked, "Are you sure about that?"

"Yes," she said. "Let's wait, and see what happens."

"Okay, so we just keep things as they are?" JJ asked. "We keep hiding?"

"Not hiding. I just think we should hold off until after I talk to Dylan," Kitty replied. "There's no reason we can't wait a little longer. And your campaign manager doesn't need a new girlfriend jumping into the mix before he even gets his feet wet."

"Are you really sure?" JJ asked. "I want this to be your decision."

Kitty nodded, and she lowered her voice. "And if we're going to keep seeing each other in secret, we'll have to be even more discreet. People will be prying into your life more than ever before. No more surprises like you pulled this morning at Graceland." Kitty pulled her hand away, and then pushed JJ's hands back across the table. She added, "And no more of this either."

JJ reached under the table and caressed her inner thigh. "I haven't checked out yet. Let's go back upstairs. I can spare ten more minutes."

"JJ please. The piano player is watching," Kitty said. "And ten minutes is honestly insulting."

Kitty took his hand and pulled it closer. He slid his fingers further up her leg and under her lingerie, then she pushed his hand away.

She looked at JJ coyly. "That will have to do for now. You have a private jet and a Yankee campaign manager waiting on you."

"That I do." JJ stood up.

Kitty smiled. "I'll be back in Nashville tonight. Call me later." She looked down at JJ pants. "And get yourself under control."

"What?" JJ asked.

Kitty gave the crotch of his slacks an obvious stare.

JJ looked down. He smiled. He was proud. He took another long, lustful look at Kitty. Then he turned, and walked away, pulling his suit coat over his bulging slacks.

"What an animal," Kitty said to herself, then smiled. "My animal."

Kitty saw him make a quick pass by the piano player before he left. The waiter came back to her table. "I hope you are staying for brunch, Ms. Stardust."

"Yes, I am, Darlin'. Bring me the house special, extra cheese and extra turkey bacon. And keep these coming." She pointed to her mimosa, and then took a lingering sip.

At first Kitty was baffled by the song the piano player had begun to play. It was more up tempo. Not the usual sweet-sounding melodies he had been performing all morning. She attempted to place the familiar melody. Then it became clear. JJ had obviously made a special request. It was the '70s rock ballad "I Was Made for Lovin' You" by KISS. Kitty noticed the piano player was smiling exuberantly and nodding her way.

It was the song JJ and she always danced to when they were first dating, and it had become one of their personal teen-couple songs for a while. Now, as an adult, it made Kitty hide her face with her napkin until it reached its thunderous, rock ballad conclusion.

Didn't I just tell him we need to be more discreet? Men!

The waiter brought her another mimosa, and she signed a CD for him. She gave him a "Benjamin" to hand over to the piano player. She felt the man deserved it for actually having a KISS rock ballad in his personal song catalog. She took another long sip of her freshly squeezed organic orange juice and champagne.

She realized now she had a few hours to kill by herself. She had a paperback copy of Patricia Cornwell's latest Kay Scarpetta crime mystery in her purse. Maybe she'd go to a coffee shop and find an isolated corner to read.

A phone rang!

It startled Kitty out of her thoughts. She felt a little disoriented. She had to place a hand on the table to steady herself.

Maybe it's time to cut back on the mimosas.

Kitty rummaged through her purse until she realized the phone she was searching for was not even ringing. The ringing phone was JJ's phone. He had left it on the table. She grabbed it and looked up. By now JJ was nowhere to be seen.

She stood, and walked across the room with the cell phone ringing in her hand.

I can't be answering your phone. What if it's your campaign manager?

She stepped from the restaurant, and walked out into the main lobby of the hotel. She had no idea if JJ went to the desk to check out, or if he left the building. He was nowhere in sight. And his damn phone wouldn't stop ringing.

Kitty walked over to the large Italian marble fountain, where the five mallard ducks were swimming. She looked at the ID on the phone and relaxed.

The ID read: Fletcher.

It's JJ calling to tell me to hang on to his phone for him (or to describe dirty sexual scenarios he has planned for me later). A yearning look came over her face. She smiled – at nothing – and realized she already missed him being near her.

She punched the answer key, and placed the phone to her ear. She almost spoke. Then she abruptly stopped herself.

It was a woman's voice on the other end...

"Did you tell her?" the voice asked.

Kitty almost hung up, then quickly – instinctively – she changed her mind.

A woman's voice?

She placed the phone back to her ear carefully – and listened.

"Hello? Hello?...It's your mamma."

Petula's voice was raspy and grating. It made Kitty's stomach clench to the size of a pistachio.

Petula went on: "I can barely hear you on this phone. JJ, are you there? I hate that phone service you have. Well, I hope you did what I told you to do and make her think it was her idea. That's how you handle that breed of woman."

Kitty pushed the phone closer to her ear.

Her idea? Breed of woman?

"Elliot and I will pick you up at the airport. I really like how he thinks," Petula continued. "And don't act all mad at me in front of him. You may think you like that woman, but you can't have some ragtag, fly-by-night, vixen hanging on your arm while you're trying to create an image of respect and gravitas."

Kitty didn't know what to do. She wanted to respond verbally, but her lungs provided no air. A part of her wanted to stop listening, but another part of her – the stronger part – wanted to hear every single word.

Petula continued, "We're going to be asking people to invest money in you, Darlin'. You have to take this seriously. These are important people. Can you even imagine showing up at a five thousand dollar a plate dinner with her? I'm sorry, but that Holloway family will always be what they are. Dullards. Common as pig tracks. Hillbillies. She dresses like a thirteen-year-old boy picks out her outfits for her. She's liable to pull out a banjo and start singing about jambalaya, or her three legged birddog. I know this is hard to hear, but you know it's the God's honest truth. And Elliot agrees entirely."

"Mommy, that lady is crying."

This accurate observation came from a sweet-looking little girl in a powder blue dress and matching ribbon in her hair. Her mother, who also noticed Kitty's distressful appearance, took the girl's hand.

"It isn't nice to stare at people," the mother said. The mother of the little girl had seen Kitty and had come over to the fountain to get an autograph and picture with the Country Western legend. She turned her daughter's face back to the ducks in the pond, as she continued to stare at Kitty herself.

Witnessing a public celebrity breakdown was spellbinding.

Kitty only marginally noticed the mother and daughter because Petula's voice dominated her entire world at the moment. It also was loud enough through the cell phone that the mother of the little girl could easily eavesdrop on some of it.

Petula continued, "It's a miracle I spoke to you before you did something reckless. You have a little of your father in you, and your brain doesn't do all your thinking. I was on the verge of a fainting spell until I heard you say the words 'you may be right, Momma'. If only your father would learn to listen to me. I am sure she can appear inviting to a lonely compassionate man like you, JJ, but she has her motives. I can assure you of that. I don't blame you. It's easy to mistake love for sympathy. I do pray you're being careful. There is an outbreak of some kind of warts out there."

Warts? Kitty's head was spinning.

Warts?

"But not a normal kind of warts," Petula continued. "I read about it in the *Ladies' Home Journal*. It's an epidemic among sexually promiscuous people. I believe they said it came from monkeys. I just have to take your word for it that you have not been having sex with her."

The mother of the little girl in the blue dress decided her celebrity picture would need to wait for a better time. "Come on honey," she said to her daughter. "Let's go check out the gift shop."

Kitty held the cell phone away with her hand. She prayed the monstrous voice would stop.

It did not.

Petula droned on, her voice a little less screeching at arms-length, but the words were quite audible: "I understand she has a pretty face and has tried to make do with that voice. Elliot said, in New York they call someone like her a bubblegum princess, whatever that means, but it sounds about right. No matter how you dress up a skunk, it still stinks. That's what my daddy always said."

Kitty threw the phone into the fountain.

Plop!

Kitty looked down into the water. Bubbles rose up from the phone. She imagined the bubbles must be carrying more insults floating up to the surface. Pop. "Hillbilly." Pop. "Bubblegum princess." Pop. "Monkey warts." Pop. Pop. Pop.

The bubbles eventually stopped - mercifully.

A duck swam over where the cell phone had dropped. It caused ripples to form behind it. The swirling water helped Kitty imagine that there was a face at the bottom of the pond. Petula's face. The face was gasping for air (having used so much of it previously).

Then the face under the water took one last desperate, expiring, gasp.

Other than the ducks paddling around and softly quacking, the water was quiet. Silent. That thing on the bottom of the pond, Kitty observed with much relief, was dead.

It didn't take Dr. Kay Scarpetta's crime solving skills to figure out what JJ Fletcher had done. He had talked to Mommy, and then asked

Mommy if she thought Kitty Stardust could impact his chances of becoming governor. *Mommy* clearly thought Kitty would. Kitty quickly surmised that was the only logical conclusion (and her logic was pretty sound). JJ had lied right to her face.

...and make her think it was her idea.
And, he did!
She briefly tried to make excuses for JJ.
He's strong.
He'll change.
His puppy dog eyes were kind of sad.
...and he's so handsome.
He loves me.
But that was only a last, pathetic effort, by the part of her – the Disney princess part of her - that wanted to deny what was staring her right in the face: He was a lying, Mommy-suckling, bastard, and that was that.

You may be right, Momma.
She made her vow right then and there. She made it to the Peabody Hotel Mallard ducks.

"I banish JJ Fletcher from my life. I banish him until the end of time!"

Kitty made one more phone call that day, from her own phone. She had to retrieve it from her purse, which she had left at the table in the dining room (right next to a fresh, new mimosa – thank you sweet Hawaiian, boxing-champ waiter). It was a call to Frankie Fairway. She asked Frankie if his offer was still on the table.

It was.
She asked Frankie if he could meet her in Nashville later that night.
He could.
The Russian Concussion delivered exactly as promised.

TENNESSEE WILDFLOWERS

4

Now six years later in the governor's bathroom, JJ still was unaware his mother had made such a phone call or that Kitty had heard any of it. All he knew was that the warmth from the shower was starting to fade, and he was starting to feel cold. He knew he'd have to get dressed soon. He really did not want to leave the bathroom today.

Until this morning at his pool, he had never actually spoken to Kitty Stardust since that day at the Peabody Hotel. He had made many concerted efforts, of course, but he had never been successful. The recent memory of her, so close, so intimate, so fiery - so angry - this morning was still monopolizing his mind.

I should have ripped those clothes off you Ruth-Adele and laid you down in that reclining pool chair, you amazing, sexy woman! It's what we both wanted!

RING!

The phone, that JJ had assumed was water-logged and dead, startled him. JJ had flung it into the trash can under the bathroom sink earlier, and had forgotten it was there. He reached down and grabbed it.

"Kitty?" JJ was surprised that he assumed it was her.

He was *hoping* it was her.

It wasn't.

"Governor Fletcher? This is *The Tennessean*. We wanted to get a statement from you concerning your son's wedding."

The Tennessean was Nashville's biggest newspaper, and the male voice on the other end had shocked JJ back to reality. He couldn't believe they were calling him already. This was *exactly* what he was afraid was going to happen.

"Who am I talking to?" JJ asked.

"*The Tennessean*."

"Your name, Son."

"Brian Logan."

"Brian, check your facts before you call me. I'm the governor. I have serious business to take care of, not pure nonsense like this."

"You're saying the story in this morning's *Nashville Sun* is not true?"

"Of course it's not true."

"Can I quote you on that? Your son Josh is *not* getting married to Dylan Fairway."

"Are you playing deaf and dumb on me, Brian? Not one damn word of it is true! You can quote me on that!"

JJ was boiling.

He threw the phone back into the trash can, hard enough this time there was no possible way it didn't break.

Immediately he realized he probably should have prepared a calm, reasoned, response. But it was too late now.

Let them quote me, the sons of bitches!

Those who have all the answers, have simply misunderstood the questions.
- UNKNOWN

PREPARATIONS

1

Petula Fletcher stood at the podium, in front of a seated group of people dressed in a wide variety of rural, back-woods clothing, dating from the late 1800s. It was the first day of rehearsals for The Cowboy Fletcher Community Theater's annual presentation of *The Shepherd of the Hills*. Theodore Westlake, a curmudgeon of a man utilizing an oxygen tank to breathe, sat behind Petula in a wheelchair. The theatrical production was a pet project of Petula's. She had seen the celebrated play about mountain people living in the Ozarks in Branson, Missouri many years ago and decided it would be a perfect holiday tradition for Nashville. Theodore Westlake was the sole investor, contributing $200,000 every year for the production. The Branson, Missouri theater group famously utilized over 80 actors, 40 horses and had a nightly - with real flames and all - burning of a cabin. Petula's production was indoors, and due to city regulations, she had to settle for 30 actors, 3 horses, and, in lieu of a burning cabin, a dry-ice machine with clever lighting. It played every Friday and Saturday nights and on Sunday matinees at The Cowboy Fletcher Community Theater to sold-out crowds from Thanksgiving until Christmas.

Also behind Petula sat Eli Lipton, a wild-eyed young man in a flowery pirate shirt, pointy Italian shoes, perilously skin-tight purple pants, a burgundy fedora and yellow scarf. He was the newly contracted director of the play. Petula had hired Eli (a little more high-priced than in years past) to add some spark to the play. Eli clasped the much annotated play in his hand. This was his big break, and he was bubbling over with excitement. Last night he had forked over a wad of cash for some obscenely expensive coke so he would feel at his absolute peak creative potential for the entire run of the play. Even now, a little bit of the white crystalline powder was clinging to his neatly trimmed nostril hairs and running down the back of his throat.

Petula looked at the crowd of eager participants who were leafing through their own copies of the play. "Thank you so much for coming out so early in the morning," Petula said. She turned to Theodore. "And thank you again, Theodore Westlake, for your continuous kind and generous support for our little production."

The sound of his oxygen tank purring was the only perceptible response from Theodore. No surprise really, as he was ninety-seven years old and stone deaf. The crowd applauded.

"And Eli Lipton. Thank you for coming all the way from Palm Springs, California Theatre for the Performing Arts. With your artistic guidance, this year's *Shepherd of the Hills* promises to be the best production Nashville has seen yet."

Eli pole-vaulted up for a carefully executed bow. Petula led the crowd in a short applause.

Florie Pettygrove and Tallulah Hicks were in the back row. Their non-speaking roles were described as Mutton Hollow Inhabitants. Florie poked Tallulah. "Wake up girl."

"I'm just thinking with my eyes closed," Tallulah replied, as she opened her eyes and sat up. She gathered her latest thoughts. "I was lamenting the death of my potted ornamentals. That new weatherman on Channel 2 didn't mention a word about a frost. He hasn't had an accurate forecast since they hired him. Even a broken clock gets it right twice a day."

Florie nodded, and said, "Did you hear Leroy Pollard's new wife gets rid of her allergies by injecting herself with hookworms?"

"Yes," Tallulah replied, despairingly, "and if you ask me she's lost too much weight on account of those worms. My hunting dog had a bad case of hookworms and we had to put him down."

Silence may be golden, but in Tennessee, gossip is King Midas. Florie and Tallulah were on even ground with most folks they knew - more than happy to keep any sensational rumors, alleged or otherwise, alive and kicking.

Florie said, "I guess you heard that Agnes Bowers was run over by the Nash Trash Bus yesterday afternoon? Right off the sidewalk, there on Roy Acuff Place in front of Studio B. She'll never walk again."

"I certainly did. And I was not a bit surprised," Tallulah responded. "Agnes Bowers refused to help her momma pay for her hip replacement surgery. What goes around..."

"Tommy Padilla is getting divorced, again."

Tallulah heaved a knowing sigh. "Tommy Padilla needs to spend less time on the bar stools and a little more time in a church pew. Of course I'm not one to judge."

"Charlene caught Tommy at The Gaylord Hotel with Fred Coffey's youngest."

"The girl who flips burgers at the White Castle? I had not heard a word about that." Tallulah said, disquieted *and* enlivened by the news.

"Yes-sir-eee-bob! But you didn't hear it from me."

"My...ohhhh...myyyyy!"

Florie poked Tallulah again. "Now be quiet. Petula is about to tell her annual joke."

Tallulah said, "I don't know why we have to be here so bleeding heck early. It's not like either one of us got the part of Granny Becky."

"We still have to rehearse," Florie replied.

"We don't have any lines."

Florie waved her to be quiet.

Petula said, from the stage, "I am just terrible at telling a joke."

Florie poked Tallulah. "See, I told you. Here it comes."

Petula continued, "But it has become a tradition here on the first day of rehearsals, so I'll do my best to summon up a good one for you."

Tallulah said, "That new director Petula hired from California sure is a squirrely rich looking guy. I guess you call that 'dressing to impress'." She squinted at the director again. "If you're trying to impress a village of leprechauns."

"Shhh." Florie poked Tallulah again.

Petula began, "There was a fellow getting up in years, and he decided he wanted to see all the well-known cathedrals in the world before he was too old to enjoy their splendor. First, he went to St. Peter's Cathedral in Vatican City. While on the cathedral tour, he noticed an odd sight. On the wall there was a telephone made of solid gold. Next to the phone was a sign that read, Calls To God – 10,000 Euros Per Minute. The tour guide explained, 'That phone is a direct line to heaven where anyone can speak to The Almighty Himself.' Next, the man visited Winchester Cathedral where he saw the exact same gold phone with a sign that read, Calls To God – 8,000 Pounds Per Minute. Each cathedral he visited he saw the same phone, with the same kind of sign. Then he came to Nashville, where he visited our very own Christ Church Cathedral. There it was again. That solid gold telephone hanging on the wall of the cathedral. But this time he noticed a surprising difference. The sign next to this phone read, Calls To God – 10 Cents Per Minute. He asked the tour guide why this gold phone only charged 10 Cents per minute. She smiled, and kindly explained to him, 'You're in Tennessee, Darlin'. Now, it's a local call.'"

The crowd laughed gregariously. Petula had delivered the joke perfectly. The introduction speech (and subsequent joke) was over, and the breakfast buffet was next on the agenda. The caterers were already removing the stainless steel lids from the breakfast trays, pouring coffee and orange juice.

"That breakfast smells good. Let's get in line," Tallulah said.

"You want to get us kicked out of the play?" Florie replied. "Hold tight until Petula gives us the go ahead."

Petula said, "I know everyone is hungry, and that breakfast smells good, but I do have an announcement to make before I let you go get in line. I'm really not supposed to talk about this just yet. President McKenzie's people, and my own son asked me to wait until they were ready to make the announcement themselves later today..."

A man dressed up as one of the Baldknobber Clan elbowed Florie, and handed her a copy of *The Nashville Sun*. Florie didn't know the man, so she ignored him. She wanted to stay focused on getting in the buffet line first. But he kept poking her, and pointing at the headline of the newspaper, until Florie and Tallulah both looked down.

Petula continued, "You know what they say, 'How do you stop a Southern woman from repeating a secret?' How do you stop a rooster from crowing when the sun comes up in the morning? Short of shooting 'em, it simply cannot be done."

The crowd laughed knowingly.

Florie, who can read faster than Tallulah, gasped, and pivoted her head up from *The Nashville Sun*. She yelled out, "Petula, stop!"

Petula, surprised by the outburst, looked out into the crowd. "Is that you Florie Pettygrove?"

"Yes, it is! Have you lost your mind, Petula?"

"I am about to make an announcement. If you have something to say, you can come up here and say it after I'm done."

"No!" Florie yelled again. "You don't mean that!"

Tallulah yelled, "She's right, Petula. You can't be serious!"

"Now you too, Tallulah. Everyone is going to know soon enough. Just let me say what I have to say. I am very proud. I don't know when I've had such delightful news to share. The people in this great state of Tennessee are going to be delighted too."

Florie stood up. She had never been outspoken, or even very opinionated, but today she was motivated by vigor she didn't even know she had. "No, we are not!"

Tallulah stood up too. She was emboldened by Florie's ire. Tallulah shook the newspaper out in front of her. "You can't be proud. It's not possible."

Florie and Tallulah pushed their way through the chairs, nearly knocking over some of their fellow cast members, Tallulah waving the newspaper the whole way. Petula stared at them with incomprehension as they clamored up onto the stage with her. Tallulah handed the newspaper to Petula.

Petula refused to look. "What in the name of Saint Peter has gotten into the two of you? It's awfully early to be drinking," she said (even though she knew personally that statement was flat out not true). "Just tell me what's wrong, please," Petula said, hoping to get back to her announcement that JJ was going to be the next vice president of the United States.

Florie's chest deflated. "Petula, it just don't make sense to me. You should be more upset. Not excited."

"Why would I be upset?" Petula reasoned. "You may not know this, but Cowboy's daddy tried to do this himself once. It's just in the Fletcher's genes. And now, it looks like someone in the Fletcher family is going to finally become everything I have ever hoped for."

"Don't you think it's a sin?" Florie asked.

Petula said, "Of course it's not a sin. I think it's all a part of God's divine plan."

"Divine plan?" Florie asked, exasperated.

Petula was getting irritated. "Yes, God's divine plan. Would you two go sit back down?"

Tallulah dropped the newspaper and fainted, crumbling into a heap on the stage.

Eli jumped up and ran over to Tallulah. He lightly slapped her face trying to revive her.

Florie reached to the stage floor, and took the newspaper from where Tallulah had dropped it. She turned, and showed it to Petula again.

Petula sighed, and reluctantly glanced at the newspaper. After a moment, she quickly grabbed it from Florie's hand.

Petula read the headlines several times. She asked, "What is this? Some kind of joke newspaper." She looked out over the crowd. Most had some awareness of what she had just read. Their smartphones were abuzz with it, and some people were reading their own copies of *The Nashville Sun*. "Where did you get this?" Petula asked Florie.

"From that guy playing a Baldknobber." Florie pointed, incriminatingly, at the man in the back row.

Petula stared out into the crowd. She saw looks of confusion, shock and revulsion. Some people were already getting up to leave the room. A separate few were smiling and nodding with approval. Petula knew she had to act fast, and she stepped back to the podium.

Petula held the newspaper up to the crowd, and said, "There is something rotten in the state of Tennessee!" Petula pulled the microphone closer to her mouth. "The news I was going to tell you most certainly was not this." She jostled the newspaper in front of her. "My son, JJ Fletcher, has been chosen by President Bob McKenzie to become the next vice president of the United States. Somebody clearly is not happy about that, and has tried to upstage this legitimate news with a pack of lies. Do not worry ladies and gentlemen. Whoever is responsible for this contrivance against my family has rattled the wrong cage. This is Petula Fletcher they're dealing with. And they have made a terrible miscalculation by picking a fight with me. Some blind little pig has just waddled right into a slaughterhouse."

Petula's plea did get their attention. Most stopped and looked back at her as she shook the newspaper again.

Petula repeated, with more wrathful passion, "Some *yellow-bellied and foolish* blind little pig has just waddled right into *a damn bloody* slaughterhouse!"

2

"You two fellas look about as flustered as a one-eyed cat trying to watch over two mouse holes," Buster Ragsdale said, with a willful calm in his voice. He knew exactly what the two men, who had shuffled up to his private property with anxious, avid resoluteness, were up to. He was already two steps ahead of them.

"Just look at your letter, and read what it says, Buster," said Attorney Lloyd Rollins. "It's a legal injunction against you and your newspaper."

Elliot and Lloyd Rollins, JJ's personal attorney, stood at the gate behind *The Nashville Sun* newspaper building. Buster Ragsdale was standing in front of the two men as four delivery trucks waited, idling, behind him. He glanced over the letter in his hand with only tepid interest.

Lloyd had called in some political favors to get a judge to issue a temporary injunction to stop the newspaper trucks from leaving the printing press. Judge Gregory Hackett was asleep in bed when Lloyd called, but the judge was a good friend of the Fletcher Family, and once he absorbed the issue Attorney Rollins presented to him, he went into his own home office – still in his boxer briefs – and had the injunction faxed over to Lloyd's home office in less than ten minutes.

The four trucks behind Buster could not leave the parking lot because Elliot had parked across the driveway gate blocking the exit.

"I want to make it clear that this injunction includes any internet versions of today's newspaper, and there cannot be any related comments made to any other press about the content of your newspaper dated today." Lloyd adjusted his tie confidently.

"My truck drivers get paid by the hour. I sure would like to get them on the road," Buster said, looking up from the letter.

"Were you not listening? Your newspaper is not going to be delivered this morning. This particular edition will not be delivered to anyone, ever. Those trucks can turn off their engines." Lloyd pointed to the injunction letter in Buster's hand. "It's all there in the papers I just served you."

"These trucks behind me? Are they the one's you're talking about?"

"Yes, those trucks, Buster." Lloyd was irritated by Buster's relaxed demeanor.

"There is going to be a lot of very upset managers at the Steak and Shake restaurants all over central and western Tennessee. And this letter doesn't mention anything about restaurant menus," Buster said.

"Steak and Shake?" Elliot jumped into the conversation. He didn't like the calmness in Buster's voice either. Elliot could see overconfidence a mile away. It was usually something he was exuding himself.

"You can't make money just printing a newspaper anymore," Buster explained. "These trucks behind us are full of the new menus for Steak and Shake. They have three new milkshake flavors, and a couple of new healthy choice options. The public's taste changes quickly, and one has to keep up with those changes."

Lloyd's cheeks began to turn flushed and both sides of his temples produced blood pulsing vessels. He already suspected he knew the answer before he asked it, "Where are the trucks with today's newspapers in them?"

Buster shrugged. "Hard to say. Those trucks left here hours ago."

"You sent your newspaper out early. You knew we were coming," Elliot said, feeling his stomach begin to churn.

"Call your drivers and tell them to stop their delivery." Lloyd ordered, handing Buster his own cell phone. His neck was bright red now. He stepped closer in a threatening way. "Every paper delivered today is a violation of this injunction."

Buster didn't accept the phone, and remained calm. "When my drivers are operating their trucks they don't answer their cell phones. It's a safety issue. That would be an actual law that they would be breaking."

"Call them on their radios," Lloyd demanded.

"Don't have radios anymore. With cell phones it's an unnecessary expense."

Elliot shook his head, flustered. "Why are you doing this, Buster? The Fletcher's have never done anything to deserve this. It isn't like you to print a story that is clearly a politically calculated lie."

"I haven't printed any lies."

"Who's your source?" Elliot asked.

"It's a solid one. I wouldn't have put it in my paper if it wasn't," Buster replied soberly.

"If it *is* the truth, you can't possibly think it will do anything but hurt the Fletcher family." Elliot was exasperated. "There is a press conference today by President McKenzie. JJ Fletcher is his choice to replace Don Summerfield. JJ truly deserves to get that position. He's a good man, and you know it. You need to go on TV and explain how you fell victim to a very clever liar. You need to do that as a friend, and you need to do that because you know the story is completely out of bounds. It is a personal matter, whatever the real story may, or may not, be."

Buster looked at Elliot. He knew the man was faithful to his boss, and he was also very good at his job. Buster knew that Elliot's determination was not going to diminish no matter what he said. He sighed. "Look, Elliot, Lloyd, I'm past my retirement anyway. There's a lot more sand in the bottom of my hourglass than at the top, which makes a man less influenced by the opinions of others. I did what I did because I feel it is the right thing to do. I actually feel like reporting important, and sometimes controversial, news is what my job as a newspaper owner is about. What are you planning to do? Arrest me and have me thrown in jail? There still is something called freedom of the press in this country, isn't there? Wait, let me answer that, *No*. But, none-the-less, if you're done, I have some menus to deliver."

"You won't retract the story?" Elliot asked.

"I'm not going to retract the story."

Lloyd said, "Then we'll see you in court, Mr. Ragsdale."

Buster motioned for his trucks to get ready to move. "Fine," Buster said. "In the mean-time, could you move your car? It's blocking private property. And when you get a chance, try out those new pomegranate milkshakes. I hear they are really tasty."

3

Georgia loved Miss Jewell's kitchen: stainless steel appliances, cornflower blue tile, a granite floor, a walk-in pantry, and more storage space than any clear-thinking person could ever use. It was the perfect room to step into first thing in the morning in a big fluffy terry cloth robe and warm lamb's wool slippers.

Georgia's morning routine could be achieved with a blindfold covering her eyes. Fill the poached egg pan with water and place it on the gas stove. Take out two thick pieces of whole wheat bread from Nathan's Village Bakery and drop them in the toaster. The coffee maker had already preformed its perking duties programmed into it the night before. Jewell would be asleep for another hour, so Georgia had plenty of time to meet the new day slow and easy. Georgia used the three and one half minutes of egg poaching time to grab the newspaper from the front porch.

She sat down in front of the big screen Panasonic TV with her poached eggs on toast and her coffee setting on a TV tray, then flipped the TV on to *Morning Joe*. Georgia had a crush on that Mr. Joe Scarborough fellow.

Joe and his co-host, Mika, were sipping their Starbucks and summarizing the latest morning's political wrangles, when suddenly Georgia was drawn away from her imaginary cable news boyfriend and his co-host. Her eyes grew to the size of Kennedy half dollars. Her attention zeroed in on the newspaper opened up on her TV tray, *The Nashville Sun*. She grabbed the paper and read the first four paragraphs on the front page before thumbing through it, trying to find the continuing story.

"Are you my maid?"

Jewell's abrupt entry into the room nearly made Georgia leap clear out of the Chippendale mahogany wing-back armchair she was sitting in.

"Lordy, Miss Jewell. What are you doing up so early?"

"Are you my maid?" Jewell asked again. She was dressed in an ivory white two tier long dress, and had a long string of pearls around her neck. She had brushed her hair and placed a carved jade hair piece in an attractive bun. Georgia hadn't seen Jewell dress herself in years.

She's wearing eye liner and lipstick too. What on earth has gotten into her?

"Yes, Sweat Pea, I'm your maid." Not being recognized half the time was standard operating procedure around this house. Georgia took no offence. "And don't you look pretty as a peacock, Miss Jewell? How are you doing this morning?"

"Well personally I'd say I was doing just fine, except all the damn doctors keep contradicting me." Jewell didn't smile, but Georgia did. She loved Jewell's dry, devil-may-care, wit. Jewell continued on, with an almost blithesome declaration, "Thanksgiving is coming up in a few days and we have a lot of things to do. We have a special guest. So we have to put on our best presentation."

"We have a guest? Is it that Mr. Ragsdale?" Georgia glanced at the newspaper. Frankly she hadn't had time to digest the whole implication of the news story opened up on the TV stand, but she knew enough to see the storm that could be brewing. And she comprehended that Buster Ragsdale might never be a guest at Jewell Fletcher's home ever again. "Maybe we should hold off preparing an extra plate for Mr. Ragsdale." Georgia looked back to Jewell, who waved her off.

"I have no idea who you're talking about. I want you to get a pad and pencil to take notes. You'll need to do some shopping."

"Let's get some breakfast in you first Sweat Pea, and then we can hold a strategy session for Thanksgiving dinner."

Georgia thought over what she was about to say next. The doctor made it clear that alarming stories, or remarks about contemporary news, could confuse Jewell and cause her unnecessary distress. But that very same doctor also said keeping Jewell up-to-date with personal, non-shocking, stories was good for her brain. Georgia loved Jewell truly, as if she were her own sister, and she tried to always follow the doctor's orders.

I don't really see the harm.

"You do recall that you have a great nephew by the name of Josh?"

"Of course I do. Josh is my brother Cowboy's grandson. He always brings me those Walnetta candies. When he was eight years old I taught him how to catch a catfish. He is over in Africa helping all those impoverished black people right now."

TENNESSEE WILDFLOWERS

Josh Fletcher hasn't been here in two years, and she remembers him perfectly. I'm here every damn day, and I'm a perfect stranger, thought Georgia.

"Your mind is a marvel, Miss Jewell." Georgia said, and sighed. She glanced at the newspaper again. "Josh has returned from Africa, it seems. And he is getting married. This coming Sunday, according to the newspaper." Georgia wasn't certain if she could rely entirely on a newspaper story as her source of such fantastic news. It was odd that no one had said anything to them about it...

But then again...it wasn't so odd when you considered it.

Jewell smiled. "I can't wait to hear the stories of his travels on that beautiful continent across the Atlantic. Josh is a very handsome, well mannered and smart boy. I imagine that there were a lot of young ladies waiting in line to be the lucky lady to marry my great-nephew."

Georgia said, "If what I'm reading is correct, that line might have had all manner of folks standing in it."

Georgia decided she had better leave it at that.

"So, we have Thanksgiving, and then a wedding the following Sunday." Jewell considered the extra chores they would need to carry out now that she had heard the news. "I need to make sure I have two dresses ready. One for our Thanksgiving dinner and one for the wedding. I always wear something bright to a wedding. A flowered print, but not too vivacious. One must never compete with the bride."

"I think you'll be safe to wear whatever you want," Georgia said. "Of course, we haven't been formally invited yet."

Georgia considered now that maybe she should have not said anything about the whole matter. Once Jewell set her mind to something, as long as she remembered what it was, it was almost impossible to steer her off course.

"A funeral or a wedding, one always goes. That's what good people do. It is my sweet great nephew, Josh. A team of wild horses couldn't keep me away."

Yep, I should have kept my big mouth shut.

Georgia looked over at the TV.

Mr. handsome Joe, if this turns out to be the spectacle I think it could be, by this time tomorrow, you may be having an early morning round table discussion with your Starbucks about the Fletcher Family right there on your TV show.

"Well, are you going to get me my breakfast?" Jewell said, expectantly. "Or do you plan on waiting until I become completely consumed with hunger and faint dead away on the Chesterfield?"

Not till the sun excludes you do I exclude you.
  - WALT WHITMAN

A HORNET'S NEST

1

Kitty laid in her bed in the darkness, slipping in and out of sleep.

Peggy Sue, sensing her master's emotional turmoil, licked her hand. It woke Kitty out of her drowsiness, and (to the little dog's dismay) a fresh flow of tears began to burst forth.

Kitty had made a solemn vow to herself to never let a Fletcher hurt her again.

I banish JJ Fletcher from my life. I banish him until the end of time!

She recalled the words quite clearly. She had kept this promise for over six years. She had pushed the memories away for as long as she could. But the damn was breaking. And now, Josh's heart was breaking too. She imagined how painful it had to be for him right now. She was too sensitive, especially when it came to people she loved. She knew that, but couldn't help herself. It came from her heart. The small act of kindness from her pet was the final straw - Kitty openly wept.

The door to Kitty's pitch black bedroom opened, and someone stepped inside. Peggy Sue growled, but stayed next to her master's side.

Estella-Jeanne asked, "Are you trying to grow mushrooms in here?"

"I'm trying to sleep, Momma."

"I brought you some honey and lemon water for your voice."

Estella-Jeanne let her eyes adjust to the lack of light, then walked over, and set the mug on the bedside table.

Kitty wiped her nose with a Kleenex. "Thank you for the water, Momma. Now you can go." Kitty turned away, tears welled up again, and she blubbered into her pillow. "Go, Momma. I need to be alone."

"Do you remember that nice young girl from Canada? The one Dylan toured with last year."

Kitty thought a moment. "Carly Rae Jepsen."

"That's the one," Estella-Jeanne replied. "She called. She wanted to congratulate Dylan and Josh, and sent them her best wishes. She said to tell you that if you need anything just call her."

Kitty blinked. "That's very sweet. Some people are so nice." Just thinking about someone offering up warm-hearted good wishes made Kitty sob again.

"Cry until you laugh; laugh until you smile; smile until you love; love until you cry," Estella-Jeanne said, recalling some old Tennessee hill wisdom passed through the ages.

Estella-Jeanne sat on the bed. She stroked the head of Peggy Sue. She looked at her daughter, and knew how much she hurt. A parent always does. "After your daddy died I sat out on my front porch and cried for six solid months. What good did it do? For anybody. I was still a widow with a little girl, a dried up milk cow, six scrawny chickens and a goat covered with ticks."

"Momma, I have to rest." Kitty blew into the Kleenex. "What am I doing? I'll just cancel the show tonight. They can do without me."

Estella-Jeanne said, "Look how much better off we are now. I have a beautiful grandson. We have mountains of money. I've even stopped stuffing cash into my mattress for when the other shoe drops." Estella-Jeanne grabbed another Kleenex from the table and handed it to Kitty. "Somewhere way back in history, some dog - plumb full of bad luck - took a piss on our family tree, and we've all lived in outright squalor ever since. But that curse has been lifted. My grandson is the first person in my family in six generations, or maybe ever, who has never known dire poverty, and all the unbearable pain and humiliation that comes with that. And he's not spoiled one bit. He's a wonderful young man."

"He is a good boy. I got lucky." Kitty honked into the Kleenex again.

"That woman is not going to hurt him, not as long as I'm breathing."

"We do not speak her name. *Or* her son's."

"I know that. But, I was thinking. What is the day after tomorrow?"

"Thanksgiving, Momma. What's your point?"

"Who owns Thanksgiving in this town?"

Kitty sat up. "The one whose name we do not speak." Kitty's interest was piqued.

"Drink your honey and lemon water, Ruth-Adele Holloway. You are going to go do your show tonight. The whole world will be watching to see how you respond to what's going on out there. And besides your son's spectacular wedding, you will be proudly speaking about, you will have another announcement to make."

"What announcement?"

"You can call all your fans on that computer, your buddies on that web thingy? Right?"

"My fanpage?"

"Yes, that thing. And you can contact them all by tomorrow?"

"It's instant, Momma. I keep explaining that to you."

"Perfect. Finally technology is working in my favor."

"Out with it Momma. What are you getting at?"

Estella-Jeanne squinted her eyes. "I think it's time the Holloway family started a little revolution here in Tennessee. Just like the Hillbilly Revolt of 1936."

"There was a Hillbilly Revolt?"

She looked at Kitty. "Viva la Clodhoppers," said Estella-Jeanne, holding her fist up in the dark. "That was their rallying cry."

"Now you're just making stuff up, Momma."

"Listen to my plan," Estella-Jeanne said. "If this doesn't send her caboose off the tracks, then I don't know what will."

Kitty listened to her mother lay out her Machiavellian plan. She let the images unfold before her in her mind.

There was no question about it. It was one of her momma's best.

2

President Bob McKenzie was not exactly at liberty to be neutral on the issue of gay marriage. His real feelings on the subject – never a huge priority – wavered between: *I don't really see the problem with it* and *it really seems to be a big problem for some people, people who opposed it in the extreme, and ones who tend to vote for me.*

That had been before. Now he had no real choice in the matter. He'd done something very bad; something his wife, Suzanne, had a very big problem with. She had never been a supporter of gay rights anyway. Unlike Petula Fletcher, her reasons were mostly on religious grounds instead of primarily political ones. But still, she didn't feel the need to make it a big priority in her, or her husband's, personal or political life. A few years ago that had changed. It became an issue that instantly advanced to the top of her passionate opposition list. An incident she witnessed had made it personal. And JJ Fletcher's gay marriage debacle in Tennessee had poured salt onto a freshly cut wound.

The incident in question – the wounding incident – occurred roughly two years ago at the DC Young Republicans' Holiday Party and Toy Drive at the Washington Marriott Wardman Park Hotel. First Lady Suzanne McKenzie walked into their luxury presidential suite to find her husband having sex with one of his interns - her nephew, Owen, from Missoula, Montana.

It could be argued that it wasn't exactly Bob McKenzie's fault. (Lord knows Bob aspired to argue *that* with his wife.) Owen had spiked the president's coconut martini with the drug Ecstasy, only half believing – *hoping!* – he could actually lure his boss of three months into a hotel room for sex. Why would a nineteen-year-old young man do that? From the first day he stepped into the Oval Office to be introduced to the president as the newest intern on staff

Owen was smitten. He believed he was in love. *He was not.* He was just a very impressionable teenage boy in the presence of an attractive, extremely intelligent, older man. Power was sexually intoxicating, and Owen was inebriated instantly. At nineteen, a boy's moral compass - if he's lucky enough to have a moral compass - is held hostage by freshly acquired bodily functions, fed on a constant diet of raging hormones. When Owen was much older, he would look back on his youthful indiscretion with shock, and embarrassment. At the time it happened - at nineteen - he was only mad he got caught.

In the convention hall, at the Marriott Wardman Park Hotel, President McKenzie, who had never taken Ecstasy (or even smoked pot for that matter) became violently ill. "It must be the shrimp," Owen said, empathetically. "We need to get you to your room, Mr. President, before anyone sees you like this." Bob McKenzie agreed. He just needed to lay down. His head was spinning. And for some bizarre reason, every single person in the room was beginning to look more than a little sexually desirable.

Inside the presidential suite, with two oblivious (and rather unobservant) Secret Service agents in the hallway, Owen carefully sat the president on the king size bed. He removed the president's shoes, and took off his tie. The president wondered why his intern was shirtless *revealing a young firm, upper body,* he noted. And why was the boy giving him a shoulder massage? One that was *really loosening him up?* Those stout, *smoldering,* teenage hands were dissolving and liberating Bob McKenzie in ways that were foreign, indescribable, and impossible to ignore. He certainly didn't feel so ill anymore. Then the full effect of the Ecstasy drug - intense sexual euphoria - overtook Bob McKenzie. The president grabbed the top of his Louis Vuitton shirt collar and ripped it open, the genuine pearl buttons flying off.

Suzanne McKenzie walked into the room at the most inopportune moment possible. Her husband was on top of her teenage nephew, pants down, lunging up and down in rhythmic, pulverizing thrusts. And while she watched - stupefied and rendered speechless - prolonged, full-throated, orgasmic moans were emanating steadily from the man she wedded twenty two years ago; moaning sounds she had never once heard in her entire life.

Owen was sent back to Missoula, with the story he hated Washington, D.C. (which pretty much was the truth). Should his mom's sister, Suzanne, tell anyone her nephew drugged her husband, a sitting president of the United States, Owen knew he might find himself serving a life sentence in a federal prison. His aunt made that crystal clear. But even with her persuasive threats, Owen didn't fret that much. He had been shagged by the commander-in-chief. He wasn't going to let his aunt rain on *that* parade. But he did keep it to himself. He wasn't a complete idiot. And he had to get busy and enrolled for next semester's classes at the University of Montana anyway.

No one but Bob McKenzie, Suzanne and Owen ever knew about what happened in the presidential suite that night. And no one else ever would. All three involved would take this entire incident to their graves. Bob had begged for forgiveness from Suzanne. He got no such thing. He tried. He explained: He wasn't gay (true). The boy drugged him with a potent hallucinogenic (true). And he could barely recall anything that had happened once he returned to the suite (not true). Suzanne did not reply to her husband's pleas. She only glared. If a picture was worth a thousand words, the stare Suzanne gave to her husband that day would have filled the entire Library of Congress. The First Lady let her husband worry about what she might do.

And worry he did.

If the subject of gay rights, gay marriage - or gay anything - was ever mentioned she made it clear that *those people* would never have a voice in the McKenzie White House. In the case of The First Lady, the entire homosexual community would pay for Owen-from-Missoula's indiscretion as long as the McKenzie's lived at 1600 Pennsylvania Avenue. Bob McKenzie was in no position to counter his wife. He would never be able to counter his wife on anything ever again. Lucky for him, they didn't disagree on that many things anyway.

President McKenzie's staff did wonder why the commander-in-chief refused to even debate the issue of gay marriage for the past two years. They made assumptions: He was a strong Christian man. He was from Alabama. He had always been very conservative. Although these observations and theories were accurate, they were nowhere close to the real reason. They did notice that anyone who pressed the issue was soundly removed from their employment at the White House. Everyone on the staff knew: the president was against gay marriage. End of discussion. Any vice president who would ever stand beside him would be against gay marriage as well.

What else did the presidential staff need to know? He was their boss, and the president of the United States, after all.

3

"Never hit a hornet's nest with a short stick," Elliot said. "That's what my grandmother always told us."

JJ looked at his campaign manager dubiously. "Your Yankee grandma said that?"

"Maybe it wasn't her, maybe it was Mark Twain." Elliot held up his hands in defense. "They both had white hair and smoked cigars. I'm just trying to tell you that we can't be taking any unnecessary risks. Not now."

Byrdie stood nearby reading her MacBook, looking up to JJ and Elliot with concern. The three of them had been locked inside the governor's upstairs office for over two hours. The Peppermint Schnapps she drank earlier, to calm her nerves, was wearing off and now she wished she had some Advil.

"I don't recall any other elected official has ever had to make statements about their children to the press," JJ said. He was putting a golf ball across the hardwood floor of his office into a ceramic coffee mug turned on its side. The little white ball went wildly astray, bouncing under his desk. He dropped another ball to the floor.

Byrdie was having trouble keeping up with all the tweets, Facebook comments and blog entries. The story about Josh's wedding plans – or lack-there-of – had set off a political wild fire. And here, at the epicenter, was JJ hitting golf balls into a ceramic mug with an image of the band KISS printed on the side.

JJ had gotten dressed in a very agreeable pressed white shirt and pants. Byrdie had noted, though, that he was perspiring enough to have conspicuous stains under his arm pits. He also had forgotten to shave, and his shirt was buttoned up crooked.

Dear God, he's got a black cowboy boot on one foot, and a brown one on the other!

She'd have to fix him up before they let him be seen in public.

When Elliot arrived, he had ushered JJ and Byrdie into JJ's office and locked the door. Elliot kept grabbing his hair in clumps as he paced the floor. Elliot explained the details about his run-in with Buster Ragsdale. The window of opportunity they had to stop the newspaper from getting out had been closed. That was that. JJ insisted on calling Buster himself, but Elliot nixed that. Attorney Lloyd Rollins had his full staff working on how to handle Mr. Ragsdale, and his newspaper. For now, Elliot wanted to get absolutely clear on the way to proceed forward without any further damage. They had to make it appear to the outside world that JJ had complete control of the story. The only problem was, at the moment, he clearly was not in control at all.

Elliot had already confirmed the press conference for noon had been cancelled. President McKenzie's office had acted quickly to get that detail out of the way. The president's people also had expressed their annoyance that Petula Fletcher had announced JJ's strictly confidential vice presidential offer to a small crowd earlier that morning in Nashville. This had been a surprising fact about Petula that Elliot wasn't aware of at the time. He'd have to deal with her for that blunder later. He was finally told that the president was going to be waiting for JJ to call the White House back personally to explain the troubling situation, a fact which was creating much of the growing stress in the room.

Calls had been placed to Josh, but they had gotten no call back. JJ's main residence across town had been visited by two of JJ's staff, and no one was found there. They also had gone to Dylan Fairway's apartment in downtown Nashville. No one was there either. All attempts to contact Kitty Stardust, to see if she knew where Josh was, had been futile. Byrdie had never seen JJ so flustered. Elliot's manic pacing and nervous hair pulling wasn't helping.

"Not everyone signed into law a statewide ban on same-sex marriage like you did," Elliot said. His voice sounded too angry and condescending for Byrdie's liking. "If your son intends to hold a public gay wedding," Elliot continued, "even if it isn't legal, it would look like you maintain different standards for yourself and your family than you do for the public."

"What should I do about the rest of this afternoon's itinerary?" Byrdie asked.

"Is it urgent?" Elliot responded. Her question clearly perturbed him.

Byrdie said, "JJ is scheduled to be in Chattanooga for a speech at the NRA's Grandmothers for Guns annual luncheon, then he has to be back here for a photo op with Miss Teen Tennessee. She's launching her foundation to eradicate world hunger. Then he has to be at the RC Cola and Moon Pie Festival in Bell Buckle late this afternoon. JJ is master of ceremonies at the Moon Pie eating contest, like he is every year!"

"We're kind of having a crisis here, Byrdie," Elliot snapped.

"I'm aware of that," she said. Elliot's snippy attitude was not setting well with her. "But I have to tell them all something."

"If we start canceling events it looks like we're trying to hide something," Elliot responded. He started with the hair ringing and floor pacing again.

JJ hit a golf ball so hard it ricocheted off the wall and smashed a glass pencil holder on his desk. JJ took the putter, and slammed it into the golf bag with the others. "Byrdie, return these clubs and get my money back."

Byrdie took a quick look at Elliot, who was nervously circling JJ's desk like a vulture. *He's no help.* She looked back at JJ.

"They were a gift," Byrdie responded.

JJ extended the golf bag to Byrdie. "Then get whoever sent them to me on the phone so I can tell them to stop sending defective golf clubs to people as gifts."

"Right now?" Byrdie asked.

"Why not?" JJ replied. His face tightened, and he added, "Is everyone planning on defying me today?"

Byrdie took the golf clubs from JJ. He kept looking at her.

"Are you going to get me the person on the phone?" JJ asked.

"Why don't I just give the clubs to a charitable organization?"

"Who gave them to me?"

"Billy Ray Cyrus," Byrdie answered. "For your birthday." Byrdie winced. She really didn't want to call Billy Ray right now.

After a moment, JJ dropped his shoulders. He said, "Maybe you should just give them to a charity. You pick one."

Byrdie sighed deeply. "Thank you, Governor. I'll take care of it as soon as possible." She took the clubs and placed them by the door very quietly.

JJ stepped over to the bar and poured a shot of Jack Daniel's. His fifth so far. Byrdie decided to start counting at three. She didn't know how she might stop him at some later point, like if the number ever got in double digits, so counting was probably a pointless activity. But she had a very bad feeling about how things were going today. So, she counted.

Elliot broke in, his voice racing, his eyes were of a man having a psychological melt down. "I think I should remind everyone what the stakes are, in case you have forgotten. We have all sacrificed a lot to get here today, none more than you JJ. This opportunity will never come around again. Ever. You have to handle this quickly and decisively. The vice presidential office is a heartbeat away from the highest office in the land. And you're getting it on a silver platter. I Googled something this morning that we all should be aware of. 30.4 percent of all vice presidents have gone on to become presidents. And everybody knows that McKenzie's got a heart condition, so your odds are a whole lot better than 30.4 percent. As political goals go, president of the United States is the goal of all goals. It's grabbing the political brass ring, JJ. The whole world would look to you for guidance and hope. And some day your face could be minted onto a coin, or an airport could be named after you." Elliot grabbed a marble paperweight of Abraham Lincoln from JJ's desk. His hand shook. "Your head could be carved into granite on the side of a mountaintop someday!" JJ and Byrdie stared at Elliot. His conviction was admirable. Elliot put the paperweight down. It appeared as if tears might be forming in his eyes. "If you had been sworn into office in 1961, then you would have been able to have sex with Marilyn Monroe. Marilyn. Monroe." Elliot shook his head at the inconceivability - the mind-boggling implications - of his own words. He repeated, "Marilyn Monroe."

Byrdie rolled her eyes, then noticed the BlackBerry in her jacket pocket was vibrating. It was set on silent, and she had let all the other calls go to the message service. She glanced at the name on the caller ID. It made her step back. She pressed her palm to her heart and looked heavenward.

"I get it, Elliot." JJ spoke with abrupt clarity. "I will call President McKenzie right now and I'll tell him that the governor's office, as well as the good people of Tennessee, have been the victim of an obvious deception. The story is a blatant lie, and I intend to get to the source of it. Whoever I find hiding there, I will make certain they are dealt with like the snakes-in-the-grass they are. Legal actions will be taken. Whoever is involved in this misinformation campaign, a deed that has undoubtedly broken state and federal defamation laws, as well as the public trust, will pay. This is personal, so I will be dealing with it personally."

Elliot nodded. This was the kind of unambiguity he had been hoping for. If JJ spoke this way from here on out, this debacle might be brought to an end in a couple of news cycles.

Byrdie held her phone out to JJ.

"No phone calls!" Elliot said abruptly, holding out his hands.

"He's probably right, Byrdie," JJ agreed.

She extended the phone to JJ anyway. "It's Josh."

4

At Jimmy Kelly's restaurant, a renovated Victorian mansion, the parking lot was mostly empty. It was just after 2:30 P.M. at the distinguished Nashville landmark. The lunch crowd had already gone and the dinner crowd had not yet started arriving.

A black Land Rover sat in the parking lot. Inside, were Rhashan and Dylan. Their eyes were focused on the front door of the restaurant. Josh had disappeared through the doors a few minutes earlier.

"Congratulations are in order," Rhashan said. "I haven't had the chance to say so to you yet."

Dylan was amazed at how silky calm Rhashan's voice always was. It was helpful at the moment because he was so nervous and anxious. It felt like his head was in a pressure cooker.

Rhashan had basically become an older brother to Dylan. Kitty's head bodyguard had been a fundamental part of Dylan's life from the first time he met him, when he was nine years old.

The strikingly large man with a gun strapped to his side had made the nine-year-old Dylan uneasy at first. At the time, Dylan believed he could protect his momma. And Frankie was still his daddy, even though he was rarely around. And when Frankie was around, he was usually in a state where he was unable to defend himself from a peanut butter jar with the lid stuck on too tight. But if his daddy was somewhat absent in the consciousness department, Dylan could take on the role of man of the house whenever it was called for. He didn't see the need to have some big brute to hang around. But soon this childish distrust shifted entirely. Dylan and Rhashan became good friends. He was spending as much time at Rhashan's guest house as he did in his own room.

Over the years Rhashan trained Dylan how to use his shortwave radios, taught him military endurance skills so Dylan could survive in the woods or in a barren Iraqi desert (as Rhashan had done), and he taught Dylan how to drive two years earlier than Kitty knew anything about. They even built a fantastic three story treehouse together. Those nights when the two of them were up until the sun rose, listening and speaking to other shortwave radio users, was a magical time for Dylan. Dylan came to also develop a deep gratitude for the man who protected his mother, especially now that he had moved out into the world where he could not valiantly protect her himself.

"Thank you," Dylan replied.
"I wish you both the best."
"It's not getting off to a great start."
"Unreasonable in-laws? I'm afraid a lot of marriages start out like that."
Dylan looked quizzically at Rhashan. "Why haven't you gotten married? I've seen those hot babes you bring back to your house, surely one of them had to be wife material?"
"Coltrane and I are just fine. Besides I like my freedom." Rhashan smiled.
"You're saying I'm about to give up my freedom, are you?"
Rhashan glanced at Dylan. He took a moment to answer. "Actually I met the love of my life a long time ago. She was my best friend. You aren't about to lose anything. You're going to be just fine."
Dylan was intrigued. "You never told me about this? What happened to her?"
"Francesca was her name." Rhashan dropped his smile. "Lieutenant Francesca Martinez."
Dylan noticed the forlorn look in Rhashan's eyes. "Oh, shit I didn't know. I've got a big mouth. I'm sorry."
Rhashan glanced down. "Her convoy was overtaken. Baghdad. No one survived."
Dylan nodded.
Rhashan didn't say anything. They both let the somber moment pass in silence.
Dylan finally said, "She was *the one*?"
"The one and only, for me," Rhashan replied.
A forest green Cadillac Escalade pulled up to the front of the restaurant. Dylan and Rhashan looked up and watched carefully. JJ

opened the door and stepped out. He had come alone; just like Josh had asked.

Dylan reached for the door handle.

"Don't," Rhashan said tersely. "Let Josh handle this."

"I want to tell him not to be an asshole to his son."

"Josh needs to fight his own battles."

Dylan nodded, sighed, and took his hand off the door handle. "I guess you're right," Dylan said. He put his finger up to a Bluetooth earpiece on his right ear.

Rhashan replied, "That is true, but that's not the only reason why. Like your mother, you have a few anger issues. I don't want you anywhere near the governor of Tennessee. Keeping you and your momma out of jail between now and your wedding day is a personal goal of mine." Rhashan noticed Dylan's preoccupation with his right ear.

Dylan, although distracted, considered Rhashan's words a moment. "You really do know Momma and me pretty well."

"Yes, I believe I do," Rhashan replied, then added, "What are you doing with your ear? Are you on the phone?"

Dylan dropped his hand, and lied: "No."

Rhashan looked at Dylan suspiciously. "What are you listening to? Are you on the phone with Josh?"

Dylan reluctantly nodded. "Sort of. He doesn't know." Dylan looked at Rhashan defensively, then confessed: "I took Josh's phone and Skyped myself. Then I put his phone on mute, and hid it in his jacket pocket."

"You're spying on your fiancé?"

"Just in case he needs help."

Rhashan repeated, "So, you're spying on your fiancé?"

"Listening. Not spying." Dylan held up his hands. "Look, I don't have any clue what he might do in a situation like this. He's under a lot of pressure."

"He loves you. You know that."

"I think he does. But what do I know. I wasn't raised like him. He's normal. He's in college. He's been in Africa in the Peace Corps for two years. He probably misses his family. And he's got more in common with them, than me. They're a pretty important family you know?"

Rhashan was shaking his head.

Dylan saw him, and shook his own head. "No, Rhashan. I'm serious. I was raised by two Country Western stars. I had no restraints, or hardly any rules. I never even finished high school. I was tutored on a tour bus my whole life. And the teacher, I might add, was a woman who didn't believe in using text books. She passed or failed me based on the color of my aura. How could I possibly know what a normal person would do?"

"You're being way too hard on yourself. You're one of the most normal people I've ever known."

"No. A normal person wouldn't have done what I did."

Rhashan waited. Dylan looked down, and clamped his hands together.

Rhashan asked, "What did you do kiddo? I bet it's not as bad as you think."

After a moment Dylan glanced up at Rhashan. He said, "When we first got the newspaper, Josh wanted to go straight to his dad. I talked him out of it. I convinced him we should go talk to momma; that we should get her to go talk to his daddy instead. I told Josh she could soften him up, and maybe make it easier for Josh to come out to him later." Dylan looked down to his hands. "But the real reason I didn't want Josh to talk to his dad was because I was scared to death…What if his daddy convinced Josh to not come back to me?"

"He's coming back to you, Dylan," Rhashan said. "You don't have to spy on him to know that."

"I'm about to ask him to spend the rest of my life with me. I need to know what he really thinks. I deserve to know. I don't know, and neither do you, if he's coming out that door and leaving with us, or if he's leaving with his father."

Rhashan sighed. He saw real fear on Dylan's face, and he knew that reasoning was not going to help. "Okay," Rhashan said. "But, put it on speaker. We'll listen together. If it gets too personal I want you to know I might turn it off."

Dylan nodded. He took his phone and flicked across the screen, and then placed it on the dashboard. They could hear scattered restaurant conversations and silverware clinking. But no Josh, or JJ. The air was tense.

"JJ should be arriving at Josh's table any second," Dylan said anxiously. He took in a deep, apprehensive breath. Dylan then added, "I would never have let myself fall in love if I'd known it was going to be this terrifying."

Rhashan understood. He replied, "Once you're there, my friend, it's too late."

* * *

When Josh had entered the restaurant earlier, he had downed the glass of beer he had ordered. He was hoping it would be the "liquid courage" it promised to be.

Parker, party of four, your table is ready! Parker, party of four!

Josh was sitting too close to the overhead speaker, and he had twitched every time the voice of the restaurant host blared out another announcement.

Above the table was a very large portrait of Elvis and Priscilla Presley, the renowned photograph taken on their wedding day. As Josh sat alone, downing his beer, he couldn't help but feel the prying gaze of Elvis and Priscilla staring down at him.

"What are you staring at?" Josh had asked of Elvis and Priscilla, with more bitterness in his voice than he anticipated, "Your daughter married Michael Jackson."

Josh switched sides of the table, so the photograph was behind him. It wasn't just the photographic image of the famous celebrities' eyes he felt staring, but several people in the restaurant were noticeably glancing back at Josh. Even a cook stepped out of the kitchen to get a look. It was so unnerving that several times Josh considered getting up and leaving.

And that wasn't the only reason Josh wanted to leave – *wanted to run*. His back was against the wall. What was he about to ask of his father? Permission? Approval? Tolerance? What was he willing to say? I'm sorry? Don't hate me?...Goodbye?

How do I tell my daddy something I know is going to break his heart?

Then he saw JJ approaching. Josh took another drink of the "liquid courage". His heart was pounding, and he wanted to just die.

A waiter walked up toward table where Josh was sitting in the back corner of the restaurant following right behind JJ Fletcher.

JJ turned and took the young man by the shoulder and smiled. "Could you give us some time? I'm having kind of a private conversation with my son."

"Oh, hello, Governor. Yes, just call for me when you need anything."

"Just bring us a couple of beers." JJ looked to see that Josh had an empty beer glass. "My usual, and another one for my boy."

The waiter nodded. "Yes, sir, right away." He quickly turned and left.

JJ sat down. Neither he, nor Josh, said anything at first. The silence gave JJ some time to look Josh over. He was relieved. His son looked exactly the same as when he last saw him.

He doesn't look gay at all!

JJ spoke first. "Don't worry, Little J, we'll sue them for slander. Whoever is responsible for this is going to wish they had never messed with our family." JJ nodded reassuringly to Josh. Josh didn't look as relieved as he expected. He looked a little sick.

"Every single person in this restaurant is staring at us," Josh said. "Don't you ever get tired of it?"

JJ looked around to witness a few people looking back. He instinctively smiled and winked at them. JJ bent in closer, and said to Josh, "If you don't smile and shake their hand they'll vote for the other guy on election day. And they'll tell everybody they know what an asshole you are. You can count on that, Son."

Josh inhaled deeply, and then said, "I'm surprised you showed up. Kitty said you were pretty upset."

JJ said, "We're calling a press conference together this evening. I'll be right there with you the whole time. You will have your chance to set the story straight. I promise you that they'll all have forgotten about you and this nonsense by next week. They went after my son, and I'm not going to stand for it...and for the record, she was the one who was upset, and I'll have to say, very confused about something."

The waiter brought the beers for JJ and Josh, setting them down carefully, and took the empty glass away.

"I shouldn't have sent Kitty. I should have told you myself," Josh said.

JJ didn't like the sound of that. "You're right. It would have been much better if you would have just dropped by yourself. You know it's safe to talk to me."

"It's safe to agree with you," Josh replied.

JJ sensed that Josh was upset. Josh could have been unduly influenced by others (probably Kitty Stardust). Petula had prepared JJ for this kind of defiant attitude earlier. She had said that most young people pass through a stage in their late teens or early twenties that make them want to rebel against their parents. It was normal. Petula had looked it up on the Internet.

"Look, Son, you don't express any of the required characteristics. I've been around all kinds of people. I've worked with those kinds of people. I know you as well as anyone, and I can promise you, you are not...you know..."

The alcohol had given Josh some much needed - as hoped - courage. He said, "There is only one *required* characteristic. I can assure you, Daddy, I have expressed it many, many times. With Dylan."

JJ looked around. He was concerned that somebody had heard Josh.

Someone had. A woman with frosted tips on her hair at a table across from them said in a callous tone to her husband in a dingy camouflage baseball cap, "That boy should show more respect for his daddy!" The husband nodded with a disapproving glance at Josh. The woman added, "Back in my day a man would have taken a switch to his son if he spoke out like that."

Josh rolled his eyes. The couple went back to cutting into their rare steaks, clanking their knives and forks onto their plates, and stuffing large pieces of meat into their mouths.

"You know, this is the restaurant I proposed to your momma in." JJ said.

"I know," Josh replied.

"What your momma and I had is not what you have with that boy. You need to know that Kitty Stardust and I have a past together. She is using you to get back at me. It's not what you think it is. She's got an ax to grind. It goes back many years, and it's why I'm so glad to have the chance to talk to you."

"I know about you and Kitty."

"No. You don't know the whole story."

Josh knew JJ and Kitty had a past, but it was true, he had never considered the full implications. "How many years back are we talking?" Josh asked.

"All the way back to high school." JJ spoke more quietly, leaning in to Josh. "I have no idea why she is so mad at me. The sex was always great."

Josh cringed. "And after high school?"

"It's been off and on. Mostly off, but I only bring it up—"

"He's my brother!" Josh cut him off. He looked deathly ill.

It took a minute for JJ to understand where Josh had gone astray in his thoughts.

"Dylan is my brother!" Josh said again. "Holy fucking shit." He looked weak. He gripped the table to stable himself. His lungs clamped. He was afraid his asthma was returning. He certainly couldn't breathe, and he felt like he might puke.

"No! No, no, no. Hell no...No! That's not what I'm trying to say. I'm certain Frankie Fairway is his daddy," JJ said. "At least I know it's not me. I was happily married to your momma when you, and Dylan, were born. What I am trying to say is that Kitty is using this relationship you imagine you have with her son as a way to hurt me. I hurt her years ago, I guess. That's what she says anyway. And now she wants to hurt me. It's that simple."

Josh slowly recovered. It took a moment. He said, "My God, I thought I was going to have to shoot myself."

JJ went on, "You do know that Kitty physically attacked me this morning? I think it's sexual rage, personally. It's gotten all pent up and twisted around for years."

"Daddy. I don't need to know about you and Kitty, and sex, and the past. I'd rather just talk about the fact that I'm gay, and how that is probably making you think you hate me right now."

JJ shook his head. "I don't hate you. Don't say that." JJ was flustered. He rubbed the back of his neck. "Her son looks like some kind of outlaw. Has he gotten you to use drugs? That's your grandmother's theory. If it is drugs we can deal with that, but you need to stay away from him."

"I love him, Daddy. I'm in love with him. I plan on staying with him for a long time. If I'm lucky, the rest of my life."

"Please. Don't say that, Little J, don't even think it."

"It's the truth. I love him. More than I've loved anyone."

"I am your father, and it's hard to admit this, but the therapist on the Internet website that your grandmother looked up said it is likely my fault. I let you grow up with too much freedom. I let you listen to all that hip hop music. I let you dabble in that strange religion with your friends. I let you join the Peace Corps. I did it because I believed you were the smartest boy in the room. Don't punish me now for giving you too much."

JJ looked at Josh, who was still attempting to process his father's Internet-derived observations.

Josh said, "I'm guessing you're talking about yoga again? And again, I'm saying yoga is not a religion. I'm standing firm on that." Josh was beginning to regret arranging this meeting. "Daddy. You are a good father. That's not what this is about."

"I think it is my fault, because when your mother died I wanted you to have everything you ever wanted. Maybe you should go back to Africa. Where was that place you were again?"

"Botswana," Josh answered, wearily.

"Yeah, that place. Give yourself a few more years of hard outdoor work to think. And just like those irritating hip hop records you loved, you're going to move on to something else. I've always trusted you, Little J. Trust me on this."

"Okay, you've talked. Let me talk. There are other things you don't know about me," Josh said.

"I think I know you pretty well."

"I'm a vegetarian."

"What do you mean?"

"I don't eat meat."

"You don't eat any meat?" JJ scratched his temple. He was very confused. "On purpose?"

"Yes, on purpose."

"I still don't know what you mean, Son? Do you have an ulcer or something?"

"I don't eat meat because I think it's disgusting and barbaric. I don't think animals should be food. We can get all the nutrition we need without killing them."

JJ was stupefied. He couldn't think of a response.

Josh noticed, but went on, "And I'm the one who totaled the yellow Humvee."

JJ shook his head. "No, Daddy said he did that."

"He covered for me. Grandpa Cowboy also covered for me when I set the tool shed on fire. He was teaching me how to smoke cigars when I was ten. And I threw a match on a gasoline can. It's a miracle we both got out alive."

JJ took a drink of his beer, and thought a moment. He said, "I'll tell you one thing, Son, if everyone stopped eating meat overnight there would be a whole lot of important industries going out of business, and a whole lot of good people would be without their jobs. No meat, no jobs. The economy would collapse. You don't have a problem with that? Because I think most Americans would have a problem with that."

Josh put his head in his hands.

JJ knew Elliot was waiting back at the governor's mansion, and the president of the United States was waiting at the White House. He had to get Josh to agree to go with him now. There was no more time for arguing. Certainly not about eating meat.

JJ said, "I have given my word that the story printed in *The Nashville Sun* is false. You are going back to the governor's mansion with me, and we are going to be speaking to President McKenzie's office, just you and me. Important people are wasting valuable time. People who have more important problems than you have, Little J."

"I'm not doing that," Josh said.

"You're going to do exactly what I tell you to do. After we talk to President Bob McKenzie, then we will be speaking to the press together, father and son. It is already scheduled. Finish your beer and let's get going."

"I've always hated talking to the press. Another thing you should know about me. And if these important people have bigger problems, like you're saying, and like they should, then why don't they go deal with them and leave me alone? What Dylan and I do has absolutely no effect on their personal lives. If I thought it did, then I would be more than happy to go stand in front of a TV and say whatever they want me to say. But Daddy, this is their problem. And my life is extremely unimportant in the big picture. My life is mine. It belongs to me."

JJ grunted an impatient sigh: "You *are* the bigger picture, Josh. The people in this state have a right to decide how things should happen. I signed a very popular proposition into law because the majority of the people asked me to do it. That is their right. I'm the governor of Tennessee, and whether you like it or not, you are my son. And you live in this state. As long as you do, you cannot marry Dylan."

Josh stared at JJ and his internal temperature began to rise. He felt it burning in his face. He understood what JJ was telling him, and it went directly to a root issue for Josh. Josh said, "You're right. I am your son. This is my home and I am proud of it. If I was a coward I'd leave and go get married somewhere else. But I love it here. I don't want to go somewhere else, someplace I don't even know, to do what I should be able to do right where I was born. That is exactly why I am going to marry Dylan Fairway, right here where my heart is, where I call my home…in Nashville, Tennessee."

JJ stared at his son. The influence was obvious to him now. Kitty Stardust was the only other person he knew who could be so damn stubborn. "Look, I didn't want to use this. Your grandma Petula gave me some information she printed out from her computer." JJ took some printed brochures from his jacket pocket. He placed them on the table.

Josh looked at them suspiciously.

"It's a program called 'Heavenly Escape'. It helps you understand how to cure these feeling you have," JJ said, trying to sound more educated regarding the brochures than he was.

"Cure?" Josh asked. "Daddy, those places are a sham. Let me guess, they charge a huge fee to provide this so-called cure?"

"It sounds like you may need more help than I ever imagined. I read these over and it is the real deal. Well, I read some of it." JJ pointed to the brochures. "The patients get treatment from a team of specialized therapists. It's like having post-traumatic stress syndrome. It's nothing to be ashamed of. The people on the back of the brochure make testimonials about how happy they are now."

"I'm your son." Josh stood up. He stumbled more than he cared to from the beers. "And the only thing that is making me unhappy right now is my family. That is all the information you need."

"Sit back down."

"My wedding will be one of the most important days of my life. I really want you to be there. But if you don't want to come and celebrate with me, and all my good friends, then don't."

"Sit back down, Josh. I mean it. Don't be stupid."

"You think I'm being stupid?"

"Yep, stupid. It sounds about right. And I'd throw in ungrateful too."

Josh and JJ stared for a moment. Josh wanted so badly to hear his father say that he'd come to his wedding, that nothing else mattered. But it was obvious JJ was never going to say anything like that.

"Stupid is a word people use when they don't have a viable, reasonable argument to make," Josh said.

"Is that what your liberal professors at the university taught you?"

"I guess so. Or it may have been my kindergarten teacher." Josh turned and walked away.

JJ shook his head. He watched him go.

As Josh passed the host station he grabbed the microphone and spoke, his voice blaring loudly to the whole restaurant: "Party of two, at table five," Josh said. "...the woman with the frosted hair and the man with the greasy baseball cap. Yeah, you. Cows are sentient beings. The cow you're eating now likely had a giant metal bolt fired into his brain to kill him. A blood and gut drenched slaughterhouse worker carved his body up into little steak size pieces. And now, that carved up piece of what was a sentient being with big brown eyes, is sitting right there on your plate; still bleeding. Take a look and enjoy it. And have a pleasant rest of your day. And next time, mind your own fucking business!" Josh shoved the microphone away, as angry tears were welling up. He took a quick, disheartened look back to where he had left his father. The tears spilled out and ran down his face. He finally turned and left out the front door.

JJ took his beer and swallowed it down. The couple at table five looked over at JJ, who could only shrug back. The wife, looking a little queasy, carefully pushed away her unfinished steak across the table. Her husband looked at his plate with some uncertainty himself.

JJ then noticed the picture of Elvis and Priscilla staring down at him.

"And who are you looking at?" JJ asked. "Your daughter married Nicolas Cage."

JJ suddenly remembered that he had a phone call waiting to be made and Elliot had a press conference planned, and he had just let Josh – the subject of the phone call and press conference – walk away.

JJ grabbed his wallet, and threw more than a sufficient amount of cash on the table.

* * *

JJ stepped out the front door of Jimmy Kelly's restaurant. He looked across the parking lot where he saw Josh approaching a Land Rover. He stepped forward, when he was abruptly cut off. It was Rhashan.

"Excuse me, I need to get past," JJ said.

"Nope," Rhashan replied.

"Who the hell are you?"

"I'm the guy that keeps Kitty Stardust safe and happy."

JJ was startled, and instantly jealous. "You're her boyfriend? That's what I kept thinking when I saw you at her—"

"Bodyguard!" Rhashan cut JJ off. "*Just* her bodyguard."

JJ was relieved. But he still needed to get past this giant of a man. "That's my son, and I need to go get him. He's going with me."

"I also keep her assets safe. That is Kitty's son, her most important asset, back behind me in that Land Rover, and you are going nowhere near him."

JJ and Rhashan stared at each other for a moment. JJ looked on either side to see if he could run around Rhashan.

Rhashan pointed to JJ's Escalade. "Do you have Triple A?"

JJ turned around to see his Escalade had a flat back tire.

"I have a flat tire!" JJ yelled.

"Yep," Rhashan replied. "And you should be happy you have three good tires left. He wanted to slash them all. He was some anger issues. I'm helping him work through those."

JJ kicked the flat tire. He stepped back up to Rhashan. "Look, this has gotten out of control. You get out of my way, and let me go get my son. I'll pay you a hell of a lot more money than whatever she is paying you. Everybody has a number, how much do you want?"

Rhashan gave JJ a cool glare. "Why don't you save your money, and buy a nice wedding gift?"

"Really?" JJ said, completely flustered.

"Really," Rhashan replied calmly. "It's very good advice. I suggest you take it."

* * *

Dylan had stepped out the door of the Land Rover, and grabbed Josh into his arms. Josh was shaking. Warm tears began to flow and soak the collar of Dylan's shirt. Josh's chest was hot and Dylan could feel his heartbeat as he continued to cry.

Josh could barely get any clear words out: "I don't want to cry."

Dylan said, "It's okay. I heard everything." Dylan held Josh tighter and kissed the warm, salty tears on the side of his face.

Josh looked at Dylan. "How did you hear everything? Were you in there?"

Dylan said, "No. Your phone is on Skype. I called myself and put it back in your pocket."

Josh grabbed his phone and verified it was on. He flicked it off. He looked at Dylan accusingly.

Dylan looked guilty. He finally said, "We've been friends for as long as I can remember and you've never been dishonest with me. About anything. I promise I'll never do something like that again. If we're going to get married I have to start acting more mature."

Josh put his cell back in his jacket pocket. "I guess I can't blame you."

"I slashed his tire," Dylan said.

"Dylan!" Josh exclaimed.

"He said you were stupid," Dylan replied, defending himself.

Josh managed a smile. "Thank you. I guess."

"I'm sorry it didn't work out with your daddy." Dylan hugged Josh again.

"Yeah, me too," Josh said, the sadness heavy in his voice.

Dylan pulled back, and watched as Josh's eyes cleared a little. "So, we're done here, right?" Dylan asked.

Josh said, "Yes, I'm done."

Friendship is born at that moment when one person says to another: What! You too? I thought I was the only one.
    - C. S. Lewis

Revenge is sweet and not fattening.
    - Alfred Hitchcock

LET US GIVE THANKS

1

A church bell rang high in the tower of Nashville's Church of the Glorious Light, a beckoning, metallic, *bong, bong, bong,* calling to all souls within its range. A sign near the main road at the entrance to the driveway read:

> FLETCHER FAMILY FREEDOM FEAST
> MULTIPLYING THE LOAVES
> NO PROFANITY, PLEASE

   Homeless people were arriving to the outdoor event. Some pushed grocery carts, others arrived alone, and others came with their whole families in tow. A few were neither homeless, nor poor, but had come to enjoy the well-publicized free meal that the Fletcher family provided to the public every year.
   The Thanksgiving soup kitchen was set up under huge canvas canopies in the church parking lot; a polished, orderly, and respectful display all around. The only sounds were shuffling feet, respectful whispering, and the clinking noise of metal utensils

serving up the various Thanksgiving food selections. The busy volunteers wore matching black and green aproned uniforms with the Fletcher Family Freedom Feast logo sewn in the top right corner. The pleasant volunteers were handing out the plates of food and drinks. Other volunteers monitored the line, making certain the hungry folks stayed orderly and remained single file.

JJ, in his trademark tight Wranglers, a white dress shirt, bolo tie and cowboy boots, and Petula, in a black Chanel dress suit and white silk scarf, stood in the center of the long line of tables. Golden oven-roasted turkeys and honey roasted hams were displayed in front of them. Petula was carving and forking over the two slices of meat allotted to each guest. JJ ladled out the turkey gravy. The other tables were filled with platters and bowls of food, with pies and cakes in Thanksgiving abundance.

Cowboy was seated in a wheelchair behind Petula with Nurse Lutkenhouse. She assisted Cowboy, feeding him the last bite of a piece of pumpkin pie, then wiped the whipped cream from the corner of his mouth. Cowboy was wrapped extensively with extra clothing and scarves to the point of his dismay. He was listening to the football game on a radio hidden from view under his lap blanket. On his dry erase board was written:

14–US 7–THEM

(and)

PIE

Byrdie and Elliot were donning aprons as well, Byrdie serving mashed potatoes next to JJ, and Elliot spooning out heaps of turkey stuffing. The weather was graciously sunny, with a slight crisp breeze; a perfect day for the outdoor charity event.

Agent Noah Applegarth and Agent Derek Cooper stood behind Petula and JJ watching over the crowd through their dark sunglasses. Periodically Agent Cooper stepped over to Cowboy and asked him how the game was going, and Cowboy would write down the current score on his dry erase board.

Only a few (nosey, wisecracking, or simply unthinking) people had brought up the now infamous edition of *The Nashville Sun*. JJ and Petula were happy to explain that the whole story was a political ploy designed and executed by the few enemies the Fletcher family had. No one protested much. When someone was giving you free food you were inclined to take them at their word.

For the past few days throngs of teenagers employed by Petula had been collecting all the copies of *The Nashville Sun* that were still left in stores and newsstands all over Nashville, and burning them. Petula had paid them $200 each (beyond the cost of purchasing all the newspapers) for the job, which did seem to help quell some of the momentum of the story in Nashville; but only a little. In spite of all of Petula's and JJ's efforts to deny the validity of what was reported in *The Nashville Sun*, to all the local and national news stations, some of the more scandal-driven cable news channels and radio stations had started to play the story in repeated news cycles. JJ and Petula had attempted to ignore these annoying news reports, but President Bob McKenzie and his staff were keenly aware. The First Lady was also quite aware, and she was exasperated and fit-to-be-tied (she was starting to believe homosexuality was some kind of virus gone-amok). The president, his wife, and his staff, were watching very closely, and utilizing instant public opinion polls to see how the nation was responding. The numbers in general were mixed, but the responses in the Red States were tallying unfavorable for Governor JJ Fletcher having a gay son - *allegedly* - and his son's plans to get married. Most news outlets were repeating the usual responses from concerned citizens and politicians: "It would weaken the institution of marriage in the United States and could eventually render it meaningless.", "It undermines religious freedom.", "It would likely lead to state sanctioned polygamy.", "If children were involved, commitment to the child would be diminished without a mother *and* a father." In the not-so-reasoned category of responses, FOX News was looping video footage of an angry pollster in South Carolina: "Gay couples allowed to get married in Tennessee," she said emphatically to the reporter, "might demand to sleep in honeymoon suites all over the country. And then, when all the beds are full, where are *heterosexual* couples going to sleep on *their* honeymoons?"

The media, in all of its forms, was doing its part to throw more fuel on the fire of the story they had begun to characterize as: "The growing outrage in America's Heartland!" The story was getting huge ratings all over the country, and as long as it stayed that way, Tennessee's hotels and motels were going to be full of reporters and their accompanying news crews looking for a new angle. It was becoming the garden variety media circus. Suddenly, almost everyone in Tennessee, whether they had actually ever met anyone in the Fletcher or Holloway family or not, were more than happy to face a reporter or a camera and express their thoughtful insight into the matter. Or regrettably – whether they were walking out of a Wal-Mart or the capital building in Nashville - make a not-so-insightful, distasteful joke.

Extra security guards Elliot had hired were stationed at all entrances to the church parking lot and had successfully kept the news reporters away from the event this morning. Petula, of course, felt unconvinced about leaving the media entirely out – with no reporters to cover it, the soup kitchen was pretty much a waste of good money and valuable time *in her opinion*.

"Only two pieces," Petula said, to a substantially overweight woman wearing neon pink sweats with Tweety Bird on the front and a tattered housecoat pulled over her shoulders. She had asked for more turkey and ham.

"Please, I'm so hungry I could eat a horse."

"It's a fairly well established fact that people eat too much on Thanksgiving," Petula replied to the woman. "And I always find my eyes are too big for my stomach."

"You're kidding me?" the woman countered back. "I'm about to keel over, so could you fork over several more pieces of turkey? And some more of that ham, please."

"There's plenty Momma," JJ said, as he reached over and gave the woman several extra big slices of turkey and ham.

"Thank you, Governor," the woman said. "Charity comes from the heart." She gave Petula a coarse glance, and added, "I suppose if you don't have one, that wouldn't apply."

As she walked away, Petula said, "It's such a beautiful day. I don't know why people have to be so unpleasant."

"Everybody gets a little cranky when they're hungry, Momma," JJ replied.

A homeless couple sauntered up, pushing a shopping cart covered with an old blanket. He wore a threadbare sweater over a dress shirt; she donned a colorful headscarf.

Petula said, "This pleasant looking couple look like they'd appreciate some good will and good food. What a lovely headscarf. Welcome to the Fletcher Family Freedom Feast."

JJ added, "I hope you're enjoying this gorgeous day we ordered up."

"Why thank you Governor, and Mrs. Fletcher. We certainly are," said the homeless man. "I always voted for your daddy, but we've been between homes now for a while, and we haven't been registered to vote."

"That's why we're here year after year," Petula said. "We come to help the people of Tennessee who have been seeing troubled times."

Byrdie looked out into the line of people, much shorter than in years past. She said to Elliot, "There sure is a peculiar absence of people seeing troubled times this year."

Elliot nodded. "You're right, Byrdie. Last year we had maybe four times as many people." He eyed the small crowd suspiciously.

"Come on by the governor's office and we'll see about getting you both back on the voter registration list," JJ said. "Now, how about some turkey and gravy?"

"Just a little pie for us today," the man replied.

The woman explained, "We already ate. I think that pecan one looks good."

"You already ate?" JJ asked.

The man clarified: "We ate over at the Kitty Stardust setup. You know, her big ol' soup kitchen that opened up about three blocks over yonder." He pointed.

"In the Piggly Wiggly parking lot," the woman said.

"Did you just say Kitty Stardust?" Petula asked.

The woman's eyes widened, excited to share. "She's got a soup kitchen over there that's as big as a damn three ring circus. Oops. Pardon me for cursing."

"You should see the crowd. I didn't know there were so many homeless people in Nashville," said the man. "We came over here for some pie because we didn't want to stand in that long line again."

Petula stared at the homeless couple in disbelief. "Kitty Stardust?" she asked again. "Are you sure it was Kitty Stardust?"

"She's got her tour bus pulled up there. She, and that other singer, sang a few songs to open up the show." The man looked to his wife. "What is that other singer's name?"

The woman shrugged, and wiped her nose on her sleeve. "Who knows? Those Country Western singers are all the same. Moving from town to town, living out of their bags like hobos, sleeping, eating, drinking, smoking God-knows-what, like out-of-control teenagers. Just a bunch of wild gypsies if you ask me." The woman shook her head. "What kind of a life is that?"

Her husband gave her a wink and an elbow. "It sounds just like our life, Honey Bunches!" He broke out giggling. His wife joined him with knee-slapping and snorting glee.

Petula was not amused. "Kitty Stardust?" she barked out, louder than before, putting a stop to the couple's snickering fest.

The woman, now a little dour from Petula's tone – but holding back giggles – replied, "It was really her, alright. She's handing out sleeping bags, tooth brushes and her very own brand of shampoo."

Byrdie and Elliot stopped serving. The mystery of the small crowd was now solved. They were observing JJ and Petula with mounting apprehension. Petula's lips pinched tighter. Her eyes grew blacker. It was unclear if she was breathing. She was clearly about to become unstable at any second. They'd all seen it before.

Nurse Lutkenhouse pulled one of the ear buds from Cowboy's ear. She bent over and whispered, "Apparently that singer Kitty Stardust has put up a soup kitchen down the street from here. Petula seems very upset about it."

Cowboy rolled his eyes. He wrote:

WHAT'S NEW?
(then)
MORE PIE

Gisele nodded, and put the ear bud back into his ear. Then she stepped over to the table to get another slice of pumpkin pie for Cowboy.

"I'll say this too," said the homeless man. "Not all those people lined up are really poor or homeless. Most of those folks there are just having a big party."

"A big noisy party," the woman agreed. "I can't take all that racket with my nerves."

Petula snapped: "Feeding the homeless is not a party!"

"And she's off," Byrdie said to Elliot.

Elliot asked, "Is there anything we can do?"

"If you're smart," Byrdie replied, "you'll just stay out of her way."

"The Fletcher family has sponsored this event exclusively for more than ten years!" Petula was roaring. She turned to JJ. "That woman is some kind of monster. She is trying to destroy us, JJ. She has to be stopped!"

"Momma," JJ cautioned. "Let me take care of this. I'll go have a talk with her."

"I don't want you anywhere near her!" Petula was snarling.

"I can handle her, Momma."

"Like hell!" Petula stabbed the knife deep into the turkey with a ferociousness usually seen only in the criminally insane. She snapped off her apron, and threw it on the ground. The scared volunteers and homeless people quickly parted out of the way, as Petula rushed through them to get to the parking lot.

"I was told we were not to use cuss words," the homeless woman said to her husband, who nodded back.

JJ turned to Byrdie and Elliot. "I am going to need for you both to handle things here." He took off his apron. "And for Christ's sakes, give them as much food as they want."

Byrdie nodded, and said, "Just go, JJ. We'll be fine." She yanked the carving knife from the turkey.

JJ took off running in the direction of where Petula had gone. Elliot yelled after him, "Look for people with camera phones JJ. Don't let your mother do anything stupid that will be on tonight's news!"

Agent Applegarth took off right behind JJ, while Agent Cooper was kneeled down talking to Cowboy, not paying attention.

JJ ran on, and waved back. "Don't worry, I've got it. I've got it."

Byrdie and Elliot watched as Petula took a swift turn from the driveway and disappeared onto the street. JJ was kicking up gravel in the parking lot right behind her, with Agent Applegarth trying to keep up.

Elliot shook his head. "He doesn't have it."

Byrdie agreed, "Nope, he doesn't."

Elliot looked at Agent Cooper who was still bent down talking to Cowboy. "Agent Cooper!"

Agent Cooper looked up. "What?"

"You might want to go after the governor and his mother," Elliot responded, and pointed in the direction of where Petula and JJ had gone.

"Oh, shit," Agent Cooper said. "Yeah, I guess I better!" He quickly scurried off.

Byrdie looked back to the waiting homeless couple. "Well now, how about that pecan pie?"

* * *

The Piggy Wiggly parking lot was swarming with people. A tour bus displayed in huge letters: KITTY STARDUST. An image of Kitty's face was blazoned above her name. In front of the tour bus were a long series of tables covered with enormous bowls and platters of food. A banner, that spanned the area above the tour bus, read:

KITTY'S KITCHEN
ALL WELCOME!

Hundreds of people, some homeless, most local Nashville folks (and Kitty Stardust fans) looking to have a good time, all stood around eating, talking and laughing. An area where a square dancing contest was well underway drew a big crowd. There was face painting for the kids, a hot dog eating contest, and plenty of other activities for young and old alike.

Volunteers in Kitty Stardust T-shirts served at busy food tables. At one table they were handing out free sleeping bags, toothbrushes, and bottles of Kitty's Glistenin' Rain hair products.

Kitty was slicing turkey. To her left was her mother, Estella-Jeanne and Ruby Billingsley, carving out the pies and cobblers, plopping whipped cream on top. Sheryl Crow, in a cowboy hat and a velvety, gorgeous, multi-colored sundress, with a button up sweater, was next to Ruby pouring up fresh brewed coffee. Sheryl, a good friend of Kitty's, and a co-producer on one of her recent albums, had been happy to come show support for Dylan and Kitty when she got the call last night. Behind Ruby was her pet pig, Minnie Pearl, in a director's chair eating some apple slices. To Kitty's right was Shandazzle, a six foot six transvestite, in five inch high heels. A long blonde wig surrounded her cinnamon brown face and a sequined ruby red dress molded to her willowy, buxom body. She spooned out cranberry sauce.

"You're looking very pretty today, Shandazzle," Estella-Jeanne said.

Shandazzle smiled, and brushed back her hair with an exaggerated fling of the wrist. "I discovered a new foundation," she replied. "Naughty Mahogany."

"They used Naughty Mahogany on me in my 'Soak Up the Sun' video," Sheryl said. She handed two cups of steaming coffee out to a couple of grateful elderly women. "Here you go ladies. Cream and sugar are at the end of the table."

Estella-Jeanne asked, "Has my daughter managed to pry that banana pudding recipe out of you yet, Shandazzle?"

Kitty forked over some slices of turkey to an appreciative, slender woman in an oversized Tennessee Titans sweatshirt, then looked toward Shandazzle. "Not yet Momma, but I will. She can't hold out forever."

Shandazzle shook her head. "Momma Holloway, she has tried. And like all others, she has failed." She plopped some cranberry sauce on the plate of an older gentleman with a baseball cap that was patched up with duct tape, who held his plate with an unsteady hand. "There you go, sir. Are you sure you've got that?" He nodded, and she said, "Thanks for coming to Kitty's Kitchen today." She continued, "Kitty sent over her charming son with his guitar to sing Shandazzle a love song. I almost broke and handed over the recipe during the third chorus. Almost." She shook her finger at Kitty. "Then she sent over her security guard, Rhashan. He was an incredible temptation. He had my shoes off. He took his shirt off. He took ahold of my tired feet, and began to rub them with his powerful hands. He told me to hand over the banana pudding recipe. If I refused, the foot massaging would stop. Shandazzle was just like Meryl Streep in Sophie's Choice. Which choice was I going to make? I have very tired feet."

"She made the wrong choice," Kitty replied. She handed out more turkey slices, then added, "Rhashan was authorized that night to go as far as necessary to get that banana pudding recipe."

"You need to give up, Kitty," Shandazzle said.

"You don't know me very well if you believe I will ever give up," Kitty said, shaking her carving knife at Shandazzle. "Someday that recipe will be mine."

Sheryl gave Minnie Pearl some fresh slices of apple. "Here you go Minnie Pearl." The pig happily accepted.

Ruby chimed in, "It is the best banana pudding I've ever had." She handed out a piece of pumpkin pie.

"I have tried to duplicate it," Sheryl added, giving Shandazzle a bewildered look. "But I can't figure out a few ingredients that make it so damn good."

"And you never will, Ms. Sheryl," Shandazzle said, emphatically. "People who want the real thing just need to come visit me more often. I'd have brought some today, but I need more than a day's notice to make preparations."

A bag lady, swaggering a little from a clear case of drunkenness, stepped up in front of Kitty. She had a giant, grimy handbag full of her life's belongings, and her long matted hair had some weeds clinging to it in spots. She said, "Well, land-a-goshen, spit in the ocean, is that really Kitty Stardust? And look over there. Is that Sheryl Crow?" Her smile revealed a few missing teeth.

Sheryl smiled, and nodded.

"In the flesh, Darlin'," Kitty said. "I wouldn't let them call it Kitty's Kitchen unless I was planning to show up here myself. How about some turkey deep fried just this morning?"

"I would love some. You know something, I started my singing career because of you. You're so pretty, and you have the voice of an angel," the bag lady said.

Kitty smiled. "You don't have to butter me up to get extra servings. But because you said that, you're getting extra servings."

The woman reached into her bag, and produced a copy of one of Kitty Stardust's bestselling books. Kitty's picture graced the cover with the title: *The Road to Happiness is Only a Country Mile*.

The bag lady said, "I read your book, this one here, and it changed my life."

Estella-Jeanne, Sheryl, Ruby and Shandazzle all sympathetically eyed the drunken woman.

An elderly gentleman in coveralls with a long white beard, supporting himself on a walking cane, took a shaky step closer and said, "I think she better read it again, and hope it changes her life back."

Shandazzle looked over to the elderly man and said, "I spend a great deal of my time in the company of drag queens, such as myself, and normally a well-timed sardonic remark like that would gain you praise and touch my heart, but sir, today is Thanksgiving. We're out here to show our respect and love for everyone."

The elderly man shrugged and said, "I'm just sayin'."

"I would love it if you would sign this here copy," the woman added, not paying attention.

"I would be happy to." Kitty handed the plate of turkey over for her momma to hold while she quickly signed the inside cover.

"You gals want to hear a secret?" the bag lady asked. "My friend swears it is the God's truth." The woman quickly snuck in a swig from a paper bag. "And if anybody knows, she would. She cleans his house. Kenny Chesney is a robot made by the Chinese."

"Is that so?" Kitty asked.

The homeless woman put the book back in her bag. She pulled the bag over her shoulder to free her hands. Estella-Jeanne handed the woman her plate of food.

Ruby scooped a piece of pie on her plate.

Sheryl offered out a cup of coffee, mindfully. "How about some black coffee?" The bag woman nodded, and took the coffee graciously, but was already looking a little dead-to-the-world as she walked on down the line, stumbling a little as she went.

Estella-Jeanne shook her head. "She's drunker than Cooter Brown and it's barely even afternoon."

"I hope she'll be okay," Sheryl added, a little dismayed.

Shandazzle nodded. "God watches over little children and drunks."

As Estella-Jeanne watched the woman waddle along, she said, "I'm sure The Almighty's got better things to do than watch over that pitiful rat's nest all day." Estella-Jeanne gave the woman a curious second look. "She said she had a singing career. Do you reckon she's somebody famous?"

"Momma!" Kitty rebuked. "That could have been us. When we were living in the hills, we didn't have two beans to rub together."

"We were very, very poor, my sweet daughter. I'll make no bones about that. But we were not fish-eyed drunk and completely off our rockers."

As if on cue, Petula Fletcher came pushing her way through the crowd.

Estella-Jeanne spotted her, and said, "It must be last call for fish-eyed drunk and off your rocker."

Kitty looked up to see Petula as she pushed a frightened homeless person aside, and placed herself firmly in front of Kitty and Estella-Jeanne.

"Well, Kitty, look who has come to darken our door," Estella-Jeanne added. "Petula Fletcher. I wish I'd known you were dropping by for a bite to eat with us. I would have made a trip to the cellar and grabbed a bottle of arsenic."

"I know what you two are up to," Petula said, ignoring the comment. "You had that story put in *The Nashville Sun* because you just won't rest until you've completely destroyed the Fletcher family name."

Kitty said, "It's a little rude to cut in front of all these hungry people, Mrs. Fletcher, when you have your own soup kitchen and all."

Ruby quietly stepped behind Sheryl.

"What is it, Ruby?" Sheryl asked.

"Oh, nothin'." Ruby's voice was a nervous whisper. "Just don't move."

"Isn't that the governor's mother?" Sheryl quietly replied back, giving Petula a concerned once over. "She looks like she's been injected with a horse syringe full of crazy," she whispered.

Ruby dipped down lower, saying softly to Sheryl, "You have no idea."

Petula glowered at Kitty and Estella-Jeanne. "Fifty miles! I have an exclusive permit. No one can feed homeless people on Thanksgiving within fifty miles of The Church of the Glorious Light. And don't claim stupidity. Although to be fair, it would be a good place to start."

"Those days are over, Petula Fletcher," Estella-Jeanne said. "We'll feed anybody we want, whenever we want, wherever we want."

"Over my dead body!" Petula replied.

Estella-Jeanne shrugged. "That might trip us, but it won't stop us."

Petula grumbled. Then she began to take the plates of food out of the hands of the homeless people and throw them on the table. "I'm sorry folks. This food isn't legal. Go over to The Church of the Glorious Light. There's plenty to eat over there."

The homeless people were not sure what to do. A few moved away, but most stood their ground.

"Go on!" Petula yelled at the confused people. "It's just a few blocks away. Skedaddle on out of here!"

"Don't go anywhere!" Kitty yelled back to the crowd. "You're welcome here. Everyone is always welcome at Kitty's Kitchen."

JJ arrived on the scene at a full run. He surmised quickly whether his mother and Kitty had done anything inappropriate. It didn't look promising. Agent Applegarth stepped up right behind.

"Hello there," Shandazzle said to JJ. "You tall drink of sweet tea. What can I serve up for you?"

JJ looked up to meet Shandazzle's gaze. "I'm not here for the food."

"Who said anything about food?" Shandazzle pushed up on her breasts and then flipped her hair.

"And here's the son," Kitty said. "JJ Fletcher."

"He's the nincompoop spawn of that thing," Estella-Jeanne said, pointing at Petula. She poked Shandazzle. "And don't be fooled by the pretty package. There's a monster inside of that man."

"A monster inside?" Shandazzle looked JJ up and down. She said, "You and I may just have a lot in common."

After a moment of sexually confused tension (on JJ's part), he forced himself to look away from Shandazzle.

"Kitty...Momma," JJ said, looking at them both with some apprehension. "It's Thanksgiving. Ms. Stardust wouldn't set up a soup kitchen so close to ours just to start a squabble. There must be some misunderstanding." He looked at Kitty. "Why would you set up a soup kitchen so close to ours?"

Agent Cooper arrived, and stepped up next to Agent Applegarth behind JJ.

JJ looked back at the agents. "We're okay. I'm about to explain the law to Ms. Stardust, and then she's going to be leaving."

Kitty took in a deep breath, then said, "Now that everyone has arrived, I'd like to make an announcement." Kitty raised her voice to speak to the crowd. "Like so many other people around here, I am tired of the Fletcher family telling everyone all over Tennessee what to do." She looked at JJ. "Just because someone in your family says something is the law doesn't mean we have to obey it. My momma and I, and all these other people, are here today to make a stand. We're here to say no more! Right Momma?"

Estella-Jeanne stared at Petula with a long pause. "If there is anything that can be done to be a burr under that woman's saddle, I'll be there."

Petula scoured. "I see...a couple of country bumpkin hicks who don't appreciate all the things our family has done for this state."

"She's right, Kitty," JJ said. "This whole display of yours seems a little petty and cold hearted toward our family. A lot of things you've recently done to our family seems that way."

Kitty's eyes narrowed. She replied, "If I did have a cold heart I'd put my own selfish desires above my own son's; like you seem to have chosen to do."

JJ noted her angry tone. It scared him a little. And oddly enough, it kind of turned him on. He was certain her glassy glare had a definite sexual undertone to it. JJ took in the scene a little more, noticing Sheryl Crow, who was even giving him an accusatory glare.

Jesus, her too? I really love her music.

Then JJ noticed someone appeared to be hiding behind Sheryl.

Ruby whispered to Sheryl, "He can't see me. Cover for me."

Sheryl had no idea what Ruby meant, but did her best. She grabbed a whole pie. "Governor, would you like a rhubarb pie to take home? Dolly Parton gave me the recipe herself, and I made these pies just this morning." She held up the pie closer to his face, moving it to the right, trying to draw his attention away from Ruby behind her.

JJ said, "No, thank you, Sheryl." He was a little disheartened. The pie did look delicious. JJ turned away, then he promptly did a double-take. Ruby was crouched down, peeking out. A look of shock spread across his face. "Mrs. Billingsley! What on earth are you doing here? You're supposed to be volunteering for me over at the church!"

Having been found out, Ruby sheepishly stepped out.

Petula gave Ruby a shocked look as well. "Ruby Billingsley! You told me your bursitis was acting up. And you couldn't tolerate the outdoor weather today!"

Ruby appeared shamed at first, but then quickly recalled her ire at Petula. "Well now that you are putting me on the spot. Your people told me that I couldn't bring Minnie Pearl to your Thanksgiving events anymore because of sanitary reasons. I told them that Minnie Pearl is not just any ol' pig, and she most certainly is not unsanitary. She is my baby. I'd never leave her at home on Thanksgiving day!"

Minnie Pearl snorted.

Petula glared. "Ruby, we had the health department complaining about that pig last year, not to mention it made some of the homeless people who were eating ham feel very uncomfortable."

Kitty shook her head at Petula. "You see, over here at Kitty's Kitchen we're a lot more open minded. Nobody excluded, just friendly, wide open arms and hearts."

Petula gave the group an acrid once over – Ruby, Sheryl, Estella-Jeanne, that pig, and then up to Shandazzle. Petula said, "Well, we can certainly see that. This... *woman* looks like —"

"Before you finish that sentence," Shandazzle cut Petula off with a lift of her already quite lifted eyebrow, "you should be made aware, and take into serious consideration, the fact that I was arrested in Pigeon Forge for attempted murder in the not too distant past."

Petula took a concerned step back.

Shandazzle leaned over the table, staring into Petula's eyes. "The charges were dropped only because they could not find the weapon." She continued, with a flip of her hair and a self-satisfied sigh, "And that's one stiletto that will never be found."

Petula regained her equilibrium, and stepped back closer. "Excuse me," Petula retorted. "Do you know who I am?"

Shandazzle replied, "I recognize who made your wig, and that's all I need to know."

Petula grabbed JJ's arm. "JJ, do something!"

JJ leaned over to Kitty. "You couldn't have a permit for this," he said. "I'm calling the sheriff to have this cluttered up side show taken out of here."

"Well bless your heart," Kitty replied. "The sheriff is right over there." Kitty coyly pointed the sheriff out to JJ. The sheriff was about thirty yards away, dressed in his usual uniform, but he was also donning a big red clown nose and making balloon animals for several children who had gathered around him.

"What?" JJ asked. "It can't be?"

"The sheriff just loves kids," Kitty said. "He waved your silly fifty mile regulation for me. He loves my music, and Sheryl's, and said we were pretty."

Estella-Jeanne added, "Good thing the sheriff is here, Petula. Otherwise these sharp knives might be a little too tempting."

JJ quickly objected, "Now, let's all be civil."

Petula glared at Estella-Jeanne. "JJ, you'd think you'd know by now, these cheap, common vagrants don't know the first thing about how to be civil!" The homeless, now log-jamming up in the line behind the scene, threw Petula some ill-boding stares. Petula continued, "But to be fair, how can they know any better, seeing how they were raised like a family of badgers up in the hills."

"Maybe I was," Estella-Jeanne replied, "poor and a little stupid once. Maybe I let you take advantage of me too. And my daughter's heart got broken as a result." JJ looked at Kitty. He wondered if Kitty was feeling contempt. It looked like contempt. But then again it could be a seething desire. It was hard to tell. Estella-Jeanne continued, "But you might want to remember, I know where you were born, Petula Fletcher. And I know who your parents are. I know where they are right this—"

"Don't you dare!" Petula broke in. She scoured, and looked a little worried. She wondered if Estella-Jeanne was bluffing. Petula's parents were far away in a retirement trailer park in Barstow, California. They were a pitiful, homespun, pair of embarrassing alcoholics, and Petula paid dearly for them to stay hidden away out on the west coast. Cowboy was the only person who even knew they were alive (at least that was what Petula believed). "I don't know what you're talking about," Petula countered. "But someone who enjoyed her luxurious wall-to-wall Berber carpeting might want to keep her mouth closed about such things."

"That was a long time ago," Estella-Jeanne said. She had heard rumors about Barstow, and Petula's Momma and Daddy, but really didn't have any proof, so she let that go. "I have a grandson now," Estella-Jeanne said. "And he is very happy. His heart is not going to get broken. Not here. Not today. Certainly not by a Fletcher. Not anymore. So you can turn your bloated, hoity-toity, above it all, sagging ass around, and hit the road out of here."

Petula's mouth dropped open. "How dare you speak to me like that." Petula looked at the group on the other side of the table with disdain. "I have no idea why, or how, you got so many people to join you today. But what I do know is that you have kidnapped my grandson. The sheriff might be interested in knowing about that. Release Josh and give him back to his family who love him. And you can keep your freak show soup kitchen. I know what happened. It's called The Stockholm Syndrome. You've traumatized Josh, using drugs and brainwashing, until he has turned against his own family. Just like Patty Hearst. I read all about it on Wikipedia!"

"Quit your jabbering, Petula. No one's been kidnapped." Estella-Jeanne had another card up her sleeve, one that even Kitty didn't know about. "But you know, I might be able to shed some light on why so many people decided to join our little freak show soup kitchen, as you put it, and not the annual event you are in charge of over at The Church of the Glorious Light. Would you like to know, Shandazzle?"

"I most certainly would, Estella-Jeanne." Shandazzle replied, playing along. "Is it scandalous?"

"Very."

"Lordy, I'm living for it."

"My grandson, Dylan, is very smart when it comes to computers," Estella-Jeanne said. "He even knows how to hack into other people's e-mail lists. Like yours, Petula. Early this morning everyone in your personal e-mail directory received a message from the Food and Drug Administration warning that the turkeys at the Fletcher Family Freedom Feast were contaminated with e-coli. He even attached photographs of some road kill to make it more funny. It made me laugh."

"Momma, you and Dylan did not do that?" Kitty asked, genuinely surprised.

A teenage boy in line wearing a Kitty Stardust hoodie remarked: "I got that e-mail. It was hilarious and nauseating."

Petula said, "That is against the law."

"And you have to admit, rather funny," Shandazzle added.

Estella-Jeanne shrugged. "If I get the gas chamber, it would still have been worth it."

JJ quickly jumped in holding out his hands. "Everyone! This bickering back and forth all stops now. The local heat-seeking reporter is locked in on us."

They all looked up to see that Rebecca C. Hooper and a cameraman were within yards, charging through the crowd.

JJ added, "I want everyone on their best behavior, and that includes you, Momma. The media doesn't need to hear any dirty laundry."

Petula took the brief moment to get in a last jab at Estella-Jeanne. "You may have acquired some money, but you're still just squirrel and dumpling eating ridge runners to me."

Estella-Jeanne quipped back, "The last time I saw a mouth like yours, it had a hook in it."

"Oh!" Petula growled. "If I had known I would ever have to see your face again, Estella-Jeanne Holloway, I would have just shot you myself."

Estella-Jeanne replied, "If I had known I would ever have to see your face again, I would have jumped in front of the bullet."

"Stop it!" JJ pleaded. "Kitty, get your momma under control."

"How about yours?" Kitty fired back.

Rebecca barged in. She snapped her fingers hurriedly at the cameraman, who gave her the okay sign. She spoke into the microphone: "This is Rebecca C. Hooper, Channel 2 News, reporting from downtown Nashville. Governor, what brings you to Kitty's Kitchen? Witnesses have said they saw you and your mother fleeing the Fletcher Family Freedom Feast at The Church of the Glorious Light." She shoved the microphone at JJ and Kitty.

JJ was a pure professional, his voice remarkably calm and reassuring: "Rebecca, this town of ours is certainly big enough for two warmhearted charity events on this lovely Thanksgiving day." JJ turned to look into the camera with a warm smile. "My Grandma Hazel always said, 'It takes more than one set of hands to pull together.'"

JJ turned back to glance at Kitty. The bitter look she was giving made him suddenly worry.

"Kitty, Governor," Rebecca cut in, "there are conflicting reports about the reality of a wedding between your two sons. Would either of you like to comment?"

JJ was quick to speak first. "Rebecca," he said. "You see, *The Nashville Sun* kind of went running with a silly story before they acquired all their facts." JJ gave the camera a firm nod. "It is what we call in politics, a big whopper. No, Rebecca, I'm afraid there's no story here, and there's no—"

"Yes!" Kitty broke in sharply. "Rebecca, there is going to be a lovely wedding between the governor's son, Josh, and my son, Dylan, at my ranch this Sunday. You are welcome to come and bring your camera crew along. A beautiful wedding is nothing to hide."

"Sunday is just days away," JJ replied. "And there is absolutely no possible way there's going to be a wedding, certainly not one involving my son."

Kitty glowed, self-assuredly. "The wedding is going to be beautiful. And it's going to be Sunday," she said to the camera. "And my dear friend, Jamie Oliver, will be serving a lovely vegetarian dinner for the guests. The *wedding* guests."

JJ smiled (but it was becoming strained). "Some of Kitty's particulars simply are not accurate. You know I've always shot straight with people of Tennessee. Take my word for it. There's no wedding. How could there be? It's not even legal in this state."

"It wasn't legal for most of the people in this country to vote at one time," Kitty countered. "But good people stood up against that senseless injustice as well."

"I'll be speaking to my son very soon. I promise he is going to make a statement that he has no intention to marry anyone right now. Certainly not this Sunday."

"That won't be possible," Kitty replied. "Josh and Dylan won't be available for comment until the day of the wedding. Next Sunday, at Stardust Ranch. If you'd like Rebecca, come on out early and I'll give you a behind the scenes exclusive."

"Really?" Rebecca beamed. "I would love that."

Shandazzle shook her head, and added, "Don't you people read the papers? It was on the front page of *The Nashville Sun*."

Petula's eyes narrowed to near slits. A rage was building in her. JJ noticed. He quickly said, "Rebecca, my momma and I have a lot of hungry people waiting for us, so we're going back to our Thanksgiving feast. But let me point out, no one has heard a word from either one of these boys. Until then, there's no story. I repeat, though, for the record, my son, Josh Fletcher, is not getting married this Sunday. I'm his father. I know him better than anyone."

Kitty retorted, "Josh is a grown man, he can make his own decisions."

"And I'm sure he'll make the right one."

"He did," Kitty replied. "He picked my son to be his husband."

An impoverished, fatigued-looking man, in dirty jeans and a USA Veterans cap, dragged up a cart with a squeaky wheel, and said, "Can you take this squabble someplace else? I'm as hungry as a tick on a turnip."

JJ said, "That's all, Rebecca, for now."

Kitty added, "And I've got a long line of hungry folks. But Rebecca, I'll plan on seeing you this Sunday."

"And one more thing," JJ threw in. "The turkeys over at The Church of the Glorious Light are perfectly fine. E-coli free, smoked, steaming, and ready to eat."

Rebecca nodded, and turned to the camera. "There you have it—"

"REBECCA!" Petula bellowed out.

Rebecca stopped. She nodded for the cameraman to turn the camera onto Petula. The violent rage in Petula's voice almost made Rebecca's teeth rattle. She imagined this could be the moment she had been praying for.

The entire crowd stopped and stared. Even Minnie Pearl stopped eating her apples and looked up.

"Momma," JJ said, attempting to settle her down. "Momma knows that in time the truth will be clear to everyone, and there is no more that needs to be said here today."

"I'd like to hear what she has to say," Rebecca responded, skillfully sounding as if her motives were impartial. "Go ahead Mrs. Fletcher, you were saying?"

"Thank you, Rebecca." Petula was breathing erratically, but her words flowed out with a focused, savage force. "I can assure you and all the good families of this state, the heart and soul of our children is in good hands. My son, the governor, will not let them down. The Fletcher family is as strong and as dedicated today to family values as we have ever been. As I stand here before God and Tennessee, my grandson will return home to his family. And then you will see for yourselves, he is a normal, healthy, well-adjusted, intelligent, strapping young man." Petula turned to look at Kitty and she placed her feet firmly on the ground. "Who can say about your son, Ms. Stardust, but nobody in the Fletcher family will ever be a sissy-boy!"

Kitty was paralyzed. The mother lion in her wanted to rip into flesh and bone, but the shock froze her. She couldn't breathe, or move.

Estella-Jeanne was not so immobilized. She began looking on the table for a weapon. Shandazzle took a cantaloupe-sized pumpkin, and handed it across to her.

It happened in the blink of an eye, but Agent Applegarth jumped into action. As Estella-Jeanne hurled the pumpkin, with the force of a cannon ball, at Petula, the young agent leapt in and swept Petula into his arms. The pumpkin grazed past Petula's shoulder, and continued on its bullet-like trajectory, until it slammed into the stomach of Agent Cooper. *Thunk!* The sudden, blinding pain doubled him over and he fell to his knees. The pumpkin plopped to the ground breaking into pieces.

JJ knew he had seconds to act. He grabbed Petula from Agent Applegarth's grip. He looked at Rebecca. "We'll be at The Church of the Glorious Light. Come on out and join us. We'll see you there."

With that, he and Agent Applegarth ushered a rattled and growling Petula away. Agent Cooper stumbled to his feet, and limped, his hands clinging to his stomach. Petula turned back and yelled, "I'll be pressing charges. You can count on it!"

Estella–Jeanne raised her fist in defiance, and yelled, "VIVA LA CLODHOPPERS!"

JJ took one quick glance back at Kitty. The look in her eyes was no longer a mystery for him. There was no sexual undertone – or overtone – of any kind. It was loathing; plain and simple. This look actually hurt. But he was helpless to do anything. He turned and quickly kept his mother in his arms, marching her away as fast as he could. JJ said, "Momma please don't talk, just keep walking."

Rebecca stepped up to get into close camera range, brushed her hair out of her face, and said, "And there you have it. Two renowned Tennessee families at war. A son is missing in action. Is Josh Fletcher a pawn in a political smear campaign against his father? Or is the governor's son picking out china down at Macy's? You'll hear it first right here on Channel 2 News. This is Rebecca C. Hooper reporting live from the Piggly Wiggly in downtown Nashville. Back to you, Linda."

We die only once, and for such a long time.
　　　　- MOLIÈRE

DON'T SHAKE THE FAMILY TREE

1

One of the freedoms of having everyone believe you were crazy (and nearly everyone in Belle Meade believed Jewell Whitecotton was, if not crazy, at least some variation of the theme) was that you could do, say, and think pretty much anything you wanted, and no one would be surprised. Least of all, yourself.

Jewell had laid the suit out over the bedspread of her cherry-wood sleigh bed. The shirt was cut up the back. The pants lay next to it. Jewell had a seam ripper in one hand, and was preparing the jacket to be ripped up the back.

Oh, my. I hate to do it. But the jacket just won't go on unless I rip out the back seam.

Jewell had found her husband Fritz's three piece suit hanging in the back of her walk-in closet were she kept some of his clothes bagged and sealed in moth balls. The person she envisioned wearing the suit now was sure to look debonair in it. Jewell needed to alter the suit because the arms of the soon-to be wearer could no longer bend to accommodate the shirt or suit jacket.

The business Jewell was in now was highly secret. She knew it had to be. She had gotten rid of her nosey housekeeper over an hour ago. She had sent Georgia out on errands. That should keep her away long enough. And Jewell was glad, in general, to have her gone. Georgia had been going on all morning about something she saw on TV. The population of the earth was over seven billion now, and, from what the people on TV said (according to Georgia) the human race wasn't going to be able to sustain so many folks for much longer. Georgia kept saying, "Something has to be done!" Jewell gave Georgia the list of errands, and told her to stop watching the TV.

Jewell had confirmed Georgia was gone by looking out her bedroom window to see her drive away in her old powder blue Lincoln Town Car. Jewell had then quickly returned to her work. All that talk about so many people had made Jewell feel lonely.

It made her miss her husband Fritz. He would have known what to say to make her feel better. He always did.

Before Jewell had left Kansas City and moved back to Nashville, her mother had taken her to the cemetery to visit Fritz's grave, one last time. By that day, Jewell had come to realize Fritz was really gone. It took some convincing, but Jewell finally accepted the truth. Fritz obviously was not around to counter all their arguments that he was dead.

At some point, while Jewell sat in a lawn chair facing the gravestone of her husband, she had the instinct to write herself a note. She had taken a gum wrapper and a pen from her purse. With that pen and gum wrapper she had tried to make some sense of the unbearable truth she was facing.

She kept this gum wrapper note in a zipped up pocket of her purse. She would find it off and on throughout her life. The message was seven words:

IT IS BETTER TO HAVE KNOWN HIM

Sometimes she didn't like this message. She'd stuff the gum wrapper back in her purse pocket, zip it back up, and angrily snap her purse closed. But she would always open her purse back up a few minutes later, take out the note and read it again. And she'd cry. But with sorrow *and* with gratitude, because she knew it was true.

Jewell smoothed out the suit jacket on her bed. She lined it up where the seam would be easy to cut.

"More than seven billion people on the earth now," she said to herself, shaking her head. "A lot of good that does me. It's not like any of them are knocking down my door to say hello."

Although his face was etched into her childhood memories, Jewell Whitecotton had never once seen the man she had planned to dine with this Thanksgiving, not until she opened the freezer in the basement a few days ago. She had only seen pictures. But they had been unforgettable photographs, because they were so important to her daddy.

Hal Fletcher had only been a teenager himself when he started taking the pictures with his parents newly acquired Reflex-Korelle camera. He had been in his mid-twenties when he stopped. He had to stop because the subject of the photographs had to be locked away, hidden from the world, in the large G.E. freezer of the Fletcher family basement.

It was usually when Hal had had too many of his rye whiskey and champagnes, what he called his Sea Captain Specials, when he would decide it was time to get out the photo album. That's when he would ask Jewell and Jackson, his only two children, to come see the prohibited photographs with him. He would carefully remove the blankets, wool sweaters and jackets from the cedar chest. The album was hidden on the very bottom. Jewell and Jackson would be wide-eyed with childish excitement as their daddy flipped through the pages. And he'd tell them once again about the adventures of Petrified Ed.

He would turn the pages, and relate to his children an exciting tale for each new set of photographs. Jewell and her younger brother would be hanging on their daddy's every word.

Hazel Fletcher usually was the one to snap them all back to reality. She would often yell out for her husband and two children; and the photobook would be slammed closed. Hal would quickly put the book back in the bottom of the cedar chest, cover it with the blankets and clothes, and then carefully lower the lid of the chest. He'd put his finger to his lips, and tell Jewell and Jackson to keep their secret.

Hazel, who knew very well all about the photo album, would pop in the room, arms on her hips, inquiring about what kind of mischief the three of them were up to. Hal and she had agreed to not share the photo album with their young children, and she suspected he wasn't sticking to his end of their bargain. Hal would hug his wife, and give her a quick kiss. He'd say: "I'm just educating our children about some important family history." Hazel would roll her eyes. She knew Hal was telling her a little white lie of some sort. But in truth, his explanation was not really a lie at all. That was precisely what Hal Fletcher was doing.

The photographs always haunted Jewell. It was like looking through the pages of a ghost story. No matter how her daddy described it, she always saw it differently. Jewell imagined that the man, who was the subject of the old photographs, must have had a very unhappy and lonely life. How she came to this conclusion was anyone's guess. The man had died many years before she was born. And not anyone in the Fletcher family, including her daddy, had any idea who the man in the pictures really was.

As she stood next to her bed, all these years later, she still was convinced the man had lived a woefully sad life. One thing she could do, to fix that, was to have him as a guest with her at a spectacular Thanksgiving dinner.

"He needs to know about family, Darling Fritz," Jewell said to the empty suit jacket. "I know you won't mind him borrowing your suit for a while. It only seems fair, him being who he is and all. I don't think he ever had a home. I just feel it in my bones. Everyone deserves love, and he needs to feel it, so he can move on. I'm going to show him what the love of a good home is like." She took the seam ripper and severed the threads up the back of the suit jacket. Jewell sighed. "Something just tells me he deserves it."

Even though it was only a notion of hers, a crazy one or not, Jewell's complicated mind and sensitive heart had stumbled onto something that was essentially the truth. If there ever was a soul who did need to know the rewards of family, and the tranquility that comes from having been loved, it was the man known in his time as Roman Stamps; the man Jewell had found in her basement freezer – a man she had known all her life as Petrified Ed.

2

Roman Stamps' entry into life was not an easy one. His conception occurred behind a backwoods tavern; basically a tin roof shanty. His mother was in the back of a horse-drawn wagon with a man she had recently met. The wagon's bare wood was painful for the young woman engaged in the drunken carnal activity. The man finally noticed and grabbed a wool blanket from inside a wooden trunk on the wagon, and placed it under the young woman's back. They continued on for another fifteen minutes. She would have enjoyed another fifteen minutes *at least* from him. But she accepted the course of events as they were, which were pretty good under the circumstances. Then they smoked some freshly rolled tobacco together in silence.

Four months later, the Cherokee woman involved discovered she was pregnant, a secret she kept from the man. He was Cherokee as well, a small cattle rancher with a family. He seemed like a good man, and she believed her unexpected news would likely destroy his marriage. She was probably right.

The woman had a difficult birth. The medical term was shoulder dystocia. But the inexperienced woman who was in charge of the delivery had no idea what had gone terribly wrong. She was not a doctor. The woman had seen a head-first birth before, which was normal, but when the baby wouldn't move any further she became concerned, then frightened. The three lanterns in the room were turned as high as the flames would go, but the light was not sufficient. She told the mother to push harder, which resulted in an even more dangerous situation. The baby's shoulder had become stuck behind his mother's pelvic bone preventing his body from moving out. The mother's deafening screams were making the frightening situation even more difficult. The baby's face was turning blue. Seconds counted. The woman reached behind the baby's neck, and pulled as hard as she could.

She saved the baby's life, but there was nerve damage to his neck. This left Roman with an arm that was rarely much good to him throughout his life. The temporary asphyxia also caused some slightly perceivable permanent brain damage. Had his mother lived she would have made certain Roman was protected from the cruel experiences associated with his disabilities. But she suffered bleeding from an internal tear near her pelvis. She should have received a life-saving blood transfusion, but in 1867, for a young Cherokee woman in Nashville, Tennessee, such a procedure was all but unheard of.

Roman was clutched in his mother's arms, his head laying on her breasts, when she died, eighteen hours after he arrived. It was the last time anyone would hold him in such a caring and loving way, even though he would live almost another sixty-two years.

Nearly all living relatives of Roman Stamps had been forced by the US government to move to Oklahoma in the 1830s, although his mother's parents were not among them. Not wanting to leave their home, Roman's grandfather and grandmother had hidden in the Snowbird Mountains at the southern end of the Appalachian chain. But before his birth, Roman's grandmother had died of cholera, and his grandfather had been murdered by fur thieves. With no close relations, there simply was no one around who wanted to take a newborn with such handicaps.

Onacona was the Cherokee name his mother had given to Roman. This fact was something he was never aware of during his entire life. He was taken to an orphanage as a baby, where he was renamed Roman Stamps, so it would be easier to adopt him out to a family. It did little to help. He was a Native American child with mental and physical challenges. Orphanages in the Nashville area were overwhelmed at that time with an unmanageable number of unwanted infants and children. And as Roman was getting older the numbers were growing. Criminal abortion laws were dramatically increasing in the 1870s, even in Nashville, Tennessee. Deadly diseases often left children with no parents. Many people were poor and had a hard time supporting themselves, much less taking on another child. It was a tough time for almost everyone in Nashville in the eighteen hundreds, but for an orphaned child in Nashville it was a time and place of little hope at all. The river port city had only been founded in 1779 and had been incorporated as a city in 1806. The orphanage Roman was in was also sorely in need of dedicated doctors, nurses, and staff. It was a frightening place where food was often so scarce the children would go days without any substantial meals. When Roman was nine years old, he ran away. His escape was never reported, nor did anyone from the orphanage ever come looking for him. His bed, a thin mattress on the third floor, was filled that very night.

The rest of Roman's life was a burdensome existence of survival from one meal to another, one camping place to a different one, and one burdensome job to the next. He often slept in makeshift tents he pitched in the woods. During the summers, he made his way traveling with migrant farm workers. During the harsh winter months, he lived in hobo encampments along the Cumberland and Mississippi rivers.

At the age of 51, Roman came dangerously close to death. Roman had been a stowaway on a boxcar during the great train wreck of 1918. He was sleeping in the third mail car on the inbound local train when it collided with an outbound express. 101 people died that day from the extraordinary accident. But Roman had been thrown from the mail car to safety. He broke three ribs and twisted his ankle, but was able to walk away before anyone noticed he was among the survivors. As was true his whole life, Roman Stamps had gone unnoticed, even in one of the worst industrial-age catastrophes in American history.

Death didn't visit him again for another ten years. He died at night, alone. His last thoughts had been about his mother. He knew absolutely nothing about her (or his father for that matter), but he had had a recurring dream about being held in a woman's warm arms. In the dreams, he could never see who was holding him so tightly, but he heard a female voice singing a lullaby. It was all he had as far as any kind of memory of love, and it had survived with him, and helped him survive, all his life.

He looked up in the night sky, with his misty thoughts of his mother. He believed it was possible that his mother was there waiting for him among the vast, star-filled skies, because he had heard stories about such things. It was a thought he had difficulty holding onto, in these last moments, because his bony, old body was so weak. Roman was laying on a blanket in a favorite spot in a small clearing near Nashville's Old Hickory Lake. He closed his eyes, and heaved a shuddery, arduous last breath. And that was that.

He was found three days after his death. Although no one could have known, Onacona was discovered on his birthday, June 6, 1929. He would have been 62 years old.

Onacona's body was taken to the Eugene Valentine Funeral Home, while authorities waited for someone to report a missing person of his description. He was not missed by anyone, so a missing person's report never materialized. He was embalmed by Mr. Eugene Valentine, and placed in the refrigerated holding room, awaiting a burial request from the sheriff's office. Due to a mix-up in paperwork, the burial request never came.

3

A stability exists for most people, a feeling of safety that is connected to others that you are surrounded by throughout a lifetime. It starts with your birth. Additions are made to the circle; and subtractions. Others may have to make adjustments to construct altered versions of it for themselves. It is a comfortable haven you can count on to be there whenever you are feeling tired or weak, or a place to share your joys. When you venture away, it's a place to come back home to. It is essential. It nourishes the soul. It is so basic that nearly every living creature who experiences feelings expresses some form of it. It is family.

For Josh, his family was suddenly gone. The argument with his father had felt hopeless, and unmendable. He felt like he was on a tiny life raft in the middle of a vast ocean. The huge ship he always knew to be his home was no longer in sight. Just an empty sea. The level of anguish, and fear, was debilitating. He was in a deep emotional collapse. A therapist once told Josh that his mother's death at an early age had created a deep need for him to maintain control. It was true. And here he was, out of any kind of control, in a freefall with no parachute. Dylan and Rhashan were in the car with him, but even they – who he knew cared deeply for him – felt too far away to fence out the sadness he was drowning in.

Being abruptly cast out from your family hurts.

"I think this is the little store Kitty mentioned," Rhashan said. He was driving the Land Rover. Josh was in the passenger seat, and Dylan was sleeping in the back, his cowboy hat tipped down over his eyes, with a Basset Hound snoozing in his lap.

The Land Rover was on a tiny dirt road that was barely one lane wide. Weeds grew high down the middle of the path. The road wound up, and up, through rolling hills. A dense forest of trees cascaded on either side – pine, ash, hickory, oak, cedar, and cottonwood – all filling every available space. An occasional deer or rabbit would scurry away into the underbrush.

They were approaching an old wooden structure, coming up on their left. Two rusting, retired gas pumps were in front. A metal sign with the trademarked emblem of a green dinosaur was swinging in the light breeze: *Gasoline – 49 cents per gallon.*

Beside the store was a large stack of firewood. Three rocking chairs were in front with whiskey barrels serving as tables; a game of checkers was half finished on one. Next to the store, a wooden porch swing was hanging from a sizable branch of a tremendous oak tree. The only things modern looking were a satellite dish on the tin roof and a neon OPEN sign in the front window. The dirt parking lot was empty other than a few weeds.

Josh pushed aside his somber feelings, and looked up. The sight of the old country store was refreshing. It felt like an escape to another time, and an escape was just what Josh needed. "It's got to be," Josh agreed. "It's the first sign of human life we've seen for over forty miles."

Dylan sat up. He looked out the window through half-asleep eyes.

"Check that out," Josh said, and pointed to a sign on the right side of the road. It was a wooden, hand-painted sign that read:

J. KENT PREYER

ARMADILLO – POP. 3

Dylan shook his head. "This looks dangerously close to one of those horror movies where boneheaded, excessively good-looking, college students take a very wrong turn, and end up watching each other die on the end of a meat hook. I hope you have your gun, Rhashan."

"I do," Rhashan said.

Coltrane jumped up in the window, looking out with excitement, as Rhashan turned into the dirt parking lot.

Josh countered the overall impression coming from the others, "I think it looks like a sweet little country store."

Rhashan added, "A sweet little country store in the middle of nowhere. My GPS device stopped reporting our location twenty minutes ago. I should point out a few things that might be pertinent to our situation. We are: a black man, two gay men, and a silly-looking dog that can no longer get onto a sofa without the aid of doggy stairs."

Josh said, "Just because we're in the boonies doesn't mean we should be so quick to stereotype people who live up here."

Rhashan said, "I saw a road sign about five miles back that said, 'This road maintained by The Army of the Confederacy'."

Rhashan pulled the car up to the front of the general store. He stopped, and parked. A sign hanging on the front porch roof read:

> IF YOU CAN READ THIS SIGN
> YOU ARE IN SHOOTING RANGE

Josh stared at the sign. He then asked (in a clear change in tone), "Rhashan, you've got plenty of ammo in that gun, right?"

"Yes, I do," Rhashan replied. "And Coltrane doesn't look it, but he does have a ferocious bite."

"I'm sorry if this sounds cold," Dylan said, "but if I hear a chainsaw, it's every man for himself."

TENNESSEE WILDFLOWERS

* * *

The store was filled with food products and general supplies. A wood-burning cook stove was stationed in the middle, with an orange glowing fire inside. There was a small hardware section in one corner. A shelved housewares section had a small supply of cast iron skillets, Dutch ovens and steamer kettles for sale. There was an area to buy enamelware coffee boilers, food mills, oil lamps, beeswax candles and lye soap. Among the delicious-looking homemade items on other shelves were: jars of strawberry, blackberry and peach jams, clover honey, sorghum and pure maple syrup, and bottles of sarsaparilla soda. Large glass bowls were filled with colorful, wrapped hard candies and pieces of pulled taffy. There was a section of glass containers marked as healing tonics, herbs, and potions. Also included on a shelf were a few large glass jars labeled, 'Vegetable Viper Stew'. A mason jar with a jumble of wildflowers was sitting on the counter near the cash register.

An elderly man and woman, both approaching the century mark, clothes worn, but recently pressed, slept soundly in rocking chairs inside the store. A bloodhound and a hunting rifle rested faithfully at the elderly man's side.

Mae Willow, a woman with seemingly ancient eyes and a wise, cheerful smile stood behind the counter. An antique brass plated register was next to her. A dusty old TV set behind the counter, on a high shelf, played a Nashville newscast at a low volume.

Dylan and Josh were approaching the counter with a loaf of fresh bread, some canned beans, a jar of clover honey, kerosene, two lanterns, candles and a twelve pack of beer.

Rhashan joined them with two mason jars full of peaches. "My momma used to can peaches just like this," Rhashan said, with a sizable smile on his lips. "Throw these in."

Mae replied, "You'll enjoy those. This year the trees were just covered with peaches, and the fruit practically fell off the pits."

Dylan dropped the cans of beer on the counter. "Oh no," he said.

"What?" Josh asked.

Dylan pointed to the television set. "Could you turn up the volume on that TV please?"

"Oh sure," Mae replied. She grabbed a remote and turned the sound up. "We don't get good reception on that old thing, but there's not much I care to watch these days anyway."

On the television screen Rebecca C. Hooper was standing in front of Kitty and JJ at the Piggy Wiggly. It was the coverage of the event at Kitty's soup kitchen from a few hours earlier. The shot on the screen cut to Petula glaring angrily into the camera.

"Why on earth is Grandma on the news?" Josh asked. There was a fearful reservation in his voice that indicated he didn't really want to know the answer to that question.

From the TV set Petula's voice erupted: "Who can say about your son, Ms. Stardust, but nobody in the Fletcher family will ever be a sissy-boy!"

The camera quickly cut to the shot of Estella-Jeanne hurling the pumpkin. It sailed past Petula (who was facing the camera, and didn't see the pumpkin coming) as Agent Applegarth tackled her to the ground. The pumpkin continued flying straight into the gut of Agent Cooper, who fell to his knees in agony.

The TV screen returned to the news desk, where Linda Chan cut in: "That was earlier today here in Nashville, Tennessee, in a story that has drawn national attention and is igniting a heated debate. The White House has issued a statement today saying that the president stands firmly behind Governor JJ Fletcher, who asserts his son is undeniably a heterosexual young man. The Secret Service Agent hit in the stomach by the projectile pumpkin is in stable con—"

Static snow and white fuzzy lines obliterated the news report on the TV screen.

Mae shook her head. "I'm sorry. Dang squirrels on the roof won't let the satellite dish alone. I'll have to climb up there and shoot them myself." She nodded over to the gentleman asleep in the rocking chair. "The last time Ernie was up on the roof he got spooked. Says he saw a tiny man covered in fur. He told me the little fella was from outer space." She sighed. "I think he's making his moonshine too strong again. You boys find everything you need?"

"Josh?" Rhashan asked. "What's wrong?"

Josh had begun to wheeze, and struggled to catch his breath. Dylan saw Josh's face was clammy and turning paler by the second.

"He's having an asthma attack," Dylan said. "A bad one."

"What do you need me to do?" Rhashan asked.

"Get him in a chair. I'll go grab his inhaler," Dylan replied. He took Josh's hand. "I'll be right back, okay."

Josh nodded. His erratic, obstructed breathing was frightening to watch. Dylan turned, and ran as fast as he could from the store. Rhashan grabbed a chair from the side of the grocery store counter.

* * *

Outside, in the parking lot, Dylan scrambled into the backseat of the Land Rover. He grabbed a backpack, and began to rummage through it. Coltrane sat on the seat next to him. "Where is it Coltrane? Where is it?" Coltrane could sense the urgency, and barked. Dylan said, "Jesus, I can't find it. Where did he put it?"

Dylan heard about people who had died from asthma attacks. Josh and he had talked about the serious nature of his medical condition a few times. And Dylan knew that any medical help, if it turned out to be necessary, would be too far away to make any difference out where they were.

Dylan started throwing T-shirts, and jeans, and socks out of the bag in a panic. He unzipped another pocket, and threw out toothpaste and a pack of disposable razors. Then he pulled out a small flashlight. He took it and turned it on, then held the light inside the bag. He pushed items aside until he saw something that looked right.

Dylan reached in, and grabbed the inhaler. He was so relieved he almost cried. "Coltrane, I got it!"

* * *

Josh was seated in a chair. Rhashan and Mae were watching him, as Dylan rushed back through the front door. Dylan ran to Josh, kneeled down and gave him the inhaler.

Josh took it, but instead of using it he laid his hand in his lap. To Dylan's surprise Josh was breathing normally.

"Use the inhaler, Josh!" Dylan said, bewildered and determined.

"It's okay," Josh replied. He looked at Dylan equally mystified, and took in a deep, clear breath.

"Are you sure?" Dylan asked. "Maybe you should use it anyway?"

"I can breathe," Josh said. "I'm really okay." Josh took Dylan's hand. "Really?"

Dylan noticed that Mae held a pint-sized, brown glass bottle in one hand and an empty spoon in the other.

"Just sit with it a minute longer," Mae said, reassuring Josh.

Dylan looked at Josh. "What did you take?"

"It's an old Cherokee remedy," Mae explained. "Usually one dose does the trick, but I'll let you keep the bottle, just in case. No charge."

Rhashan said, "Look, I am personally responsible for both you boys, so we're going back into town and getting you to a doctor."

Josh shook his head, "I'm really fine. Seriously."

Mae assured them, "You do what you need to do, but I can promise you, I've never seen a case like his this tonic didn't cure. And I'm ninety two."

They all looked at Josh. He took in another deep, clear breath. "I feel great."

"Okay," Rhashan said.

"You boys up here to do some hunting?" Mae asked.

"We're just on a little vacation," Dylan explained, evading the whole explanation.

Mae put the lid on the bottle, and gave it to Josh.

"From the law?" Mae asked, looking over Dylan's tattoos. "These days that's half the customers I get up here. Hunters, and people hiding out from one law enforcement agency or the other. A family of six came through this morning. Said the Federal Marshals were hot on their trail. Cute little kids. I don't ask questions."

"We are hiding, but not from Federal Marshals," Josh explained. "Kitty Stardust sent us up here. Actually, you might be able to tell us what road we need to turn down to get to the house where she used to live."

Mae's face lit up. "My mind is as slow as molasses these days!" She looked at Dylan. "You're Estella-Jeanne's grandson, Dylan. Why didn't you say so? Estella-Jeanne called this morning. She told me to give you the star treatment." She snapped her finger at Rhashan. And you're the man who looks like Paul Bunyan's bigger brother, but with darker skin. She told me all about you boys. Now that I know who I'm talking to, I'm going to give you three cases of those peaches, and some bottles of Ernie's whiskey to take with you." Mae smiled again, a bittersweet nostalgic look in her eyes. "Estella-Jeanne's momma was an old dear friend of mine. We grew up together here in Armadillo. We used to skip school, just the two of us, and go smoke grapevines in my daddy's barn. This mountaintop sure has not been the same since Estella-Jeanne and Ruth Adele left." Mae looked at Dylan. "Your grandpa and grandma are buried in the cemetery right next to the old church. You should go by and take a look and say hello. Their grave markers are right by the huge oak tree split in two by lightening. You can't miss it."

Dylan nodded. "I'll go check that out."

Mae nodded back, then looked at Josh, "From what I understand, you must be Petula Fletcher's grandson?" She gave Josh a sympathetic pat on the shoulder.

Josh nodded. "I'm Josh. And yes, Petula's my grandma."

"I'm Mae Willow. Born on this mountain. And I'll die on this mountain. You're the ones causing all that hullabaloo down in the big city," Mae said. "It's a pleasure to meet you."

"Pleasure to meet you too, ma'am," Rhashan said.

"Same here," Dylan added.

"Thanks for the medicine," Josh said, holding up the bottle.

"Glad to help." Mae shrugged. "Personally, I can't imagine why anyone would mind if you young men got hitched. My Lord, I've been married to Ernie over there for over sixty years."

They look over at the two people surprisingly still sound asleep. Even the hound dog was snoring.

Mae gave a charitable nod in the direction of her husband. "He may not look like much. But, all these years later, we both still manage to keep each other happy. There are many a good songs played on an old fiddle."

"They don't wake easily," Dylan observed.

Mae nodded. "They don't have their hearing aids in. Ernie lost most of what was left of his hearing when his moonshine still exploded a couple of years ago. That old hound dog can't hear neither. You could fire a civil war cannon between the lot of them, and not one of their eyes would flutter. That's his sister sitting next to him. She never did marry. Too mean. Ernie and I have been through thick and thin together, and in this very short life, if you find someone to do that with then that's all that really matters." Mae winked. Her eyes - years of wisdom beaming from them - stared at Josh and Dylan. "My daddy was a white man married to a pure blooded Mapuche woman. He met Momma when he was traveling in South America. Both of their families cut them off for good. Never spoke to them ever again. Told them their love was cursed and doomed. Momma died three months after Daddy, seventy-one years after they met, and just as much in love. I wish somebody could explain to me how that was doomed?"

Josh and Dylan nodded, with smiles that said, *thank you*.

Mae said, "Now let me draw you a map to Estella-Jeanne's home. And per her very instructions, if any nosey reporters come poking around asking about you, I'll send them to the old Turlington home place. Nothing out there but poison ivy and copperheads."

Mae walked over to a dusty shelf, and grabbed a pen and paper. Dylan and Rhashan stepped up to pay for the goods on the counter.

Josh began to get up from the chair, when he noticed that the woman in the rocking chair - the one who had been sleeping so soundly - had opened her eyes. She was staring at him. The color of blue was unmistakable - the color of Bluebell flowers. Josh thought a moment, then glanced over to the jars on the wooden shelf across the room. He got a chill, and experienced a slip in perception that caused him to become slightly dizzy. He sat back down. An image of his mother floated into his mind. Her face was smiling, and she was telling him an extraordinary magical children's story about a woman and some rattlesnakes.

Even though he already knew the answer, Josh pointed to the large mason jars on the counter, and asked, "Mae, can you tell me, is that rattlesnake stew in those jars?"

4

Josh told the woman – who turned out to *really be* Rattlesnake Calliope – the entire story, exactly the way he remembered his mother telling him. Calliope (hearing aid now in), Mae's sister-in-law, found the story of her catching rattlesnakes, and making a stew of them, charming, "...and slightly embellished. It sounds exactly like the kind of engaging and sweet story your mother would come up with." Calliope and Josh both felt as if they had witnessed seeing a ghost. For Josh, it was seeing a woman his mother had described in revered, larger-than-life, detail over fifteen years ago. For Calliope, she saw the face of her dear friend in Josh's. He did look amazingly like his mother.

Dylan and Rhashan had gone ahead to the Holloway home place and let Josh spend some time with Calliope. They were happy to get the house opened and set up while Josh had a visit with someone he had discovered was a close friend of his mother's.

"Your momma was a special person, of course much younger and idealistic than I was. She found beauty in people and things I frankly had no time for," Calliope said.

Josh replied, "I am a lot more like you on that count."

"My daddy always told me to try and find 'the good and the God' in every person I met," Calliope said, with a shake of her head. "I finally told him one day, 'After years of trying, Daddy, I'm going to have to look elsewhere.'"

Josh smiled. He had reached a similar distrustful conclusion about people himself.

Calliope had taken out an old shoebox of pictures. They had gone outside the store to sit in the wooden swing hanging from the oak tree nearby. While Calliope sorted through the mostly black and white photographs, Mae had brought them some much appreciated hot apple cider and a tray of homemade oatmeal cookies. Josh tried to imagine his mother telling the story of Rattlesnake Calliope. It was sometimes hard for him to bring up an image of her in his mind, or to actually hear her voice, but today, for the first time in a long while, he was honestly feeling his mother close to him. And he was having an easier time seeing and hearing her than ever before.

After extensive sorting, she came up with the photograph she was looking for. It was a picture of Josh's mother holding a bundle of wildflowers, with Calliope, both standing in front of the oak tree. It appeared to be the precise spot where Calliope and Josh were now swaying in the swing.

It had gotten late in the evening, and fireflies had begun to appear just above the grassy lawn. Calliope had looked out over the yard in astonishment. "I have never seen fireflies come out this late in the year." Then, she sighed. "Isn't that funny?" she said, and looked at Josh with her illuminating blue eyes. "Your momma loved fireflies."

Josh looked at the photograph of his mother, and then watched the tiny balls of glowing yellow lights drifting and bouncing magically as far as the eye could see. He tried to picture his mother standing there, where she was in the photograph. She likely had enjoyed watching fireflies as well, from right where he was sitting. The swing wasn't there at the time, but Calliope confirmed that his momma and she had indeed sat in a couple of wooden chairs, pretty much in the same spot, drinking iced tea and admiring the fireflies.

"I remember this day," Calliope said, as she held out the picture to get a good long look. "Mae was the one who took this picture of us. Your mother came up here, on what she said was her one of her personal, and strictly confidential, vacations. She didn't even tell your daddy about them. He thought she was out shopping at the mall, or taking in a movie with her friends. She said she would often start out with a plan like that, but she would call her friends and cancel. Then she'd drive on up here. For someone who was so fond of people, she sure would take any chance to get away from them." Calliope smiled. "I guess we all are full of contradictions?"

Calliope handed the picture to Josh. "This is yours now."

Josh shook his head. "I don't want to take your only picture of her."

"I don't really need reminders of the past anymore. These days I pretty much am looking forward to whatever comes next." She winked, and took a drink of her apple cider. Josh didn't see any signs of her approaching *whatever comes next*, even though she had told him she was nearly a century old, but he didn't say anything.

Calliope thought back, and said, "Your momma said her favorite thing in the whole world was a wildflower. Nothing brought her more joy than finding a new one, one that she had never seen before. She said she felt the same way about people too."

Josh took the photograph, and let his hands rest down in his lap. After a peaceful moment of time had passed, watching the fireflies and listening to the birds chirping in the trees, he asked Calliope, "Did you make that stew inside the store? If you did I'd like to buy some."

"Oh no, Honey. I did make that. But it's been jarred up, and I simply won't have you tasting my stew unless it is fresh made. Snakes are all hiding in the rocks now. This spring I'll catch a fresh batch, and you come back. I'll give you some of that."

Josh nodded. He could easily imagine making a trip back up. He was really starting to enjoy the peace and quiet far away here in the Tennessee hills; and the good company.

"I promise I'll make it just like I did for your momma. You keep that picture. And remember your momma was a beautiful, truly extraordinary person, because that's the God's honest truth of it."

Life is what we make it, always has been, always will be.
- GRANDMA MOSES

TIME FOR DINNER

1

"It is unprofessional, Cowboy," Gisele explained. "And a little silly."

Nurse Gisele Lutkenhouse held a peeled banana in her hand. She was looking disappointed at Cowboy on the bed, his lips tightly closed, with a look of unwavering defiance on his face. Gisele looked to see if they were alone, then she licked the banana from bottom to top, pausing at the top for a little smooch. Her lipstick left a little red kiss on the banana. She looked at Cowboy for a response.

He opened his mouth.

"You have mischievous twinkle in your eye, Mr. Cowboy Fletcher," Gisele said, shaking her head. "You are truly incorrigible sometimes, but I believe your heart is in the right place. Otherwise I'd go right out that door and they'd send one of those other nurses back here to take care of you."

Cowboy shook his head, but smiled as he took a sizable bite of the banana.

Petula walked into the bedroom carrying a big, sleek, black Chanel handbag. "How's the love of my life?" Petula asked. She went to stand next to Gisele by the bed, and smiled at Cowboy. She kissed his forehead and took his hand into hers. Cowboy squeezed Petula's hand three times. Only Petula and he knew that was their private message for: *I love you.*

"Cowboy is radiant and rosy today, and a little contrary. So I would say he is feeling pretty much his old self," Gisele said, then added, "He has not had a bowel movement in a while, so I have been forcing some extra fruit and fiber into his diet."

"Do what she says, Cowboy," Petula said. "You don't want another castor oil enema now do you?"

Cowboy shook his head.

"Nurse Lutkenhouse, could you give me and Cowboy some time alone?" Petula asked. "I bought some new coffee beans. They're down in the kitchen if you want to make some coffee."

"Oh, sure," Gisele said. "Just come get me when you need me." Gisele dropped the banana peel in a waste can as she left the room.

Petula adjusted Cowboy's pajama collar. "Well, you do seem to have some color in your cheeks," she said. "That nurse does seem to have the healing touch." She brushed his hair back from his eyes. "It looks like JJ is going to need our help after all." Petula looked up, scrutinizing the past in her mind. "All those years ago I should never have tried to pay Estella-Jeanne Holloway to keep her daughter away from our son like I did. I should have just hired that man from El Paso to kill them both like we joked about." Petula contemplated the thought for a moment more. "Oh well, it's too late now to dwell on the things you should have done."

Petula walked over to a large oil painting of Ronald Reagan. The painting was hinged on one side and she opened it up to reveal a safe in the wall behind it. Petula whirled the combination. "Remember when we were younger, Cowboy? There was so much hope for this country. The first time I saw you, when you were speaking in Knoxville. You were giving a speech on the importance of getting involved in political causes, the virtues of American idealism, breaking up unions, and other important issues. Every word you said had consequence. I knew I was watching the future president of the United States." She pulled open the safe, took out several ample-sized stacks of hundred dollar bills and placed them into her handbag. She turned to Cowboy. "And if you had done all the things I told you to do, Cowboy, that is exactly what you would have become."

Cowboy watched her. She was probably right. He knew it. He heaved a somewhat remorseful breath.

Petula continued to take out more stacks of cash. "I've been doing my homework on President McKenzie's wife, Suzanne, and I discovered she collects rare Hummels. It's a well-guarded secret because there is some controversy about some of her figurines having a connection to Adolf Hitler." She closed the safe and spun the combination. "I'm certain that story is a fabrication made up by enemies of Suzanne McKenzie. The First Lady is a strong, smart woman, and strong, smart women always have loads of enemies. Don't I know that, Darlin'?"

Petula zipped up her handbag and walked over to Cowboy. She pulled his blanket up around his shoulders. "A nun approached me earlier today and told me I should be sainted for what I am doing to save our grandson's soul." Petula shook her head and continued, "I told her she had the wrong idea about me. Saving souls was her boss's job. My job is to save my son's damn political career." She looked up and eyed the mounted head of a lion on the wall. "Oh, I almost forgot."

Petula walked over to an immense mahogany gun cabinet. The collection of rifles was behind thick security-glass sliding doors. She reached up to the top of the cabinet and grabbed a hidden key from under a stuffed bobcat. She unlocked the cabinet and slid the door open. Inside were over fifty rifles of all makes: Ruger, Marlin, Nosler, Weatherby Vanguard, Remington, Winchester, among others. She grabbed one of the larger Winchester hunting rifles.

A phone was ringing in a distant room. She ignored it. "I had to sign up Ruby Billingsley to help me out. The bank is foreclosing on her house, so I offered to help her out if she helped me out. She insists on lugging that pig along with her everywhere, so I'm likely going to regret it."

Rosalita, a house cleaner in a work dress and white apron, quietly stepped in. She had a phone in one hand and an ostrich feather duster in the other. "Mrs. Fletcher?" Rosalita asked tenderly, taking note of the rifle in Petula's hand, "I know you said you didn't want to speak to anyone, but this is about Miss Jewell."

"Jewell?" Petula asked. She laid the hunting rifle down on a writing table and took the phone from Rosalita. "Hello?" Petula said into the phone. Her curious tone changed instantly. "Dear Lord, not YOU!"

Buster Ragsdale was on the other end. He said, "This involves Jewell, so don't hang up on me dear Petula."

Petula motioned for Rosalita to go. The woman obediently scurried away, closing the door quietly behind her.

"I don't have time to talk to you right now, Buster," Petula responded bluntly. "I'm a little busy trying to save my family from the burning house that you set fire to."

"Oh, my dear, I think you'll pencil me in." Buster didn't sound daunted.

"I'm hanging up now," Petula said.

"Petrified Ed," Buster said confidently.

Petula faltered. She pulled the chair from the writing table and sat down.

Buster finally said, "Are you still there, Petula Honey?"

"He's a myth," Petula snapped. "Just a stupid legend; some ridiculous long-forgotten lie about my husband's family."

"Is it now?" Buster asked, not really looking for an answer.

"I've got a lot of things to deal with Buster." Petula was becoming intolerant. "I've forgone sleep. I've forgone food. I don't remember the last time I've had a drink...of anything! And today..." Petula inhaled deeply: "...on a day I should be celebrating my son's good political fortune, *today* I was forced to have close personal contact with people I find utterly abominable." She paused a moment, then spoke forcefully, "So, listen Buster Ragsdale, stop digging into my family's past!"

"This kind of found me," Buster explained calmly.

"Shouldn't you be retired and out fly fishing or something?"

"I'm at Jewell's now."

"You're not welcome there. You should leave."

"I probably should leave. I wasn't invited by Jewell. Georgia called me," Buster said.

"Time is wasting. Tell me why I am still on this phone. Is Jewell alright?"

"Jewell has made an amazing Thanksgiving dinner. She's just fine. I cannot say the same thing about her guest."

"Her guest?"

"Let's just say he's legendary," Buster replied.

Petula thought it over thoroughly. She said, "Cowboy's father swore what you're referring to was taken care of a long time ago."

"Maybe Hal Fletcher should have been more specific."

Petula's mind covered all possible scenarios. None of them were good. She said, "If you're making this up, Buster."

"The last time I saw this fellow, it was in old photographs down at the newspaper office. He was riding in the back of Hal Fletcher's pick-up truck on Halloween night. It must have been around 1942. I believe he was dressed up as King Tut."

"I'll be right over," Petula said. "Don't you dare call anyone else."

Petula turned the phone off. She looked at Cowboy accusingly with a huff of exhaustion. Cowboy wrote something on his dry erase board. He pushed it up for her to read:

WHAT?

"It's not a what, oh Light of My Life. It's a *who*," Petula replied, getting up and grabbing the rifle. "A stiff, long dead *who*, that, if my memory serves me correctly, is the mandated property of The National Bureau of Indian Affairs." She opened a drawer and grabbed two large boxes of hunting rifle ammunition. "Cowboy, is there some reason why the skeletons in your family's closet have to all come falling out on me at the same time?"

Cowboy wrote on his board:

I LOVE YOU PET

A smile spread across his face, the same charming face she fell in love with so many years ago.

He's a little worse for the wear, she thought. *But not too bad.*

"Darlin', I promised," Petula said, "for better or for worse, and lately things have been trending disproportionately for the worse. And sometimes I think you take my love for granted." She sighed. "But I'll be damned if I don't still love you too."

And she did.

2

Elliot Pendleton opened the passenger door to JJ's Escalade and scooted inside. Byrdie was behind the steering wheel. Elliot attempted to pull the door, but it was difficult to get it to close. He had to pull it hard, and even then it made horrible scraping noises.

"Thanks for coming," Byrdie said. "I wasn't sure if you should see this, but I was afraid I might need your help at some point."

Elliot kicked at an empty bottle of Jack Daniel's at his feet. It clanked with other whiskey bottles. "Help doing what exactly?" Elliot asked. "Where is he?"

"Just pull that door hard to get it to close. It's freezing in here." Byrdie pointed ahead out the windshield. Elliot looked in the direction her finger was aimed.

"Jesus, what is he doing out there?" Elliot asked.

Elliot pulled the door partially closed, which was the best he could do. He and Byrdie were looking at JJ out in the middle of a harvested tobacco field. A huge barn was next to where they were parked. It was just after sundown and the full moon illuminated JJ in the dusky darkness. He was kicking dried out tobacco leaves into the air with his cowboy boots. From head to toe he was covered in mud. He was also yelling and throwing fist jabs in the air. He was far enough away in the field that it was impossible to hear his actual words, but it wasn't hard to imagine what most of them likely were.

"It's what is known as a Fletcher fit," Byrdie explained.

"I went home to take a shower and get some clean clothes. I was gone maybe thirty minutes," Elliot said. "What happened?"

"Well, you might have noticed before you left JJ was drinking a little heavily," Byrdie said. "I tried every possible way to stop him, but I couldn't talk any sense into him, so I came along to drive." She then added, "Josh used to come out here to the barn when he was in high school, when he and his daddy had a big argument. So JJ being desperate for anything, hoped to find him out here."

"Okay?" Elliot was still needing further explanation.

"He searched the barn and Josh wasn't there. Then when he was getting back inside the Escalade he dropped the flashlight on the ground, and when he bent down to pick it up the wind blew the door closed and it hit JJ on the head. That was the final straw. He started kicking the door, and of course it kept flinging back at him. He kicked the door until it stopped coming back." Byrdie sighed. "He's been kicking and yelling ever since."

Byrdie and Elliot watched helplessly as JJ held both hands up in rage and yelled at the moon. One boot apparently got stuck in the mud between the tobacco rows. JJ pulled, and his foot popped out of the boot. This made him even madder. He grabbed the boot with both hands and yanked it from the mud, then flung it as hard as he could.

"From what I hear it runs in the Fletcher men to throw these fits," Byrdie said. "I've actually witnessed JJ throw a Fletcher fit twice before." They watched as JJ pulled off his remaining boot and flung it through the air. "This is the worst I've seen," Byrdie added.

After a moment, Elliot said angrily, "He needs to disown his son. Publicly and privately. It's the only chance JJ has now." He shook his head, and added, "I don't know Josh that well, but what he's done to his own father is unforgivable. Senator Tony Hamilton is on every news channel saying that he isn't afraid to say that he and all three of his sons are proud to stand up for the sanctity of marriage between a man and a woman. He's chomping at the bit to be vice president."

"It seems unfair," Byrdie said sincerely, "to have to choose...'*Know well what leads you forward and what holds you back, and choose the path that leads to wisdom.*'"

"Who said that, your grandmother?" Elliot asked.

"I'm pretty sure it was Buddha," Byrdie answered. "But, then again, they both wore muumuus and ran around without shoes."

Elliot gave Byrdie a splinter of a smile, but his glower quickly returned. "President McKenzie has some liaison arriving first thing in the morning," he said. "I'm sure he's coming to give JJ an ultimatum." Elliot stared at JJ with growing concern. "How long does a Fletcher fit usually last?"

Byrdie stared ahead as well. JJ kicked the muddy rows of tobacco in his socked feet. "He's been going about thirty minutes. I think he's got about another fifteen minutes left in him. Of course that's just an educated guess."

Elliot watched and nodded. "I guess all we can do now is wait."

A jack rabbit leapt away from JJ, bouncing in high arches across the field.

"Yep," Byrdie replied. "I believe that Jack Daniel's bottle has some left in it." Byrdie pointed to a more than half full bottle among the mostly empty ones at Elliot's feet. She said, "You might as well finish it off while we wait."

Elliot looked between his shoes, and bent down for the bottle. "I thought my friends and I drank heavily when I lived in New York City." Elliot twisted the top off the bottle. He said, "But I had no idea what heavy drinking was until I got to Tennessee." He swung back the bottle and took a long drink." He let out the burn from his lungs and offered the bottle to Byrdie.

She shook her head. "If I wasn't driving I promise I'd join you," Byrdie said. "A Fletcher fit is not something that should be watched sober." She watched JJ another moment, and said, "Oh Lordy, hand it over."

3

Buster Ragsdale and Petula Fletcher sat across from each other at a divinely set Thanksgiving dinner table. Jewell had taken out her Royal Copenhagen blue fluted porcelain dinnerware and her best silverware for the occasion. A large golden turkey sat on a platter surrounded with apple stuffing. Giblet brown gravy, buttery mashed potatoes, glazed baby carrots, sweet potatoes with marshmallows, cranberry sauce, baked bread rolls, all surrounded the centerpiece of fresh flowers, candles, and miniature pumpkins. Cloth napkins were rolled into fine silver napkin rings and wine glasses lined up neatly next to empty plates.

Buster and Petula were drinking some pricey Bordeaux. They stared at the guest seated at the head of the table. He looked debonair in the nice suit Jewell had put him in. It was a little large for him though. He hadn't been a big man in life, but Roman Stamps was skinnier than ever now, as he had been dead, embalmed and mummifying since 1929.

Buster and Petula had been staring for quite a while in silence. Words just couldn't be found.

Georgia had called Buster earlier in the evening. She had been frantic and begged Buster to come over as fast as possible. When he arrived Buster had found Georgia with a Bible in one hand and rosary beads in the other. Between Hail Marys, Georgia explained how she had arrived back from a long list of errands to find the dried up dead man sitting at the head of the table.

Buster had stepped up closer to Petrified Ed, looking close, then reaching out to touch his face. He nearly jumped out of his shoes when Jewell yelled from right behind him, "Mister, if you're looking for a conversation with him, you're wasting your time. He's deader than that alder wood chair he's sitting in!"

After Buster took a much appreciated seat, and got his heart back under control, he established that Jewell had discovered Petrified Ed in a basement freezer a few days ago. She had felt sorry for the dried up old gentleman, who she recalled quite well as Petrified Ed.

Jewell had been busy today. She had gotten up well before dawn and pulled out Petrified Ed's body to let him thaw a bit. Then she moved to the kitchen, and began preparing the dinner. Georgia believed there was no real guest coming, but helped Jewell cook and set the table anyway. While Georgia was out on errands, Jewell got dressed. Then she went to the basement with her deceased husband's suit (the one she had cut to fit over the rather stiff arms of her guest). She dressed Petrified Ed and carried him up the basement stairs. He wasn't heavy, she explained, and no stiffer than she felt some days. Jewell positioned him in the chair at the head of the table, served him a large plate of steaming hot food. She adjusted his tie and wished the dead man a very happy Thanksgiving. Jewell was enjoying a plate of food herself when Georgia had arrived back home. As Jewell described it: "Georgia saw Petrified Ed and let out let out a bloodcurdling scream that could have woke up the dead."

Buster noted that it apparently hadn't.

Jewell told this story with a calm clarity that had even convinced Buster she had done something – if not normal – certainly something that seemed as if it were a sweet gesture. Georgia was not so consoled, and she gladly went to stay with her sister across town until Buster gave her a call when things had returned to normal.

Buster immediately realized two things:

One – He needed to protect Jewell as best he could from her own innocent, but what would surely be misunderstood, undertaking. No matter what her will had dictated, if the police and a few psychiatric doctors got involved, Jewell might be forced into a nursing facility for what she had done.

Two – He had Petula Fletcher right where he wanted her. This second point was like a gift sent to him from heaven. He'd been worried about the inevitable legal battle Petula was sure to pursue against him and his newspaper, and now he might have the trump card he needed to thwart her – sitting right here at Jewell's Thanksgiving table. With JJ's political career in such jeopardy, Petula would do anything to prevent yet another Fletcher family scandal from seeing the light of day.

Buster had put Jewell to bed. Luckily, all her Thanksgiving cooking and preparations had exhausted Jewell. She gratefully went right to her room without any disagreement. After she put on her nightgown and laid down, Buster sat next to her bed and held her hand. Jewell closed her eyes and whispered, "He's okay, now. He can move on." Then she fell fast asleep.

"So Buster," Petula finally uttered, as she pulled her eyes away from Petrified Ed. "Now that I'm here, what do you want?"

"Call off the lawyers," he replied. "I'm retiring, but my staff would like to keep the newspaper going. They have families to feed, and our paper is barely surviving this new technological age. If we have to fight you and your team of lawyers, we'd probably have to shut down once and for all."

"You would deny me that pleasure?"

"I think Jewell's guest here has given me the leverage I need."

"That's all you want?" Petula asked.

"Let's see where this conversation goes."

"The damage has already been done," Petula said with disappointment. "Crushing your little newspaper would have been a personal joy for me, but forgoing my own happiness to save my family from public humiliation seems to be the burden I carry in this life." Petula looked at the dead man at the end of the table. "I think I know a guy who can get rid of a body for a fairly reasonable fee."

"Yes, a body," Buster replied, then added, "How on earth did Jewell find this particular one in a storage freezer next to some boxes of Aunt Viv's Frozen Fruitcakes? If I remember the story as it was reported at the time, Petrified Ed was buried in a Cherokee burial ground under the supervision of the Chief of the Cherokee Nation. And yet here he sits tonight. If our old friend is here, then who is buried at the Sacred Oak Cherokee burial ground?"

Petula gave Buster a tired sigh. "Well it is kind of a family secret, as you probably can imagine."

"I figured that," Buster said. "But now that the secret's out?" He nodded over to Petrified Ed.

Petula looked at the dead man at the end of the table again. He did look pretty snazzy in his suit, *considering*. She was baffled, and asked Buster, "Why did Jewell dress him up and sit him at the head of the table? I hope this doesn't mean she's finally taking a turn for the worse?"

"Actually when she explained it to me I found her motives fairly lucid and not that unreasonable," Buster said. "Jewell said she felt her family had done a bad thing and she needed to correct it. She said she also felt there was no one on earth better to share a special Thanksgiving dinner with than an actual Native American. Jewell kind of harks back to the old stories of Pilgrims and Indians sharing corn, furs and fishing tips together."

Petula mulled it over. "I suppose she's right." Petula took in the scene of all the food. "Jewell went to a lot of trouble to make him such a special dinner," she said. "It's kind of tragic that he's dead and couldn't enjoy it."

"So how about that family secret?" Buster smiled. "I'm dying to hear it."

Petula poured them both some more wine. "Yes, I suppose there's no reason to hide anything from you anymore."

Buster knew the basic story, as the local media had covered it pretty extensively at the time. For ten years Roman Stamps laid in the refrigeration room in the basement of the Valentine Funeral Home with no one taking much notice. During this time Eugene Valentine's boy, Vernon, and Hal Fletcher, both gangly unrestrained teenagers, were pretty much always getting into some kind of trouble. The Valentine family lived above the funeral home. The two story columned mansion renovated in 1922 into the magnificent Southern gothic mortuary had plenty of room to raise six children upstairs. Eugene's wife, who helped with the bookkeeping, flower arrangements, and soothing the mourners, liked having the family business and the family home in one manageable place.

Vernon and Hal were a couple of handsome mischievous boys who were almost never seen apart, and everyone in the area knew them well. Most enjoyed their youthful antics, but others felt like their parents should have taken the switch to them a whole lot more than they did. Friends of the boys often stayed overnight at the Valentine home, and it simply came with the territory to speculate about what was on the bottom floor of the house. Nighttime trips down to the funeral parlor guided by Vernon and Hal were an essential part of the sleepover. Truth or Dare took on a whole new, terrifying, level of consequence when you stayed over at the Valentine house. Many never came back for a second night.

A night visit down to the region of the dead included everything from laying in an empty coffin, holding a séance, telling ghost stories, or the ultimate kind of dare; taking a peek under the sheets. To see the stiff, blue remains of someone recently deceased was truly a teenage terror that no future experience would ever duplicate (or would anyone want it to). A few times the fun and games ended badly. An especially unfortunate one was on the night that Vernon's girlfriend – at the time – had to be taken to the hospital to be treated for mental trauma. The poor girl had been lead into the basement refrigeration room and was told to pull the sheet off of what she believed was her dead math teacher. Instead, it was Hal hiding underneath the sheet. And when he sat straight up, the girl leaped backward over a metal table (where her dead teacher, Mr. Walsh, really was laying) and blacked out completely. After she regained consciousness in Nashville General Hospital, she understandably broke up with Vernon. He was kind of expecting it.

Stealing the keys to the funeral home's Packard Henney hearse and driving it to the newly opened Ellison Place Soda Shop was a fairly regular mischief-making maneuver for Vernon and Hal. Hanging out next to a real hearse while eating burgers and fries and drinking milkshakes made the boys *kings of cool* – for a short time. They would have *fun, fun, fun* until Eugene Valentine showed up and took the Packard Henney hearse away.

Vernon and Hal were unavoidably the center of attention wherever they went. To them it felt like their personal responsibility to keep others entertained. They were often scolded by their parents, or some other adult who disapproved, but this rarely did much to dampen their spirits or slow them down. They were having too much fun. The possibilities were only limited to the imaginations of Vernon and Hal, which had very few limits.

It was only a matter of time until Vernon's and Hal's prankish personalities would lead them to the John Doe abandoned in the secondary refrigeration room in the basement. For them, it was like two gold prospectors stumbling upon the Mother Lode.

During the 62 years Roman Stamps was alive he never attracted any attention whatsoever. He never sought it out. But in 1939, a decade after he took his last breath – and even though not he nor anyone would have desired this kind of attention – Roman Stamps was going to finally have his moment in the sun (or in this case, the moon).

Vernon and Hal only knew Roman as the John Doe their father kept in the rarely used back refrigeration room in the basement, the one reserved for the unusual occasion of overflow in the main refrigeration area. This happened when there was a bad multiple car accident, a brutal flu year, or a rare tragic incident like the gun shootout at the Riggs National Bank and Loan in the summer of '36. The room in the basement was also utilized when someone very well-known died and the huge number of extra flower arrangements needed to be refrigerated until the day of the funeral. Otherwise Roman Stamps was alone in the cold darkness on a small table in the back of the room sealed up in a somewhat airtight oak oblong box. Nobody minded. He took up very little space.

The first time Roman Stamps made his appearance was on Halloween night 1939. The Valentine family always made a big spectacle on all hollows eve. Their house was decorated from the lawn to the rafters, and it was a must-see stop for any trick-or-treaters. Vernon and Hal watched from a tree branch eating bags of candy as children dressed as ghosts and vampires walked up to the windows of the funeral home. On this particular night in 1939 the children took pause. They saw a new decoration that hadn't been there in years past. A shriveled, tanned, tall, skinny, mummified-looking, man stood in the window dressed up as the pirate Long John Silver. Vernon and Hal had never been prouder as they made scary ghostly calls from high up in the tree, and laughed when the young ones took off running in fear. Crowds of children gathered to see the terrifying - real-looking - Halloween apparition in the Valentine Funeral Home window that year. Adults took notice as well. It was a little *too* real looking.

When asked about it the next day, Eugene Valentine explained that his son Vernon and his buddy Hal Fletcher had done an outstanding job of Halloween decorating with a simple Halloween mask and a mannequin they stole from the closed-down Stoval's Department Store.

Eugene gave the boys a lecture on respecting human life (even in death) and then he himself came up with the name that stuck for years to come. He said, "Your pirate looks like he's dry as a mummy.

I'd even go so far as to say he's petrified." He nodded and patted his son, Vernon, and Hal on their backs. "Yep, what we have here is someone I'd call Petrified Ed." They all three laughed until Vernon and Hal fell on the floor and grabbed their stomachs. The name stuck. And Petrified Ed was how he was identified from that day forward.

The next year Petrified Ed made an appearance in the window dressed up as Tarzan. Sherlock Holmes came the following year. By the fourth year the boys decided to up the ante. At midnight, they took Petrified Ed, now dressed up as King Tut, on a ride through the neighborhood in the back of the family's Ford pickup truck. Over the next several years this night ride drew more and more attention. There was always speculation on whether it was a "real" dead man or not, but that was part of the thrill.

Even after they started college, Vernon and Hal always made sure to be home for Halloween. It was their big night and they couldn't let their devoted fans down.

One Halloween night a person watching the spectacle of Petrified Ed was Chief Joseph Black Hawk. This time Petrified Ed was taking his wild ride through the streets of Nashville as Superman, his red cape sailing nobly in the wind as the pickup truck made its way past hundreds of smiling spectators. Chief Black Hawk wasn't smiling.

Chief Black Hawk visited the Valentine Funeral Home the next day with a representative from the Cherokee Nation Tribal Court. A few skin and hair samples were taken from Petrified Ed, and Eugene Valentine was put on notice.

What was reported next in the press was that Eugene Valentine was sent a certified letter from the American Civil Liberties Union from New York City ordering him to render the body of Petrified Ed to the local Council of the Cherokee Nation for a proper burial immediately.

As far as anyone knew, that was exactly what he did. At least, as far as anyone outside of Eugene Valentine's immediate family knew.

The director of the Native American Heritage Commission in Nashville received a body in a sealed wooden casket from Eugene Valentine as requested. This casket was buried under the strict guidelines of the Cherokee Nation at the Sacred Oak burial ground west of Nashville. As reported to the press at the time, it was a beautiful and sacred ceremony honoring an unknown man in the respectful Cherokee tradition.

"What wasn't reported?" Buster asked.

Petula was dismayed at having to repeat the tale she had been told by her husband. Petula hadn't thought of the crazy story in many years, and it didn't sound any less bizarre today: "What wasn't reported was that Eugene, Vernon and Hal Fletcher didn't like the ACLU telling them what to do."

Buster said, "And I take it, since our friend here is sitting at Jewell's table now, Eugene and the boys gave them a different body?"

"Cowboy said his daddy Hal and Vernon threw a couple of sacks of potatoes in that wooden casket, and with Eugene's help, they sealed it up tight. Then they hid the real Petrified Ed where he wouldn't be found for a very long time."

"And why would they do that?" Buster asked.

"Who knows? Pride. Mischievousness. Stupidity," Petula answered. "If that chief would have just asked Eugene for the body himself, Eugene would have likely complied. But by getting the ACLU involved, he and those boys felt strong-armed. They weren't about to kowtow to some New York lawyers. After all, the ACLU commanding a Southerner to do anything is bound to get under anyone's skin." Petula shook her head distastefully. "Eugene and the boys found the whole prospect unacceptable and offensive."

"Dressing up a dead body as fictional characters and driving him around Nashville to cheering crowds isn't offensive?"

Petula said, "From what I hear, a lot of people came out to watch. Back then that's what was considered light hearted entertainment. Frankly, what I've seen on TV today is a whole lot more offensive to me. And Cowboy told me there were people who didn't find Vernon's and Hal's midnight Halloween caper entertaining at all, so who knows. It's history now."

Buster motioned to Petrified Ed. "Well, it appears you and I have a date with history. And I have to say, you are fairly accurate about those days," Buster said. "I have looked through the archived photographs of Petrified Ed they have filed at *The Tennessean*. There are quite a few of them. And people were lined up all over Nashville to take a look. They didn't looked too offended to me." Buster sighed. "You're right. We live in a very different world now."

"Yes," Petula agreed. "And I am not so excited about how things are today personally. But I still have hope."

"And so now we're left to deal with our poor old dead friend ourselves," Buster said.

Petula shrugged. "I'll give my guy a call. I can trust him."

"To do what?" Buster asked. "Throw him in a landfill somewhere? That is not happening on my watch. My grandfather was Cherokee."

"Well, do you have a better idea?" Petula asked.

"You and I will do it," Buster replied.

"Are you crazy?"

"He's a human being. At least he was, and being dead doesn't make that any less important. He deserves to be buried with his ancestors," Buster said firmly. "There's an old Cherokee burial ground near my farm east of here. We'll bury him there."

"I have a lot on my plate right now, as you know," Petula said, "and the ground outside is likely frozen at the moment."

"Fair enough. I'll put our friend here back where Jewell found him and put a new lock on the freezer. But as soon as the ground is thawed, you and I are going to do Petrified Ed right. Someone laying him in a final resting place with respect has been a long time coming."

Petula sighed. She saw no justifiable reason to argue with Buster. Petula looked over the table covered in a spectacular feast. "Well, I for one, am starving."

Buster looked it over too. "It would seem wasteful not to enjoy Jewell's amazing Thanksgiving dinner," he said.

"Ah, I'm sure you've eaten with a lot worse company than this, Buster," Petula surmised, nodding to Petrified Ed. "Lord knows I have."

Buster paused, then nodded. "Pass those candied yams. They've been calling my name ever since I got here."

4

"We could just call it off," Dylan said.

Dylan and Josh were laying snug, bodies interlaced, inside a cozy two-person sleeping bag on top of a blowup mattress. Being so close together had unburdened them emotionally and they were enjoying the temporary refuge that comes when two allied souls lie next to each other. They were in an upstairs bedroom of the old Holloway house. An oil lantern was next to them on the floor giving the room a soft glow, burning low enough that the walls and ceiling of the unfurnished room were undefined. The moonlight shined through two bare windows, and with the wind blowing through the undulating trees outside the room appeared to be fluid and dream-like.

Josh silently thought about the words Dylan just uttered. It was not something he expected Dylan to say, and he didn't have a ready response.

Estella-Jeanne had considered selling the house and the surrounding land a few years ago (neither she nor Kitty wanted to come back and live there) so she had kept both the outside and inside regularly cleaned up, and the lawn tidy and well-kept. She had asked Dylan if he had any interest in the house or property. He didn't. As recently as six months ago she had come up with a crew of workers to completely replace the damaged roof. All the furniture and curtains had been removed and the house completely repainted years before. The one thing that remained unchanged from the time Estella-Jeanne lived there with her daughter, Ruth-Adele, was the wall-to-wall Berber carpeting, which had very few visible stains and was holding up quite well.

Two months ago Estella-Jeanne had a sudden change of heart about selling her old home place. The night before she had awakened after a vivid dream where her deceased husband had walked with her through the house room by room holding her hand. When they arrived at a mirror in the hallway she noticed they both were young, the age they were when he died, and that a tear was running down his cheek. The dream visit from her husband, and a profound gut feeling, made her change her mind about selling the property. She certainly didn't need the money from the sale anymore. Calling the realtor to ask her to take the property off the market had been an easy decision to make.

Rhashan had gotten a roaring fire going in the fireplace downstairs earlier which heated up the house to a toasty and comfortable temperature, but it had now burned down to embers. He had fallen asleep hours ago in his sleeping bag that he'd thrown down in front of the fireplace of the living room. He'd woken up twice to add some wood to the fire, but now was in a deep sleep with Coltrane's head resting across his legs.

Upstairs the considerably cold mountain air was slowly seeping into the bedroom Dylan and Josh were in. Dylan was happy he had put down two thick blankets on top of the air mattress, and saved one to throw over the top of the sleeping bag. Unlike Rhashan, Dylan and Josh were wide awake.

"The wedding?" Josh finally asked. "You want to call off the wedding?" The fact that Dylan would even suggest such a thing ultimately left him irritated.

"Well, yeah," Dylan replied. "We could postpone it until things are better with you and your dad."

"And let ignorance prevail? What would that prove?"

"Nothing. But I don't want our wedding to have this cloud hanging over it and I can't stand to see you so unhappy."

"I don't want it hanging over our wedding either." Josh pulled closer to Dylan, maneuvering his arm over Dylan's chest. He ran his fingers over Dylan's fine chest hair and nuzzled his head on his shoulder. Dylan smelled of musky sweat, cologne and wood smoke from the fireplace. They'd all three gotten a hearty workout collecting wood and splitting kindling for the fire. Josh savored the sweet smell of Dylan - *his man*. It was satisfying, comforting and arousing.

"You know this house isn't as bad as Momma makes it sound when she talks about it in her shows," Dylan said.

"You mean you've never been up here?" Josh was surprised.

"Momma didn't really care to bring me I guess. I don't think she has fond memories of this place. She says the good old days were not really that good to her. She talks about it in her shows all the time. One of the stories is about an old bull who always escaped from the neighbor's farm. It would chase her miles down the road every time she had to go catch the school bus. Rain or snow he was almost always there ready for the chase, and he'd run after her all the way to the school bus door. And all the kids would be cheering for either the bull or for her. And she talks about these twin red-headed girls that lived up here; she called them the Gruesome Twosome. They were twice her size and evil as hell. Momma was like a toy for them to play with. One time they tied her to a wooden sled they had leashed to a goat. Then one of them slapped briars under the goat's tail and smacked him with a board, just to see how far he'd go before Momma could get herself free. So the story goes."

"My God," Josh said.

"I'm surprised she likes animals as much as she does," Dylan pondered.

"Or people," Josh added.

"She's full of crazy stories like those." Dylan searched his memory for another one. "Oh, this is a good one. When she was really young there were a couple of geese named Rasputin and Larry who would hide behind the barn and then attack her when she'd ride by on her tricycle."

Josh asked, "She remembered their names?"

"Oh yeah," Dylan said. "When she ran away they both chased her and bit her on her butt, which, she says, is where the expression getting goosed obviously comes from. To escape Rasputin and Larry she'd run up and climb into the barn loft where she'd have to stay until they wandered off."

"Okay, I might never come back up here either."

"Yeah," Dylan said. "She says in her shows that she tells and retells all those stories because she heard somewhere that those who forget the past are doomed to repeat it."

Josh laughed. "I love your momma." He thought it over. "That barn you're talking about has got to be the barn Rhashan and I went in to look at. It's really big," Josh said. "I was thinking that recording studio you wanted could easily be built right in that barn."

"Oh no," Dylan said firmly. "We are not moving up here."

"Why not?"

"Are you kidding me?"

"It's peaceful and quiet," Josh responded. "And it's beautiful up here."

"There's no plumbing or electricity," Dylan countered. And then added, "Or a Bevmo."

"We could put up solar panels. And there is plumbing. Rhashan and I found a well and a septic tank. The pipes probably have roots in them. Rhashan said he could fix that. And who needs Bevmo? We've got a real moonshiner living right down the road."

"When did you and Rhashan go looking for wells and pipes? And start conspiring behind my back?"

"You were taking a nap."

"I better stop taking naps." Dylan reached over and kissed Josh, who responded with a vigorous kiss in return. "But with you around I can't seem to find time to get any decent sleep." Dylan pulled Josh in closer, turning to his side so their naked bodies were entwined. He looked at Josh adoringly. "I am so happy you're coming on the tour. You have absolutely no idea how lonely I've been. The other guys are sick of hearing me complain about it. You'll be surprised. We're not in that shitty converted old school bus anymore. This bus has private sleepers, a bathroom and a kitchen. You're going to love it. Oh, and Kevin had a baby, so his wife is with us now."

"There's a baby with you on the tour bus?"

"Yeah. I was worried at first, but she doesn't cry much. She's a lot less noisy than when Zach had that damned Cockatoo. You'll be surprised."

"You guys don't have Captain Jack anymore?"

"He flew out the bus window. Remember I said we were opening for Keith Urban last summer. We were in south Florida and it was hotter than hell. Keith was on the bus one night after a show and opened one of the windows. Out he went. We never could find that stupid bird. I guess Captain Jack is still somewhere in the palm trees outside Miami. Keith felt horrible and offered Zach the money to replace Captain Jack. Thank God Zach accepted a new guitar instead."

Josh smiled, then asked, "So these sleepers are private?"

"Yep," Dylan said, kissing Josh again. "As private as you can get. Nice and cozy. We get the master sleeper...Back to my original point. In Tennessee we're not getting a piece of paper saying we're legally married anyway. Saying we're married isn't going to change anything. We'll still be together. We can get married some other time. Maybe even in another state."

"Just last night you slashed my daddy's tire. Aren't you still angry?"

"I'm mad as hell. But I would do anything to make sure you're happy."

"Nope. We're getting married. I am done with hiding. Completely done."

"Okay. I just needed to hear you say it."

Josh kissed Dylan again, tenderly inching across Dylan's face to his ear. "You should go check out that barn," Josh whispered. "A quiet studio out here in the country. Think of the music you could make."

"There's no need to think about anything," Dylan whispered back. "We're not moving up here. Just keep doing what you're doing to my ear. It's driving me crazy."

Josh continued.

It was driving him crazy too.

The supreme happiness of life is the conviction that we are loved.
   - Victor Hugo

THE BEST LAID PLANS

1

Wendy, a white and chestnut brown suri alpaca, looked up to see what was causing the clamor on the other side of the wall of her pen, a high enclosure constructed of beautiful multicolored river stones.

A cowboy hat flopped over a security camera posted on top the wall, effectively preventing it from doing its job of monitoring for intruders. Two hands grabbed over the top, one right after the other. Wendy saw JJ Fletcher throwing his leg over the wall, then hoisting his other leg over. This intrusion was very irritating for her. Wendy quickly fired up into attack mode, running to the wall fully prepared to bite the pair of cowboy boots dangling uninvited into her private territory.

JJ had done his homework and was prepared. He pulled an apple from his jacket pocket and held it down. "Here you go, crazy alpaca creature. It's a treat. I read on Wikipedia this is your favorite."

It was true. It was one of Wendy's favorites. The instinct to bite into the intruder's feet was instantly replaced with the instinct to accept the tasty snack. She reached up and grabbed the apple from JJ's hand. To her joy several more apples were produced from the stranger's pockets and dropped onto the ground. JJ also had a bag of Crockett Creek Beef Jerky in his jeans pocket for the dogs that roamed the grounds of Kitty's ranch that he was sure to encounter.

JJ had done a Google Earth search on Kitty's ranch and discovered the alpaca pens were the weakest point in the security of Kitty's property. There was a fire road that curved into a "U" right past this point. He easily had hidden his dark green Escalade behind a thick grove of evergreen trees. His cowboy hat was now covering the only visible security camera, and he was fairly certain it was the only one in the area. He jumped to the ground. It was a soft landing, and he didn't want to look down to see why it was so soft. He knew.

JJ had come to Kitty's ranch a desperate man today. He felt completely crazy breaking into her private property through an alpaca cage. The whole situation with Josh, and Kitty, and the president of the United States did have all the right ingredients for crazy making. So here he was, the governor of Tennessee breaking and entering, and it appeared standing in a pile of alpaca poop. He looked at Wendy chewing happily on one of the apples and decided it was safe to make his move.

This in-depth investigation into ways to break into Kitty's ranch had been done many times. Those times over the past six years were a different variety of crazy. He was crazy in love with her and wanted to see Kitty any way possible. JJ had never gained the courage to follow through with his plan of a surprise night-time visit to Kitty's bedroom. He had gotten as far as purchasing the apples for the alpacas and the bags of beef jerky for the dogs and parking on the other side of the wall. But he never left his vehicle. He knew he very likely would have been shot before he ever reached Kitty's ranch house anyway. Her head of security had a military background, and was very loyal to his boss. (JJ had recently had this theory confirmed.)

On the many occasions he had sat there alone parked behind the evergreens he would often ponder his overwhelming, nerve-racking, incessant attraction to Kitty. Were they star-crossed lovers drawn together by universal forces larger than themselves? Sometimes he convinced himself Kitty was some sort of demon that was sent to incapacitate him where he was weakest – in his loins.

Most times he just figured it was a severe case of desperately wanting what he couldn't have.

He never reached any conclusive answers there in the darkness, but with his vivid imagination and his right hand he would often reach a fairly satisfying temporary resolution. And, of course, once the tension was curtailed, he had some pretty good apples and beef jerky to eat afterwards.

Today, in the broad daylight, he felt very exposed. JJ knew that huge security guard of Kitty's was going to quickly realize one of the cameras was blocked. (JJ couldn't have known Rhashan was not even on the property, or that the person in charge of security today – a Russian immigrant named Olga – was more of a threat to JJ's life than Rhashan ever could be.) He would have to act quickly. He also was nervous because he had no real plan for when he got to Kitty's actual house. All he knew was that President McKenzie had sent a very serious spokesperson named Walter Houseman to Nashville this morning. Walter was very clear and officious (in fact, JJ had thought he was an acrimonious prick in an excessively starched, pressed suit – an observation Byrdie later told JJ she totally agreed with). "President McKenzie chose you because he believed you were his ally. It is time to prove your allegiance to the president, or your lack thereof." Mr. Houseman had said, then added with a smug, chafing tone, "It's not like you're the only concubine in the royal chambers." (Yep, he was a prick.)

JJ had felt instantly badgered, but he figured the D.C. schmuck was hired precisely for his badgering abilities. Mr. Housman told JJ he had twenty-four hours. Not a minute more. JJ promised he would deliver exactly what President McKenzie needed. His plan was to find the only person who knew where Josh was, Kitty. And being desperate and feeling crazy, this was the only way he knew to have this goal achieved.

And here he was in a pen with an alpaca doing the only thing he knew to do to realize that promise. JJ reached through the fence from the inside and felt around for the clasp to Wendy's pen. He found it, pulled back the latch and opened the gate.

* * *

Kitty sat in her bedroom dressing chair and stared at her mirror. Her mind was in such a whirl she didn't see her reflection at all. Friedrich, her Pilates instructor, was coming in a few minutes and she had slipped on her workout clothes, and had just sat down to put on a light application of skin rejuvenating neuropathies to her face. She had no idea, of course, that JJ Fletcher had broken into her property only moments earlier and was sneaking past trees and bushes, throwing out beef jerky to her dogs, quickly approaching her house. If she had, she would have likely bolted the house down tightly and grabbed her loaded gun. But she was deep in thought about nothing else but the wedding.

She was going over and over the plans in her mind, thinking back to make certain she hadn't misses any important details:

She had spent the evening before contacting everyone on the wedding invitation list personally. There was no time for formal invitations or waiting for RSVPs. It was a small list that Dylan and Josh had written down before they left. She had even secured last minute flight arrangements for Josh's friends Kasia and Mosi. The only guest on the list she couldn't get a full confirmation from was Josh's Great Aunt Jewell. She had spoken to someone by the name of Georgia, who had told Kitty, "I'll do what I can. But with Miss Jewell, every morning she wakes up, God bless her, her brain is under new management." Kitty told Georgia not to worry, that she would save a spot for them both in the front row, as Josh had requested.

Kitty had called her friend Jamie Oliver and he was flying in from Essex to handle the vegetarian menu. David Lebovitz was sending one of his finest bakers from Paris to prepare the wedding cake. Fernando from The Primeval Florists was handling the flowers. Jimmy Snow, her hairdresser and friend of the past twenty years, was doing her hair. Francisco Costa was shipping overnight three dresses for her to pick from. He flawlessly knew the right dress for

Kitty, and he had her exact measurements because he'd just designed her dress for the Academy of Country Music Awards in April. Kitty knew she could trust him to make her look wonderful (and was secretly gratified there was no bride's dress that she'd be in competition with on this special day). The boys had picked muted gray suits of slightly different tones from Alexander McQueen. Instead of registering, the boys had requested contributions to Kitty's Critters-In-Crisis as wedding gifts. The photographer and videographer Kitty used for her own photo and video shoots were handling the recording of the event.

At 10:27 P.M. Kitty had a sudden outburst of emotion and called her momma. They talked for two hours about how she was losing her baby. Estella-Jeanne softened the depressing truth by reminding Kitty that she might have grandchildren some day; that gay couples had children all the time now. Or, if it came to it, she suggested Kitty adopt a child from some foreign country "...like half those other celebrities seem to do." This seemed to help ease the pain a little. Kitty fell asleep with wedding planning books all over her bed.

She awoke at 6:20 A.M. and leapt right to work. While she was exercising on her treadmill, she called Jimmy Snow to discuss whether her hair should be up or down. She had worn it up in her most recent video for her new single, "Daddy Baptized Porter Wagoner" (an old-style country standard, already a huge favorite at the top of the country charts, based on a true story about a dear friend of hers whose grandfather really did baptize Porter Wagoner). Jimmy suggested her hair being up, told her not to worry, and begged that she let him go back sleep.

POW! POW!

Kitty was startled out of her thoughts instantly, nearly dropping her face cream and leaping out of her bedroom dressing chair.

POW! POW! *The gunshot blasts went off again, and they sounded closer.*

Peggy Sue, who had been sleeping on the bed, jumped up and burst into a barking frenzy, spiraling around in circles.

"What in Sam Hill is going on out there, Peggy Sue?" Kitty stood up and carefully edged toward the bed trying to see out through the curtains. She was almost to the bed reaching for the gun hidden under her mattress when she saw his face.

"God's sweet body and blind my eyes," Kitty said with a discouraging sigh.

JJ waved at Kitty through the glass. He seemed desperate, motioning eagerly for her to come over to the window. Kitty reluctantly walked over, unlocked the window and pulled it open. Peggy Sue was right behind barking ferociously.

"Let me in! She's shooting at me!" JJ said anxiously.

JJ was standing at the top of an extension ladder. She thought, *The yard man cleaning out the gutters yesterday must have forgotten to put it away.* Kitty looked out from her second story window down to the ground. Olga was standing below with a Russian semi-automatic in her hand.

"Tell her who I am, Kitty," JJ pleaded.

Olga pointed the gun at JJ and yelled up, "One more move comrade, and Olga will have clean view of sky through your ass."

JJ pulled closer to the ladder and held his free hand over his buttocks. He looked to Kitty with alarm.

"What are you doing way the hell up here?" Kitty asked.

"I just need to talk to you," JJ replied.

"Miss Kitty, this man was peeping in window," Olga said. "In Russia we shoot such people."

"Hold your fire, Olga," Kitty said. "...for the moment!" She turned to Peggy Sue. "And you quiet down and go sit on the bed." The dog stopped barking, but stood her ground. "Go get on the bed, Peggy Sue. He ain't worth biting." The dog snarled, then slowly went and jumped on the bed, but kept emitting a low growl from her new perch.

"Speak," Kitty said to JJ. She yelled down, "Olga, you can stop shooting, but stay alert!"

JJ looked down at the Russian woman. The gun barrel was still pointed straight up. "Okay, I'll get to the point." JJ looked back to Kitty.

"Keep it short," Kitty said bluntly. "My Pilates instructor should be here any minute and Friedrich charges me extra if I'm late."

JJ rolled his eyes, then said, "President McKenzie has a very pushy asshole-of-a-man sitting in my office right this very minute. If Josh doesn't make a public statement either tonight or tomorrow morning on my behalf, that asshole of-a-man will be flying back to Washington, D.C. and my extraordinary opportunity to become vice president of the United States will be going back with him," JJ said. He was visibly exhausted through-and-through. "You're the only person who knows where my son is, and you don't return phone calls."

Kitty stared at JJ with little empathy. She said, "Instead of attempting to bully your son into conforming to the president's big plans for you and everybody else, why don't you invite President McKenzie and his lovely wife to Josh's and Dylan's wedding? Then maybe President McKenzie would see what real family values look like? I'd be happy to have two extra plates set for them."

"Jesus, Kitty. Would you take this seriously? This isn't a game," JJ said. "People can get hurt."

"People have already been hurt, JJ," Kitty replied. "And you better believe it when I say, I am taking this very seriously."

"I can't find my son anywhere, and neither can anyone on my staff, or the police," JJ rationalized. "For all any of us know you and your son have Josh drugged and locked in your basement."

Kitty glared at him.

JJ glared back.

Kitty finally responded, "That sounds perfectly reasonable. I think you have solved the mystery of your son's disappearance. Maybe Scooby-Doo, the president, and you can now have me arrested and hauled away in the Scooby-Doo Mystery Van. Even better, he's the president, have the FBI or The Bureau of Alcohol, Tobacco and Firearms come here to my ranch for a siege like they did in Waco or Ruby Ridge. Because I can't think of anything more threatening to national security than some woman in Nashville, Tennessee planning a Sunday afternoon wedding. Until they arrive, if you don't mind, I am going to go do my Pilates exercises. I fell asleep on top of a Martha Stewart wedding planning book and I'm a little stiff." She reached for the top of the window to slam it closed.

"Wait!" JJ said, pleading again.

Kitty paused.

"I want to ask you a question," JJ said.

"Okay, shoot... Not you Olga!" Kitty yelled down quickly. She and JJ looked down at Olga.

Olga was holding the gun with one hand and reading her cell phone with the other. "Let Olga know if I need to shoot. I read text from my sister in Vologda."

JJ dropped his confrontational demeanor. "Are they really in love? I don't see how it can be possible, but are they?"

After a moment of skepticism, Kitty saw JJ was actually trying to be sincere. Kitty sighed and released her grip on the window. "They are really in love, JJ."

"Real love?"

"What other kind is there?"

JJ took the possibility in, mostly for the first time. His face looked forlorn and after a moment of staring at the ground he looked up to Kitty. "What am I supposed to do?"

"If he really thinks you're the best choice for vice president, then he surely respects you enough to let you disagree with him on some issues. Josh is your son, what more could President McKenzie expect from you?"

"Elliot says that for some reason McKenzie and The First Lady are notoriously anti-gay. This White House doesn't even discuss the issue, and *The Nashville Sun* has now made it my personal can of worms. And it's not just them. We have polling numbers that indicate the public is not with our sons on this either. Some right wing religious organization has even threatened to burn down the governor's mansion if I don't get Josh on TV denouncing his deviant lifestyle."

"All the more reason Josh and Dylan need us on their side," Kitty replied. "You don't give up just because you're outnumbered or outgunned." Kitty added, "I did talk to Josh and Dylan on the phone. Josh saw what you and your mother said on TV. It was seriously devastating to him."

"You talked to him?"

"Yes."

"Is he still mad at me?"

"Extremely heart broken and crushed is more how he sounded to me."

JJ sighed and shook his head. "I still don't know how I feel about this yet."

"The wedding is in two days. That gives you some time to decide."

"You should have seen him at Jimmy Kelly's," JJ said. "It was like he hated me."

"Come back here on Sunday with a nice gift and that will be a good place to start fixing that," Kitty replied.

"Can't they just do what they need to do and keep it a secret?" JJ was getting frustrated again.

Kitty looked at JJ for a moment and could see that he was in utter anguish. He reached for her hand, and she let him hold it. "Finally after all these years I have gotten up here to your window," JJ said.

"I figured that was you parked outside the alpaca pens off and on all these years."

"You knew I was out there?"

"Whatever you had on your mind, I didn't want to hear it."

JJ appeared hurt. "All I have ever wanted to say was how much I love you."

Kitty yanked her hand back.

"What's wrong?" JJ asked. "Why is everyone so mad at me?"

Kitty's glaring, angry stare returned. "Here is the lesson you need to learn, JJ. It is a fairly obvious truth that when you're in love, when you're really in love, you want to shout it to the rooftops. You want the whole world to know. The neighbors, the sun and the moon and the stars, God, and everybody. You don't want to hide it. Things that hide, things that are secret, do not survive long in this world. They wither and die. Things that hide are afraid. I am not afraid. Your son is not afraid. But you are." She grabbed the top of the window. "So don't say you love me!"

Kitty slammed the window closed.

JJ yanked his hands back in the nick of time, over compensating with his elbows. He lost his balance and reached back for the window ledge. He missed and grabbed again, but was too far away. And backward he went.

"For the love of Jesus!" Kitty yanked the window back open and reached for JJ, but he was already in a free fall. Kitty watched helplessly. It was like a scene from a movie – his legs and arms flailed, time seemed to slow down, he drifted in the air – his hands grasping, his legs pedaling. Then he hit the ground on his back with a resounding *thud*.

Olga stopped reading the text message on her phone and stepped over to look at JJ.

"Is he breathing?" Kitty yelled down to her.

JJ was motionless. Olga looked closer, then stood back up. "It not look good!" she yelled back up to Kitty.

"Do you know CPR?" Kitty yelled again.

Olga held the gun up. "No CPR in Russia!" She shot the gun in the air.

POW!

JJ opened his eyes. He didn't know where he was at first. He took in several deep breaths trying to regain his senses and understand where the loud bang had come from.

Olga yelled up, "He not dead."

JJ saw Olga with the gun and scrambled up to his feet, grabbing his back with both hands. He staggered and backed away from Olga, frightened.

"Good enough for me," Kitty said, and slammed the window closed.

JJ took a few minutes to regain his ability to stand up straight. He and Olga stared at each other. She didn't seem to be warming up to him.

"I don't suppose you know where my son is, do you?" JJ asked, still grimacing in pain. "He has blond hair, wears glasses, kind of my height."

She ignored him. "Olga go and let Pilates trainer into house. Olga let you out through front gate."

"I'll just go out the way I came in." JJ sighed. "I'm parked back there and I have a very unpromising future I have to go face." JJ turned and walked back toward the alpaca pens. "And an alpaca who is going to be very mad because I just smashed the last of the apples with my ass."

Olga yelled after him, "Do not forget hat. Hat is blocking camera!"

"I got it," JJ yelled back.

Olga shook her head. "Crazy Americans."

2

Petula's head was tipped back to see through her bifocals. She was looking inquisitively at a porcelain figurine of a little boy climbing a wooden fence with a long necked goose nosing up at him. He was wearing butterscotch-brown lederhosen and an ivy green pointed hat. The figurine characteristics, based on the work of German artist Sister Maria Innocentia Hummel, were unmistakable. Petula's large Chanel handbag was crumpled on the marble countertop next to her.

A tall man in a neatly pressed suit stepped up on the other side of the counter with a Whiskey Toddy in his hand. He produced a hand-carved wooden coaster and placed the drink down in front of Petula.

Never looking away from the chubby boy figurine, she took the drink. "Thank you, Mr. Symonds. I have had an excruciating day." She strained the words out with a long exhale. "I don't believe I could take one more catastrophe this year."

"M'mm h'mm," Mr. Symonds replied, crossing his arms. He was as cold as a marble statue.

The antique store was immense in size. It was impossible to determine where any walls existed. It seemed to go on forever in every direction. There was not an inch of space from floor to ceiling that wasn't occupied. Although it was cluttered in appearance, the merchandise was all immaculately clean with hand-written glossy white tags tied with a string on each item. There wasn't a spider web or dust bunny in sight.

"You'll find that the figurine is in pristine condition," Mr. Symonds said passionlessly. "There were twelve in the original series."

"I think The First Lady would absolutely love this, don't you?" Petula asked as she took a sip of the Whiskey Toddy. "Her husband is doing my son a spectacular favor and I want to get The First Lady something very special."

"Only seven survive today," he explained. "My sources tell me it is true that Mrs. McKenzie has the other six in her possession."

Petula lit up. "How lucky am I? And to find it right here in Nashville." She looked at Mr. Symonds with a hearty smile.

"Finally something is going your way," Mr. Symonds said. His lips curled up, but it wasn't a smile.

Petula looked at him briefly. She felt a cold chill rippling off of him, but she didn't understand why. She tried to recall if she had met him before.

"It *is* a one-of-a-kind find," Mr. Symonds added.

"How did you come to own it?" Petula asked. She liked this impeccably dressed man in a paisley red bow tie. He had handsome round tortoise shell eyeglasses. His brown skin appeared flawless, not a blemish in sight. She noticed that his fingernails were trimmed, his fragrant cologne was not too brash, and he appeared to have perfect diction with just the right portion of Southern inflection. She wondered again if his narrow, glassy stare was intended for her.

"The owner would like to remain anonymous."

"Really? Why?" Petula asked.

Mr. Symonds pinched his lips. "Perhaps you're not aware of the past associated with these particular Hummels? Honestly, I find the fact that The First Lady collects them as rather odd, and some people could easily find it un-First Lady-like."

"The other figurines in this set are kept inside the White House in the presidential bedroom," Petula said. She shook her head confidently. "Exaggerated tales like the one I imagine you are referring to are just gossip to further smudge The First Lady's good name. I hope you aren't the kind of man who believes such nonsense."

"I purchased this one from a man in New Orleans," Mr. Symonds explained with authority. He turned the figurine around and studied it for a moment, then continued. "He was a very handsome, distinguished man with a pencil thin mustache. He was a World War II veteran. He told me how he had smuggled this figurine, with the other six Hummels, over the border of Germany into Austria. He had to sneak them out under the cover of darkness, you see, because the seven figurines were hidden inside a foot locker he had stolen from the bedroom of Eva Braun."

Petula absorbed the information with some initial revulsion.

Mr. Symonds continued, "Upon further reading of an unauthorized biography I discovered that Chancellor Hitler publicly claimed that Sister Hummel's chubby boy figurines were an abasement to the virility of the German male, but privately he thought Hummels were winsome and well crafted. He had one of his assistants secretly go to porcelain shops in Munich and buy them for him when there were new releases. Eva and he had just started to collect some of their favorites when The Allies began to march in."

Petula contemplated this story a moment longer with a slight repellent look on her face, but quickly recovered. "Well, I drive a Mercedes and no one seems to mind that." Petula finished her drink and placed it down carefully on the coaster. "So how much do I owe you? And please remember it is ungentlemanly to take advantage of a Southern Lady."

The man took a pen from his shirt pocket and wrote a number on a piece of paper, then turned it around for Petula to see.

Her posture stiffened. "This is not the amount we discussed on the phone last week."

"No, it's not."

"It seems quite inflated."

"It is."

"Now, you are not going to raise the price just because you know how much I want it, are you?"

"Nope." Mr. Symonds' eyes narrowed. He pulled down his glasses and stared at her over the rims with a flat gaze. Petula pulled back. He then wrinkled his nose and puckered his lips as if he had just bitten into a lemon.

"Why are you looking at me like that?" she asked. She blinked several times. She was truly perplexed by the man's ongoing look of animosity. She said, "I'm starting to get the feeling you don't like me."

Mr. Symonds replied, "Trust your instincts."

Petula glimpsed more closely at Mr. Symonds. She stepped nearer and squinted her eyes. "Do I know you?"

A sudden complete transformation occurred somewhere inside Mr. Symonds. His stiff, pragmatic persona was replaced by a swaggering, gleaming, statuesque entity of grace and ferocity. He became taller. His chin flew back. His hand swished back and forth until it was pointing up into the rafters.

Petula stepped back in alarm. She almost spontaneously yelled out.

Mr. Symonds pronounced, "There is nothing to fear but my beauty itself! ...I am Shandazzle!"

Petula grabbed an antique china cabinet for support. She looked around the store. Petula hadn't noticed until now how many pristine, exemplary items there were, and there wasn't a hint of dust in sight. The lighting was warm and not harsh on the skin. Petula said to herself, "And that is Cher playing over the sound system."

It was so obvious she didn't know how she missed it before.

"Oh, I get it." She looked at Mr. Symonds with hint of scorn and a little smirk. "This *is* an antique store." She added a knowing, irreverent nod in his direction, "You're that *friend* of that horrible woman, Kitty Stardust."

"We are not only very good friends," Mr. Symonds replied. "I *do* Kitty in my show."

Petula nodded. "And it appears, just like her, you thumb your nose at honorable society by embracing a culture of willful subversion. I suppose it feels good to openly ignore the very rules of conduct that keep our enduring civilization flourishing and morally above-reproach by dressing up in clothing designed for the opposite sex. All when the good Lord clearly made you a man. But why am I wasting my breath, if you associate with people like Kitty Stardust, I guess I shouldn't be surprised."

"M'mm h'mm." Mr. Symonds took a lingering look up and down at Petula. "A rich, old, Southern heifer wearing shoes that are over a year out of fashion. And she's uppity, intolerant and insufferable. I guess I shouldn't be surprised either."

"I'm a guest in your store," Petula shot back. "And here I was thinking what a respectable looking man of color that was standing here in front of me. I guess you really can't judge a book by its cover!" She stepped closer. "And for the record, one of the rules that a real woman follows, that you probably wouldn't know about, is to keep her family together no matter what it takes. And keeping my family intact, safe and respectable is exactly what I am trying to do. You are either with me or you're against me."

"You know, the young people in this country, and all over this planet, are just waiting for people of your considerable age to finally die off so they can live in an unbigoted sublime utopia of their own making." Shandazzle looked skyward. "We have a dream. A Shandazzling dream. This dream is for a world filled with splendorous color, unabated flamboyance and unreasonable fabulousness." Mr. Symonds looked back at Petula. "And for the record, you are either with us or you're against us."

Petula was undaunted. She gave him a dismissive wave. "Well I'm not dead yet." She stepped back to the counter and reached into her handbag. "And thankfully I have higher hopes for the youth of the world than you do, or I would go find a tall, sturdy oak tree and hang myself from it." She produced a bundle of hundred dollar bills. She looked at Mr. Symonds unbothered and slightly impatient. "I know when negotiation is no longer in my favor," she said. "So let's not waste any more time. I assume cash will be fine?"

Mr. Symonds answered, "Cash will do." He smiled. Cash payments and feeling victorious always made him feel jovial. Petula counted out the crisp bills on the counter.

He said, "Would you like that gift wrapped? Free gift wrapping today for any merchandise once owned by the world's most notorious dictator and his lover."

Petula replied sourly, "I'm in a hurry, just put the damn Hummel in a box."

Small is the number of them that see with their own eyes and feel with their own hearts.
  - ALBERT EINSTEIN

NOWHERE TO RUN

1

"Keep going! I'm okay," Dylan yelled ahead to Rhashan and Josh. Dylan wasn't technically jogging anymore, but thrashing forward in a headlong rush flailing his arms as if he were drowning. If he didn't stop soon he was going to plunge into a nosedive.

Rhashan was leading Josh and Dylan on a morning run. The county fire road that cut through the dense woods provided an ideal trail. Coltrane was palpitating with excitement, bouncing from tree to tree marking them along the way and sniffing out any field mice or moles hiding in the underbrush. They had been running just over three miles and Rhashan had not broken a sweat. This was well below his normal jogging intensity. Josh was in pretty good shape, average for a young man his age who suffered from asthma. Dylan, on the other hand, was what Rhashan called in the Navy – *Sea Green*: turning pallid, deluged with flop sweat, and quickly approaching the point of puking.

"Let's take a breather," Rhashan called back. He knew Dylan had been pushed as hard as he could. "We can stretch our legs the rest of the way." Rhashan slowed down his stride and winked at Josh. "Josh has asthma and we don't want to push him too hard."

Josh started to contest, but then caught Rhashan's eyes. "Oh, yeah," Josh said, glancing back at Dylan. "I better slow it down." He dropped down to a slow trot, feigning some breathlessness for effect.

Dylan caught up to Rhashan and Josh in a badly contrived spirited gait. "Are you sure?" Dylan looked gravely ill, but was fake-smiling. "I can go a few more miles."

"Coltrane needs to slow down too," Rhashan said. "He gets over excited and overheated."

Dylan stopped and grabbed his knees for support. "Thank you, Jesus!"

Coltrane started barking. He was leaping forward and then running backward, and repeating the bizarre maneuver. All three men looked through the thick bushes and brambles to see what had gotten Coltrane so flustered.

"Look," Josh said. "It's a little bear."

A bear cub about three times the size of Coltrane was about ten yards into the brush beyond the trees. The bear was not frightened, but clearly curious about the strange creature leap-frogging forward and backward, and yelping at an octave she was not familiar with at all. Being a young girl, the bear wondered if this new creature was something she could play with like her two brothers, who were just behind her about thirty feet. Then she remembered something new she had discovered over the past few months - sometimes the playful furry creatures in the forest turn out to be yummy treats that she could share with her siblings - like that frolicsome white-tailed deer they had for dinner last night. She raised up on her back feet and stood tall to get a better look.

Rhashan ran and grabbed Coltrane. He saw the two other small bears foraging in the weeds behind the original bear, now standing on its hind legs watching them. Rhashan's veteran military skills switched into gear. He surveyed the area 365 degrees. He saw a weathered old church about a quarter mile away. The road they were on curved in the opposite direction, although it probably made its way by the church eventually. It was impossible to know for sure. They were closer to the church as-the-crow-flies. They'd just need to cross through the thick underbrush, which included a lot of blackberry vines - which promised to rip up his new jogging suit. It was hard to find a jogging suit in his size that didn't swish when he ran. This really pissed Rhashan off as he glared at the thorny blackberry briars everywhere. But the danger they were in could possibly be mortal in nature. A mother bear was nothing to take lightly. He was further concerned because he had left his gun back at the house. Being an Iraqi War veteran he should have known he should always expect the unexpected.

He kept trying to hold Coltrane's mouth closed, but it was a vain enterprise. Coltrane had seen a bear and some evolutionary spark inside the dog had begun to burn – *Sound the alarm! Sound the alarm! Sound the alarm!* Why drawing all attention to oneself was your predisposition (as a small canine with legs that barely kept your stomach off the ground) when you spotted a creature who was higher on the food chain than you were was not clear. That was debate material for evolutionary theory classes. But whatever the genesis of his instincts, Coltrane was going to bark. And there was nothing on this earth, short of his own death, that could stop him.

Sound the alarm! Sound the alarm! Sound the alarm!

"We have two choices," Rhashan said, as he kept struggling with his frenzied dog's muzzle. "With bear cubs there will be a mother right behind. Conventional wisdom says to roll into a ball and remain still."

The seriousness in Rhashan's voice made the situation unambiguous. Up until now Josh and Dylan had been seeing the bear cub as a rare and pleasurable brush with nature. The tone and look on Rhashan's face said that was not the situation they were in. They both nodded at Rhashan, ready to do whatever he told them to do. Rhashan continued, "But I have a dog in my arms, that I paid seven hundred dollars for, that will probably not stop barking no matter how much I try to hold his stupid trap closed, so I think we should consider our second option. There is a church about a quarter mile over there, and if we run straight to it, we might make it before the mother of these three cubs catches one of us."

And mauls that unlucky bastard to death, Rhashan thought, but didn't see the need to say out loud.

"Of course we don't know if we can even get inside the church," Rhashan reasoned. "It could be locked or possibly worse, have no door left on it at all."

"What mother bear?" Josh asked innocently enough.

Rrrrrrooooaaarrr! – came the answer to his question from deep in the woods.

On her hind legs, behind the other smaller bears, was the mother. She was an American Black Bear roughly 210 pounds. She was in a sour mood because it was time to find a cave for hibernating, and that always put her in an irritable funk, especially with teenagers in tow. Her small ears were set back, her huge paws were lifted out in front of her, and her narrow muzzle was whiffing the air – and she appeared to not be pleased with what she had gotten the scent of. Her daughter and two sons noted her frightening growl and stood firm in place. Momma bear rarely made this kind of roar, but when she did a smart bear cub knew to pay close attention. Something consequential was going down.

"I vote 'No' on the rolling into a ball," Dylan said. He hadn't had the chance to catch his breath from the morning jog, and now he was forced to stagger for even more air as his adrenal gland began flushing stress hormones through his body like an out of control espresso machine.

"Yeah," Josh agreed. "We go for the church." His heart was racing too. He kept his eye on the momma bear. She was not moving yet, just staring at them and making gruff, scary-sounding, warning noises.

"Do we walk calmly trying to not look like prey?" Dylan asked. "Or should we just run?"

"Run," Rhashan answered. "As fast as hell."

The momma bear dropped down to all fours and started covering ground immediately. Rhashan bolted first, then Josh and Dylan were off after him like shots out of a rifle. They were all three tearing along with white-knuckled fear, vaulting above the brambles like gazelles racing across a meadow. The briars lacerated their jogging pants and eventually their legs as well, but they didn't feel a thing (that burning pain would come soon enough once they stopped running). In the overgrowth were weathered and crumbling tomb stones they had to negotiate and leap over like Olympic hurdle jumpers. Dylan briefly saw an oak tree split in two and thought: *Grandpa and grandma I'll have to come say hello at a later time!* Josh tripped once, but was back up on his feet like a professional athlete. In fact they were running faster than any of them, including Rhashan, had ever run in their lives.

The momma bear was bounding through the underbrush gaining ground on her human quarry. Her cubs were struggling to keep up, fumbling and somersaulting along. They were mostly clueless as to what was happening, but they knew they didn't want to be left behind. Whatever Momma was going to do was sure to be savage. The three cubs had never seen their mother so deliriously angry. She was seething. They had all three believed it was going to be another boring day of foraging for grubs, roots and berries. *Boy, that turned out wrong!*

Rhashan, clutching tight around his dog, was closing in on the door of the deteriorating stone church.

Yes! There was a door!

As expected, Coltrane was uncontrollable and barked the entire flight through the woods and old cemetery. Rhashan had managed to hold him, but the dog had not made the task easy. The church door was closed. Rhashan took one fast look back at the large bear bounding toward them, grabbed the knob of the door, and shoulder slammed it hard. To his wondrous relief, the door flew open.

Josh and Dylan were essentially airborne as they sailed through the church door right behind him. Rhashan hurled the door closed, dropped to the floor with Coltrane still in his arms, and braced his back against it. He felt the impact of the mother bear hitting the decaying old door headlong from the other side. It felt like a cannon ball hit it, the sound like a thunderclap. The door held, and Rhashan stayed in place with his back tightly braced. He heard the sound of the bear outside bellowing. He imagined that wallop to her head was throbbing pretty severely.

Josh and Dylan turned around. It took a second to become convinced the door had held and that there was no voracious bear anywhere in sight. Once that was established they both dropped exhausted onto the plank wood floor. Their lungs were in a frenzy to capture as much air as possible and their hearts hammered against their chests. (The nightmares of them reliving what had just occurred would haunt all their nights of sleep for months to come.)

Rhashan surveyed the room. The small stained glass windows were intact and there were no other doors for a bear to find and enter through. They were evidently, thankfully, safe. The mother bear bumped against the door a few more times, but she was not really trying. Likely, from her point of view the threat had been thwarted and sealed off. Rhashan could hear the mother bear making howling noises that sounded like a child bawling. There were more sounds, some rustling of footsteps and spry sounding yelps - likely the little ones arriving on the scene. Rhashan imagined that had things been only slightly different for the three of them (four if you counted Coltrane), the little bears would be gleefully doing their part to help their mother rip one of them to pieces right about now. And then, like the little cubs they were, would be jealously fighting over the good parts.

Rhashan released Coltrane, who had thankfully stopped barking. The dog sniffed anxiously at the bottom of the door. Rhashan stood up and looked out the small glass window of the church door. The mother bear had laid down and was surrounded by her three cubs. The three little bears were frolicking and jumping on their mother. Rhashan had hoped she was up and moving around, but she looked like she was tired out and was not looking to move on anytime soon.

"Is she out there?" Dylan asked, sitting up on one arm.

"Yep," Rhashan said. "The whole family, and they look like they are planning to stay a while."

The church, a single room building, was mostly empty. It had a vaulted ceiling that arched high above them. There were seven rows of pews and a pulpit in front. The wood planks on the floor had splintered apart in places. Amazingly, considering the age and neglect of the structure, the stained glass windows were still intact. A plain wooden cross hung on the wall above the pulpit.

"It's probably because of the death defying ordeal we just went through together, but I have to say this church is one of the most divine places I have ever seen in my life," Josh commented. He looked around the room, never lifting his head off the floor.

Rhashan added, "I will have to say I was praying fairly intensely for the door to be unlocked. So if that was divine intervention, thank you."

The three of them rested for awhile. Regaining a sense of balance again required less talking, and more intake of oxygen.

"It's pretty amazing what a mother would do to protect her children," Josh said finally.

Rhashan agreed, "Yes, it is."

The sentiment wasn't lost on Dylan. "I think I'll call Momma and tell her I love her." He looked at the others. "I don't guess anyone has their phone?"

"No," Rhashan replied. "It's back at the house with my gun." After a moment of consideration he added, "Along with our food and water."

"I thought I saw you bring a bottle of water?" Josh said to Rhashan.

"I gave it to Coltrane about twenty minutes ago," Rhashan answered. "While I was waiting for you guys to catch up."

"Ouch," Dylan said. "That was directed at me wasn't it? Okay, Josh you were right. As soon as we get back to civilization I'll hire a personal trainer to join us on the tour bus." Dylan looked around the church, taking it in as if he was recalling something. "In her shows, among all her stories, Momma talks about how she learned to sing in a one room church house. I guess this has to be it?" Dylan said.

"I imagine it is," said Rhashan.

Dylan, Josh and Rhashan rested in the peaceful dim light filtering through the stained glass windows of the church. It felt good to just lay still and enjoy the quiet for a while. With what was waiting just outside, there was little else they could do anyway.

2

Kitty was power walking on her treadmill going over her exhaustively detailed list of wedding plans on her iPad when Olga abruptly barged into the room. There was a heightened sense of urgency on Olga's face which was almost always the case with Olga.

Kitty slowed the machine down to listen, noticing Olga had a large manila envelope clutched in one hand.

"Yes, Olga?" Kitty asked.

Kitty attempted to see what the package might be, and saw words written on the side:

URGENT FOR KITTY STARDUST'S EYES ONLY

"Did someone deliver a package?" Kitty asked.

Olga outstretched her arms in a fully disconcerted way. Kitty sighed. She knew that when Olga did that, time would have to stand still for a while. And it was a terrible mistake to try and hurry the Russian woman along because it would just lead to even more details or unrelated topics. The last thing you wanted was more details or unrelated topics.

"Olga wash that silly looking dog," Olga said exasperated.

"Peggy Sue." Kitty nodded.

"Every morning she get into Iris garden and dig up bulbs. I work so hard."

Kitty stopped the treadmill completely. She held onto the handrail and patiently waited. "Yes, you do work very hard."

"Every morning she dig up Iris bulbs. She get into stickers and she get more fleas. Every morning I give her bath."

Kitty stepped off the machine and wiped her face with a towel. "I see you have a package that looks like it might be urgent?" Kitty instantly knew she had made a mistake. She had sounded impatient and Olga had clearly noticed.

"Urgent?" Olga huffed. "Urgent is what doctor say Olga need for these knees of mine. Urgent surgical procedure, he say. There is no time for procedure on knees I tell doctor. Olga must go to nursery to buy more bulbs. Olga must go to animal clinic for special flea soap. Olga must replace fresh flowers in whole house, up and down stairs all day long. I cut bunions off my feet this morning. Crazy doctor want to charge Olga for such things. I have too much work to do..." she shook her head dismayed, then got back to her point, "So...I washing silly dog in kitchen sink and phone start ringing, ringing,

ringing. No one answer. *Where everyone is?* asks Olga. I answer phone and it is that crazy Englishman Jamie Oliver again. He ask me if eggplant is in season here in Nashville. I say, who am I? I am Olga from Vologda, Russia, not Google. I am busy with dog bath, look it up yourself Englishman!"

"The package?" Kitty tried to reach out for it, but to no avail.

Olga nodded tersely, "I get to that very soon. I go back to washing dog in kitchen sink. Now doorbell ring, ring, ring. *Where everyone is?* asks Olga. I say to silly dog to stay put in sink and I go to front door. There is package on ground outside but no person anywhere. I look and look. I see no one. So I go grab package and silly dog run out the front door. She covered from head to tail in shampoo."

"Is Peggy Sue outside?"

"I am certain she in Iris garden again digging up bulbs. Dog never listen to Olga."

Olga finally handed the package to Kitty. "My English not so good, but I think, may be important."

"Yes, I see that. Could you go get dog from garden...I mean *the* dog from *the* garden?"

"I go find silly dog and run new bath. I work so hard. My knees and my feet, oh, they hurt so much."

Olga limped out of the room. Kitty wiped her face again with the towel and looked over the package. It was odd that nothing but those few words were written on it. It looked like it was written with a black marker in a childish way; big square letters. There was no postage. She debated if it was safe to open it. But after some thought, she figured it must be something related to the wedding plans and ripped off the top and pulled out the contents of the envelope.

There was a cover letter, which looked as if it were typed on an old typewriter, which was odd. And behind it were four color printouts – they were photographs.

Kitty thumbed through the photographs, growing more confused and concerned as she did, and then returned to the letter on the front. As she read the letter she sat down on the edge of the treadmill. Kitty's hands were shaking. She shuffled back through the printouts. She looked more closely this time, making certain what was in the images was real. She looked at each one carefully, and it made her feel nauseated and terrified.

She whispered, "Dear God, this can't be happening."

From what she was looking over in her hands, Kitty drew a sudden, shocking connection. She jumped up, dropping the papers and the envelope to the floor and turned around to grab her iPhone which was resting in a charger on the treadmill.

Kitty held tightly to the phone, attempting to stabilize her violently shaking hand, and yelled into its voice recognition receiver: "Call Dylan!"

* * *

In the smaller of the upstairs bedrooms of the old Holloway house the theme song from the TV series *The X-Files* suddenly filled the air. It was coming from a cell phone attached to a charger sitting on the inside window sill. The other end of the charger cord extended out under the slightly opened window to a small solar panel that had been attached to a three-legged base placed on the outside roof. The phone played the theme song five times before it subsided. The phone belonged to Rhashan.

In the larger bedroom there were two other cell phones. Now one of them was going off – the Blondie song "Call Me". It was sitting on the floor next to the air mattress bed. This phone belonged to Dylan. It continued on for several minutes before it stopped. The other phone was in the pocket of a jean jacket hanging on a wooden coat rack by the door. It vibrated, and the sound of an elephant trumpeting repeatedly filled the room. This was Josh's phone. After a few minutes it stopped.

* * *

All the calls were from Kitty. She cycled back through the three cell phones many more times while she was driving (fairly erratically) in her silver Tesla Roadster through the streets of Nashville. Kitty was looking at her cell phone when she turned onto the street that led to the governor's mansion. She was so engrossed, she had to swerve her car to miss hitting the Nash Trash Tour Bus. She heard the squealing of tires and saw, in her rear view mirror, the bright pink bus bank sharply to the right, likely flinging the tourists - enjoying the famous Nashville comedy tour - out of their seats. Then the bus jumped onto the sidewalk, nearly sideswiping a STOP sign; then righted itself back on the road and kept going. She hoped no one inside the bus was hurt. "Dear Lord, didn't they just accidentally hit a pedestrian last week? I hope the girls are okay," Kitty said to herself, thinking of her two friends who conducted the musical comedy bus tour of the city. Kitty felt horribly bad that she didn't have time to call them or go check on them, but at the moment she simply had other concerns that were far more pressing. "I'll have to call Sheri Lynn and Brenda Kay later and explain...and apologize."

Kitty kept driving and redialing her calls to Dylan, Josh and Rhashan. With each call not being answered Kitty became more filled with dread. Hundreds of horrifying scenarios had impregnated her mind. Of course, she never imagined that Dylan, Josh and Rhashan were trapped inside an old church with a tempestuous, irritable mother bear and her cubs outside – the church where she first began to sing when she was a little girl.

She had spoken to all three of these men several times over the past few days, so she knew their cell phones had service available at the abandoned and isolated old house that she used to call home. Rhashan had told her they had a solar powered charger they were all using to keep their phone batteries going. Kitty was feeling queasy, overwhelmed and approaching a state of pure hysterical panic. Considering the contents of the envelope sitting in the passenger seat of her car, her apprehensive concerns were reasonable ones for her to have.

Kitty was like almost everyone who lived in the city of Nashville. She felt their city in America's heartland was a safe harbor from a world that often seemed fraught with dangers, unpredictability, wars and senseless tragedies of all sorts. The good natured persona and the feeling of family that the world associated with the Country Western music industry was actually something that was essentially true. Country folks took care of their own. Once in a while (usually an especially long while) Nashville would be struck with a shocking blow. When the Country Western entertainer Stringbean and his wife Estelle were violently murdered at their home near Ridgetop, Tennessee, the brutality had been earth shattering at the time. Stringbean and his wife had been an essential part of the Nashville family. Stringbean was a regular at the Grand Ole Opry and on the hit TV show *Hee Haw*, and he and his wife were truly two of the most kind-hearted people in Tennessee. To this day it is almost impossible to imagine that the crime ever occurred. But thankfully the event was far from ordinary, and in the end the crime brought the music community even closer together.

Kitty's feeling that life was essentially good was a certainty generated from the circumstances and influences of Tennessee, the place where she was born and lived. Danger and evil were *out there* somewhere. But now she didn't know what to believe. She was honestly more scared than she'd ever been in her life.

3

JJ Fletcher crept down the upstairs hallway of the governor's mansion with stealthiness, being careful to stay on the carpet runner, which was quieter. He had managed to break away from Elliot for a few minutes. He had Byrdie fake an important phone call which gave him the opportunity to step outside his office and shrewdly sneak away. He needed some time alone. Elliot was a bundle of nerves, his delirious eyes looked like two cherry-bombs ready to explode. JJ's own nerves were brittle and frazzled, and Elliot's testy grumbling was making it worse. He and Elliot had convinced Walter Houseman that JJ was doing everything humanly possible to contact Josh, and Mr. Houseman had thankfully gone back to his room at the hotel to wait. But with no Josh to be found, the only option that looked plausible anymore (and looked as if it might salvage JJ's chance-of-a-lifetime political opportunity) was for JJ to disown Josh to the public and make an iron-hearted speech voicing his vigorous support for marriage in Tennessee remaining between a man and a woman. Elliot had written this very speech and had it ready for JJ to give. So far JJ had refused to even look at it.

It didn't help that the fall from the ladder at Kitty's house had wreaked havoc on his back and his spine was throbbing like hell. The whiskey he had been swigging all morning was only dulling the anxiety and pain. The propensity to use alcohol to ease, or possibly erase, any and all pain was something he came by honestly from both of his parents. But today JJ actually had an instinct to hold back, and to not fully drown away his pain and sorrows. He *really did* miss his son. Drinking that personal pain away just didn't feel right. Something inside him was brewing, and he couldn't identify it exactly. But there it was, something impending - something imminent - and it didn't feel natural for JJ. It felt like something entirely new.

JJ looked behind him. He wasn't followed. JJ had arrived where he wanted to be. He opened the door to Josh's bedroom and slipped inside. Once inside the room he quietly closed the door behind him and sighed with relief. Elliot wouldn't find him here now.

The room was dimly lit. The window shades were open and the natural light was soothing. JJ didn't turn on the light. He liked the momentary feeling of peace the softly lit room offered.

JJ looked around Josh's bedroom. The housekeeper kept it clean, which was primarily just a weekly sweep of the wooden floors with the Bona mop and a good dusting. Even though the bed hadn't been slept in by anyone in years, the sheets and pillow cases were changed twice a month. Josh had only used the room briefly before he left for Africa. JJ still had his original home on the north side of Nashville and Josh used his room there as his primary escape when he was finishing up his final year of high school. He attended the University of Tennessee in Nashville, so Josh had never actually lived away from home until he had set foot in his one-room shanty in New Xade. This room, in the governor's mansion, was mostly a sophisticated showcase. Josh helped move some things over, but Byrdie had organized the set-up of the room with the interior decorators who had redesigned the entire governor's mansion when JJ had moved in. Since JJ was a single man with only a son, the changes were mostly making the home more masculine. The previous governor had a wife and two young daughters. The decorators had set up Josh's bedroom to reflect a proper teenage boy and had asked Josh to bring some of his belongings to personalize it. They had displayed Josh's trophies, some lacrosse gear – Josh's stick, helmet, and shoulder pads. A couple of cowboy hats hung on the wall. There was a framed poster from the documentary film *Jane's Journey* about Jane Goodall hanging on the wall. Josh had brought some personal photographs too.

JJ had been in the room several times over the years but had never noticed until today an item on the table next to Josh's bed. It was a framed photograph of Josh and Dylan. They were in ski gear. It must have been from the trip Josh had made to Sun Valley, Utah before he went to Africa. JJ knew Josh had gone with a friend, but forgotten who it was.

JJ sat on the bed and picked up the picture. Josh's blue eyes gleamed, his honey-colored blond hair was pulled down around his face with a ski cap. Dylan Fairway had an undeniable eye catching face, his skin slightly suntanned and his hair was long like his father Frankie's. He was adorned entirely in ski attire but for a black cowboy hat. His eyes crinkled at the edges, and that smile was unmistakable – JJ saw Kitty's unrivaled, ravishing features...*that beguiling smile*...in Dylan's looking back at him from the photograph.

Both boys were beaming from ear to ear.

How did I never see it before?

Josh had also hung a picture of his mother on the wall above his chest of drawers. The woman in this photograph was holding a small baby in her arms. JJ had taken the picture himself. Josh had found it when he was fourteen years old. It was in an album of photographs that Josh's mother had saved. Josh asked to have it enlarged and framed. JJ looked at his wife's blithesome expression. When he snapped that photograph there was no hint of anything but joy ahead. How far away that day seemed to him now.

"He's really gone," JJ said to the photograph on the wall. "What am I going to do now?"

His wife stared back at him. Her calming countenance suggested there was nothing to be worried about. That smile of hers - from so many years ago - could not have been more incongruent with how JJ felt. But there it was. And in truth, her smile did seem to soothe JJ's anguish a little.

A little.

In the faint light, and with the comfortless ache JJ was feeling in his heart, he started to have such an unquenchable need for his wife that he almost convinced himself he heard her voice.

You promised.

There was a chill flowing across his skin. He looked around for its source, but saw nothing that could explain a cool breeze from where he was sitting.

That was not her voice. That was not possible.

Lordy, JJ, get control of yourself.

JJ shook off the ghostly sentiments that had clearly gotten the best of him. He thought he needed to go face Elliot again, and figure out a way to salvage this problem with the president without Josh. His son apparently had no intention of helping his daddy out, and that was painfully clear now. Josh was steering his own ship now. JJ put the photograph of Josh and Dylan back on the bed stand and sighed deeply. *Maybe being alone in Josh's room wasn't such good idea after all.*

And here comes that chill again.

You promised.

There was a slight knock on the bedroom door and it startled JJ.

Byrdie slowly and quietly opened the door and stepped inside, and JJ's gut reaction was to object. He didn't want to be interrupted yet. He needed a few more minutes to get himself centered again, to prepare for the hostilities that were waiting. Then he saw that Byrdie's face was full of trepidation.

"I'm sorry to interrupt sir," Byrdie said. "There's someone here who has to talk to you."

"What's wrong, Byrdie?" JJ asked. He knew Byrdie well. Something had truly unnerved her.

Byrdie started to speak, but thought better. Instead she pushed the door open to let someone else inside.

JJ couldn't believe his eyes. It was the last person on earth he expected to see. Kitty was wearing jeans and a plain light blue T-shirt. She had on a light amount of makeup and was wearing a baseball cap. In her hands she held a manila envelope. Kitty was shockingly beautiful as always, but, like Byrdie, her expression was ill-boding.

"I'll leave you two alone."

Kitty reached for Byrdie's hand. "No, please stay Byrdie." Kitty looked at JJ in a way that made him feel extremely apprehensive. Kitty continued, "We're going to need someone with a sound head in here with us."

Byrdie nodded.

"Kitty, what's going on?" JJ asked.

"I came over here as fast as I possibly could," Kitty replied. "I've been getting emails and phone calls ever since that article in *The Nashville Sun* was printed. And I have seen a few people say pretty horrible things on TV about me and you; and our sons for that matter. But I had been ignoring them. Rhashan told me not to engage with anyone, so I've tried not to." Kitty looked down. "Well, for the most part. I did call Fox News and tell that malicious Michelle Bachmann to go suck on Satan's pitchfork. That may not have been a good idea." Kitty shrugged, clearly over-fatigued by recent events, and sat down on the bed. "I had no idea JJ. I am so sorry. It's your mother." Kitty handed the envelope to JJ.

JJ took it, but he didn't know what she expected him to do.

Kitty's eyes welled up with tears. "I swear JJ, I never could have imagined something like this would ever happen."

Byrdie was frantically calling numbers on her BlackBerry. She kept listening, but by the look on her face, she wasn't getting any kind of response. This was of no help for JJ to understand what was going on.

Kitty said to JJ, "You were right. Someone was going to get hurt."

JJ asked, "What on earth are you talking about?"

Kitty pointed to the envelope. "It's all in there." JJ looked at the envelope as Kitty explained it to him, "Your mother has been kidnapped."

JJ looked at Kitty. The information in that one sentence was too bizarre to completely grasp at first. "What do you mean?" He asked, even though he didn't expect Kitty to repeat what she said.

"Someone dropped this off at my house this morning. It's a short note with some demands. And then there are some photographs." Kitty looked from the envelope to JJ. "They look real to me, JJ."

JJ opened the envelope. He thought – was hoping - Kitty had made a mistake.

"JJ, I can't get in touch with your mother." Byrdie met JJ's gaze. "With those pictures and the fact I can't get her, I think we have to assume what Kitty has is real."

"And there's another problem," Kitty added. "I have been trying to call the boys and Rhashan but none of them are answering their phones. They're all at my old home place. We have to get up there as soon as possible. I think something may have happened to them too."

JJ pulled out the contents of the envelope to catch up with what Kitty and Byrdie had obviously already gone over. He stared at the pages with growing disbelief. He leafed through them several times. Four were color printouts of Petula tied to a chair. Her mouth had a gag tied around it. She looked terrified, and there were marks on her face. It looked like cuts and bruises. The images were not perfectly clear. The camera they used, or possibly the printer, was not the best quality. But it was Petula.

The first paragraph that JJ read from the letter was short:

We have Petula Fletcher. If our demands are not met exactly as outlined below in 24 hours, she will never be heard from again. We only deal with JJ Fletcher and Kitty Stardust. Anyone else, including the police or the FBI, get involved and the deal is dead, and so is Petula Fletcher.

It went on to explain their demands.

Kitty said, "I came the second I got it. It didn't look like a prank to me."

Byrdie added, "I made some quick calls to verify this before we came to you, JJ. I've been trying to call her phone. Your mother's not answering it. I also called the house, and the nurse there said Petula never came home last night. I didn't explain why I was calling. I didn't want to upset your father."

"That is Momma," JJ said. He shuffled back through the photographs. "I'm sure of it." Then he read the rest of the letter. "This is what they want?" He asked, astounded.

Kitty nodded. "And I can't get Josh, or anyone else up there, on the phone."

"They're at your place in Armadillo?" JJ asked. He felt a little betrayed by this revelation. His own son was staying in the house he used to come and pick up Ruth-Adele Holloway in his pickup truck. In a way, he realized this was a logical place for their sons - under the circumstances - to go hide. It *was* in the middle of nowhere. "That's where Josh has been this whole time?"

"Yes," Kitty replied. "But now I don't know where they are. Normally I could get them on their phones. It doesn't make sense why they aren't answering."

"I should get my security people on this," JJ said.

Kitty responded, "I think we should do just exactly what they say. The time they marked on the letter is already over three hours ago. We really don't have a lot of time."

"Maybe I should tell Elliot," JJ said.

"No, JJ," Byrdie said. "You and Kitty go. I'll handle Elliot."

"What are you going to tell him?" JJ asked.

"I'll tell him as much of the truth as he needs to know," Byrdie said. "I'll tell him you found out where Josh was hiding, and you are going to go talk to him."

JJ thought a moment. "What if Josh refuses to do what this letter is asking him to do?"

"He'll do it," Kitty said assuredly. "That's his grandmother. I'm not worried about that. I just can't understand why not one of them is picking up. I can't imagine a reason, nothing good."

JJ quickly thought it over. "Then you're right. We better get up there and find out."

4

"Okay, the bears have been gone for over thirty minutes." Dylan was looking out the back window of the church. The stained glass distorted what he could see outside, but he was still able to get a pretty good view of the woods, enough to see that a momma bear and her offspring were not among the trees and tombstones of the old cemetery. "I think we should be okay."

Coltrane was curled up on the floor half asleep near the door. Rhashan looked at him. "What do you think Coltrane?" he asked his dog. "Is it safe?"

The Basset Hound moved his eyes in Rhashan's direction, but didn't move.

"I'm not going to lie," Josh said. He was laying on his back in one of the wooden pews. "I'm thirsty, I'm hungry, and this pew is making my back and my ass hurt. But I think we should give it another fifteen minutes. I want to be as sure as the sunrise that those bears are long gone before I go stomping back out into the woods."

"Yeah," Rhashan nodded. He was looking out the little window of the front door. "I think I'm going to agree."

Dylan nodded and stepped away from the window. He walked over to the pew and lifted Josh's legs and sat down underneath them, and then placed them down onto his lap.

Josh cringed a little. "Ouch, watch where the blackberries got me."

"Oh, sorry." Dylan placed his hands softly on Josh's legs. Dylan was lost in his thoughts.

"What?" Josh asked him. He put his arm behind his head to get into a better position to see.

"What do you mean?" Dylan asked.

Josh smiled. "Your mind has wondered out to sea about something."

"Oh, yeah," Dylan acknowledged. He said, "I was just thinking about another story Momma always talked about."

"Yeah?" Josh said prodding for whatever it was.

"So if this church is really here," Dylan said, considering the possibilities, "then that means Momma's stories about the Wampus Swamp Cat out here are probably true too."

"The Wampus Swamp Cat?" Josh asked with a dubious look.

Dylan nodded, "She said the Native Americans up here used to tell stories about it. Some said it was like a malformed mountain lion or a panther, but it was twice that size. And it could stand on its hind legs. It would kill cattle and sheep, and people's pets. Momma thinks she saw it several times.

"Your momma saw it?" Josh asked. "The Wampus Swamp Cat?"

"Grandma Holloway said she saw it too," Dylan added. "They said it had glowing yellow eyes and smelled worse than a wet skunk carcass. You never wanted to hear the Wampus Swamp Cat cry out, they said. The sound of it would make the ground shake and it would make people kind of wig out."

"Wig out?" Rhashan asked.

"They would hear voices, and have visions and stuff. But the scary part is that when it howled, or whatever you call the sound it made, before the sun went down the next day, at least one person within the earshot of the sound would always die some kind of horrible death."

Josh and Rhashan looked at Dylan hoping to see a joking smile or a wink, but oddly, he was still lost in his thoughts.

Dylan said, "So, I was thinking, for some of the people buried here in the cemetery the sound of that Wampus Swamp Cat might have been the last thing they ever heard."

"Okay Dylan, I need for you to come back into the room with us. Your momma was just kidding you," Josh said, reassuring himself. "I mean people are always telling crazy stories like that, especially up in the hills like this."

"No, not Momma," Dylan disagreed. "She told that story as if it were the God's truth. She still does."

Josh thought it through. He said, "I see no need to validate any more of your momma's stories. The church was real. That's good enough for me."

"I second that," agreed Rhashan. "After a momma bear and her cubs, I really have no desire to meet a momma Wampus Swamp Cat and her kittens. Whatever they may be; especially if their baneful meow is a harbinger of a horrible pre-dawn date with death."

Dylan nodded. "Yeah, I guess you're right."

The three men didn't say a word for quite some time. The wind swept through the trees outside, birds and bugs chirped, and the old church made creaking sounds. Earlier these sounds seemed normal enough, but now for all three men the sounds were starting to sound unearthly and malevolent.

"The wind sure makes some peculiar sounds out here in the woods," Rhashan observed.

"Yeah, it sure does," Josh agreed.

Rhashan added, "And I sure wish we had a flashlight or a lantern. This old church is kind of dark."

"A cell phone sure would be nice right about now too," Josh said.

Coltrane lifted his head and sniffed the air as if something did not smell quite right, and then he started to whimper.

Dylan looked at Coltrane with unease. He shook his head. "I am really sorry I brought up that Wampus Swamp Cat."

"No shit," said Josh.

"Yeah," Rhashan agreed. "Jesus, I swear I keep hearing a damn cat purring right outside the door."

"Me too," Dylan agreed.

"I don't think I can stay here another second," Josh said, nervously glancing at all the windows.

Rhashan stood up. "I think it's time to make our move!"

Things are beautiful if you love them.
— JEAN ANOUILH

Was blind, but now I see.
— JOHN NEWTON

THE WALLS CAME TUMBLING DOWN

1

The Cadillac Escalade made its way through the rough road and steep inclines that roped through the Tennessee hills. The trip had not changed much since the last time JJ had driven it when he was a gangly teenage boy driving up to see his girlfriend in his pick-up truck. He remembered every bump in the road and hairpin turn, and for all the time and the recent unfortunate events, JJ was still happy to be with her again. Some people, no matter what happened between them, or how much time had passed, when fate brought those people back together it was like time hadn't passed and they'd never left each other's side. For JJ Fletcher, that's how it felt with Kitty.

They had decided JJ should drive. Kitty continued hoping beyond hope to get an answer as she cycled through calling Dylan, Josh and Rhashan. But no one ever picked up.

At the start of the drive they discussed the best way to comply with the demands made by whoever had written the letter. Kitty had called and gotten Rebecca C. Hooper on the line. She turned the phone over to JJ, who explained to Rebecca as much as he could. Rebecca promised she would be waiting for him to call her back. She agreed to have equipment and the station ready to make a breaking news announcement. She wasn't sure if she could guarantee that it would go live (not knowing what she was reporting), but she told JJ she would do whatever she could to make it happen. It wasn't prime time, so she would likely be able to pull it off.

"You remember the way?" Kitty asked. She stopped dialing for a moment. It was frustratingly pointless.

"Yeah," JJ answered. "I could drive it with my eyes closed."

"Sorry, of course you know the way." Kitty was despondent. "I don't know what I'm saying. I just need to know they're okay."

They had passed the general store a few miles back and were only about ten minutes from the house. It occurred to Kitty that she should have called Mae Willow, the owner of the little store. She might have had some information about the boys' whereabouts. If they weren't successful finding out anything at the house, then Kitty would have JJ go back.

There was a fork up ahead, one road went to the Holloway homestead and, if you hung to the right, the other road went down to the church where Kitty had essentially began her singing career.

She had been seven years old, and the crowd was made up of seventeen local churchgoers. She sang "I'll Fly Away", while two blue-haired ladies in handmade, strawberry-red polka dot dresses backed her up on piano and tambourine. The Mount Sinai Church parishioners clamored to their feet, and sang right along. Little Ruth-Adele knew, as she watched that small church group join her with such joyous elation, that she had found her calling. The ability to make other people rise to their feet in joy with just the sound of your own voice was the most fully gratifying feeling she'd ever felt. It still was. The one room church was finally shut down in 1987 when a church member tragically died from a rattlesnake bite during a Sunday morning assembly. The newly installed preacher had thought bringing back the age-old tradition would stir up some much needed spiritual passion and fill up some of those empty pews. But if he'd asked other practitioners of this dangerous activity ahead of time, he would have known to de-venom the rattlesnakes behind closed doors before bringing them out to the congregation.

"Does Petula have any prescriptions she can't live without?" Kitty asked, genuinely feeling concerned for a woman she had honestly felt no concern for whatsoever her entire life. "The kidnappers might not even be aware of that."

"The first thing that comes to mind is alcohol," JJ answered. "I've never seen Momma go for more than a day without some kind of hard liquor. Her purse is full of prescription bottles too. God knows what those are."

Kitty said, "At some point we may need to call her doctor to find out if there is any that she can't survive without."

"And then what?" JJ asked. "We don't exactly know how to contact these people."

"I guess you're right." Kitty sighed. "I just don't understand what would make anyone do something like this."

"Angry, provoked people," JJ answered. "People who don't think anyone is listening to them can become unreasonable." JJ let her sit with that a moment. "The last time I talked to you I believe you were kind of unreasonable."

Kitty started to object, but then didn't. "Okay, I'll admit it. I can be unreasonable. I did feel bad not calling for paramedics when you fell off the ladder."

Mentioning it made JJ reach around and massage his shoulder. "That fall did hurt." He took in a heavy sigh. He asked a question he'd been wanting to ask for a long time. "Why didn't you ever call me? I mean for all these years? What did I do?"

Kitty couldn't believe it took such a long time to finally confront him with the facts. "You asked your mother if you should be seen with me in public, or date me, or something along those lines." She paused, seeing JJ needed more. Kitty added, "Remember when you left your phone at The Peabody?"

He thought back. "That's where I left it?" JJ said, finally remembering.

"Yes, it was. And your momma called."

JJ rubbed his face hard. "Awe, hell. She swore to me that she never said anything to you."

"She probably didn't realize that she did. When I picked up your phone I never had the chance to speak. But she did. She told me everything she ever believed about me, and every horrible thing I ever believed about myself. And after all you and I had been through together, you agreed with her and you took her advice."

"I never meant for you to know about any of the crazy notions she had in her head about you. I don't know why she always feels like she has to butt into my life."

Kitty said, "Probably because you let her, JJ. Have you ever thought of that? And that's not the point. What she thinks, or thought, doesn't really matter. It shouldn't have mattered to you…All I cared about was you…and being with you."

JJ took the last turn that led up to the old Holloway homestead. A hill continued on up about a half mile further, then it dropped over to the top where the house stood.

JJ was about to explain that he was sorry, but Kitty cut him off.

"Do you have any ideas who it could be?" she asked.

"I've been trying to think of who, and I have a few ideas," JJ answered. His apology would have to wait, which was okay with him. He wasn't good at it. "My office has been getting some pretty heated phone calls and e-mails from some religious groups, and extremist groups. Elliot spoke to a few of them, but I doubt he told me everything. He said they were nutty fringe people, and he wasn't that worried. So I figured I shouldn't be either."

Kitty stared at her cell phone. It never felt so useless. She looked up. "There they are!" Kitty yelled out. "Slow down!"

Kitty's outburst almost made him swerve off the road. JJ looked out the windshield. Josh, Dylan and Rhashan were at the side of the road, watching them. A Basset Hound was standing with them. They must have heard the car coming up the road.

Of course they heard us coming. There's no noise but the crickets out here. JJ thought.

He slowed the car down to a stop.

"Thank God!" Kitty opened the door of the Escalade, and was immediately yanked back down. *The seatbelt!* She unsnapped the belt, and jumped out.

JJ put the car in park, and turned off the engine.

He was about to get out of the car to join them, when he noticed Josh look at him. He was talking to Kitty. JJ could clearly make out the words on his son's lips. "What is *he* doing here?"

JJ was so happy to see Josh he had forgotten that they were not on good terms – by any stretch. They all four were staring at JJ. He reached for the envelope that had the pictures of Petula and the letter, then looked back out the windshield.

Jesus, they're looking at me like I'm some kind of monster.

He realized he had a lot to explain. And he realized that none of it was going to be easy, not just the details about his mother's desperate situation, but the kidnappers had demands that had to be met.

No, this was definitely not going to be easy.

JJ opened the door and stepped out.

2

Rhashan had the best phone for the Skype connection with Nashville's Channel 2 News station. They were able to use a tripod he had brought with him. The camera on his iPhone was set to go. The sun was behind them, and Josh was standing in front of a solid background of evergreen trees. The lighting was nearly perfect under the conditions. The wind was negligible on this side of the house, so the sound check was clear.

Rebecca had gotten a small team together for the broadcast – her favorite cameraman and her best hair and makeup guys. This story, whatever it turned out to be, promised to go international in High Definition and she was going to be ready. She brought in some IT computer guys who worked with Rhashan to make sure the Skype connection was optimal. Getting the okay to go live had been easy with the station owner. The story about JJ Fletcher and his son's alleged gay wedding had become a big news story all over the country. The small group in the production room, including the station president, were ready to go live. Every television tuned into Channel 2 in Tennessee and the surrounding states were about to have *Divorce Court* interrupted by a *Breaking News Story*. The president of the United States had been notified as per JJ's request (as it had been demanded in the kidnappers' letter). President McKenzie and his staff were watching from a laptop computer set up in the Oval Office.

Anticipation in the news station was at maximum.

Josh had quickly changed from his running clothes into some jeans and a nice coral red polo shirt and combed his hair. Kitty applied a light face powder to Josh's face to reduce any glare. She never left home without the shine-eliminating powder in her purse. Josh had memorized the section of the letter he was required to read verbatim. The time requirements of the kidnappers made it impossible to get back to Nashville, so the setup outside the Holloway house was the best they could do and most expedient.

Rhashan was standing ready at the camera phone making final adjustments. He was using Dylan's phone to speak with the team at Channel 2. All was ready. Josh was clear on their monitor.

JJ, Kitty and Dylan watched standing right behind Rhashan.

Dylan's arms were crossed and he felt his throat closing up. When he heard what the letter was demanding of Josh he was furious. Kitty had to take him for a walk to calm him down and make him see there were no better options. He didn't calm down, but did agree to let Josh do what he needed to do.

Josh had said very little. He quickly agreed to read the section of the letter as it was called for. His concern for his grandma prevailed over his own needs. Deep inside though, he was angry, defeated and resentful. But he had no choice but to follow through, and quickly. Whatever his beliefs or convictions, he had to relinquish and defer to the whims of others. He hated that. He had taken a swig of the tonic Mae had given him when he changed his shirt and thankfully his breathing was clear.

Kitty was equally conflicted. She hated obedience or conformity of any kind. Once, when she was nine, she couldn't get a heavy winter coat unzipped. She had panicked and screamed uncontrollably until her momma cut her free with her big stainless steel sewing scissors. That's exactly how it felt when she had to be subservient to anything she considered illogical or foolish. *Trapped.* It made her want to scream uncontrollably. She took Dylan's hand. If there was going to be any screaming, it would have to wait for a more appropriate time.

JJ was well aware that he was having his personal and political needs met, even though it was not the way he would have envisioned. Ever since he had arrived at the old Holloway home he had felt the disdainful glances his way from everyone, even Kitty's security man. Through all the dire looks, he just made sure they all kept moving at a quick pace. That's all he could think to do.

But he also felt something else. It was a calming *something else.* It was in the sound of the wind, he decided. Yet he couldn't place the sound. It reminded him of a mandolin.

You promised.

Yeah, it has to be the wind, JJ thought.

Rhashan looked up to the group, held up a finger for quiet. He then pointed to Josh with three fingers up.

Josh nodded and looked into the camera.

Two fingers...

One finger...

"My name is Josh Fletcher. I am the son of JJ Fletcher, the governor of Tennessee. I have been unwilling to speak until now about the growing controversy over myself and my family. I can no longer remain silent. The feelings people have when they are my age can be confusing, and that has been the case for me. Recently, I questioned my sexual preference, but I have come to realize I was under the influence of people who held beliefs and ideas that are not true for me. I apologize for not addressing this personal problem sooner."

Dylan broke from Kitty's grip. He was crying as he walked away, disappearing behind the house so he couldn't see Josh. Kitty cast a brief look at JJ. He met her eyes, and noticed her lips were taught. She was holding back tears of her own.

Josh continued, "It is now, and has always been my father's strong character that has helped me and guided me. It has been his strength that has helped me now."

Josh flashed his eyes to JJ. Josh's jaw was twitching, and for a moment JJ thought his son was not going to finish. JJ had a hit of anxiety pound him in his gut area, but it quickly subsided.

Someone just touched my shoulder.

JJ quickly turned around to look behind him. It *had* been someone's hand on his shoulder. He was certain of it. But no one was there. Just the road and the dense woods on the other side. He turned back around. Josh was talking into the camera just as he had been. JJ unconsciously placed his own hand on the part of his shoulder he had felt someone touch him just a moment before. He dropped it just as quickly. It made him feel uneasy. At that moment, as he tried to rationalize - and dismiss - the fact he had felt the touch of someone's hand,

someone who clearly was not there...

JJ almost fainted from a sudden shift in awareness, and for the moment JJ was no longer present with the others.

JJ thought back to when he was standing in front of a full length antique bronze dressing mirror. Josh and he were standing side by side. Josh was very small. They both were wearing suits and the room was cold.

God, please help me remove this damned barrier between me and my son.

The voice was his own and it was vivid and clear. It was the morning of his wife's funeral. He had completely forgotten ever saying those words. All these years later. All these long years later and...

It was gone!

...It *was* gone.

The barrier - whatever it was - was not there anymore. How it happened he, even later, would not be able to say. The only strange part for JJ - as he looked over at his son Josh, no longer a little boy, but a young man - was why there had ever been any kind of wall between them in the first place. JJ remembered holding his wife's hand as she lay in a hospital bed. The diagnosis of leukemia had been a belated one. The doctors had missed it. They thought she had a severe case of the flu and had sent her home with promethazine-codeine and Tamiflu. Then a lab report had come back that had caught the rampant white blood cell count, and her doctor had called JJ at home in the middle of the night. The call was on a Tuesday, and she had been pronounced dead a mere two days later. Josh never saw his mother in the hospital because she had requested that her young son not be brought to see her until the blood transfusions and chemotherapy were completed – they were frightening looking procedures, she imagined, for a child, and would be too difficult to deal with. Hell, it was frightening for her and JJ. She never thought for a moment that she might need to say goodbye. JJ had been told differently by the doctors, but he couldn't bring himself to show anything but hope to his wife. He had not been able to bring himself to believe the doctors anyway, so the hope she witnessed on his face had been real. That last day, in the last hour, she had opened her eyes. JJ bent down and took her hand. He said to her, through tears, "I promise I'll take care of him." She didn't verbally respond, but her eyes said that she'd heard him. And she *had* heard him. He knew it. She attempted a smile – her last heart-felt gesture of her love for him – then weakness overtook her. Her face relaxed into a barren, emotionless emptiness that JJ felt he himself was falling into. It seemed like this immense plunge into the void lasted for a very long time, and just as suddenly, it felt as if it ended impossibly too soon. Then he knew he was alone in the hospital room. More alone than he had ever been.

That memory of that last moment with his wife, and then of that request he had made in front of the mirror a few days following with Josh at his side, connected.

A promise and *a prayer.*

And now here he was watching Josh doing something that was purely and simply no longer acceptable for JJ Fletcher. He was not living up to that promise he had made to someone who trusted him emphatically the moment he had made the promise to her.

He knew now something about Josh he didn't understand before. He knew something about himself he didn't understand before. Josh was exactly the same today as the day JJ had made that long ago promise to his dying wife, and he would be the same the last day JJ spent on earth as well. Josh was his son

my beautiful son

and that was a fact that could never be changed. Ever. It was so simple. But then the answers to the biggest questions in life often are.

I promise I'll take care of him.

JJ felt centered again. He looked at Josh, who wasn't looking at him, but was looking into the camera. JJ searched around to see where Dylan had gone. He was still nowhere in sight. JJ looked over to Kitty. She wasn't looking at him either. But he felt like someone was. He felt it all around him.

I wonder why no one else feels this?

JJ looked down and saw the letter in his hand. And everything suddenly seemed very wrong. But he knew exactly how to fix it. He never felt so certain of anything in his life.

"Please do not hold my father, a truly honorable and faithful governor of our great state, responsible for my errors," Josh continued. He was calm and convincing. "There is not now, nor will there ever be a wedding between myself and Dylan Fairway. Any stories to the contrary are entirely false. I am a heterosexual man. I am proud of that fact. I thank you for allowing me this time to clarify my point of view. Again I apologize for all the problems I have caused, and I hope this rectifies all those problems quickly and decisively." Josh stopped. His message was done.

JJ walked over and stood next to Josh. He kissed his son on his forehead and ran his fingers through Josh's hair. JJ looked into the camera. "Keep that going," JJ said to Rhashan. "You too, Rebecca."

He looked across to Kitty. She was confused. JJ wasn't supposed to say anything. He noticed Dylan was walking back to join his mother. Dylan likely wanted to console Josh. Of course he would after what he had just gone through.

"Thank you, Josh. Well done." JJ put his arm around Josh's shoulders.

"Do you want me to stay?" Josh asked.

"Oh, you're not going anywhere," JJ answered. JJ looked into the camera. "I am JJ Fletcher, the governor of Tennessee. What you just heard was my son reading the contents of this letter." JJ held up the piece of paper. "He did an excellent job of reading it. Of course he did. He's my son. But I'm afraid it's just a letter written by a group of people who have kidnapped my momma, Petula Fletcher." JJ caught Josh's shocked look. JJ looked back up confidently. "Beyond his name being Josh Fletcher, not one word of this letter is true." JJ stood firmly, he began to speak with a kind of fiery, serious clarity. "What is true, is that my son here is getting married, tomorrow at the home of a dear friend of mine. I hope they find it in their hearts to let me come. I've got to give my son away, after all. That's what any truly loving father would do."

Dylan was now standing by Kitty. "What is going on here?" He whispered to her.

Kitty shook her head. "I have no idea," she whispered back.

"My son, Josh, is marrying Mr. Dylan Fairway, a handsome young man born right here in Tennessee," JJ continued. "He comes from fine stock, and I hear he can shoot the wings off a mosquito sitting on a raccoon's back at twenty yards." JJ gave Dylan a confident nod, then continued," I, as a Tennessee man myself, could not be more proud to have Dylan become a part of the Fletcher family. And I am excited to have a member of my family become a part of the Holloway family. It's about time." JJ looked at Kitty, and nodded, then looked at Dylan. Kitty was still too perplexed to do anything, but Dylan smiled back appreciatively. JJ continued, "Here is a message for the cowards who have my momma. It is one of her favorite political assertions: *Some blind little pigs have just wondered into a slaughterhouse.* Get ready. Tennessee's best, and the best in the FBI will be coming for you. You have made one hell of a mistake kidnapping Petula Fletcher, by the way. You hurt one hair on my momma's head and you will be suffering the direst consequences our legal system has to offer. I'll make certain of that." JJ softened his tone a little. "And furthermore, I am pretty sure there are many other people in this beautiful state who would like to, as a good friend of mine put it, show off what you have for each other. You most likely want to have the privilege of getting married too. This state doesn't offer that for you today. But it will tomorrow. I am issuing an executive order this afternoon that will make all marriage in our state, no matter what the gender of the couple, fully legal starting as soon as I can get it written up. A Fletcher is not a hypocrite. If you are a father or mother listening to this, and someone in your family, your church, your community, or your government, tries to drive a wedge between you and your own son or daughter, tell them, like I am about to tell them, including you, Mr. President." JJ pointed at the camera. "Kiss my ass. Nothing is more important than your own child. Nothing." JJ looked into Josh's eyes, and he mussed his hair again. "Life is never going to give me anything else as beautiful as this boy right here." JJ pulled Josh in more tightly. "And if you can't understand that then you are no friend to the idea of family. Certainly not any family that truly loves one another."

JJ looked at Josh, "Do you have anything you'd like to say?"

Josh cleared his throat. He quickly cut his eyes across to Dylan and Kitty, who had mutual stunned expressions on their faces. "No," Josh replied. He looked back at the camera. "I'm good."

"Then I guess that's all for now," JJ said. He motioned for Rhashan to stop the camera. "Thanks Rebecca. And thanks Rhashan, that's a wrap."

Rhashan disconnected his Skype link and then stared at JJ, just as confused as everyone else on his side of the camera.

"What did you just do?" Kitty asked JJ. She stepped carefully his way.

JJ kissed Josh on his forehead again. "I don't know. But it sure felt good." JJ shrugged. He appeared to be riding on a pretty good high.

All eyes were still on JJ. Waiting for some other shoe to drop. But it was becoming evident that it wasn't dropping.

"I think," Dylan began, then altered his words. "No, I am sure, he just told the president of the United States of America to kiss his lily white ass."

Kitty walked up to JJ. "No, really, what just happened?"

JJ shrugged, "I'm not sure myself."

"I can tell you one thing for certain, there are people out there right now who are going to want to kill you," Kitty said seriously worried. "And did you even consider what someone might do to your mother now?"

JJ thought it over. "Well...you're probably right."

Kitty looked at JJ with concern. She tilted her head and squinted her eyes. "It doesn't bother you that some perfect stranger might have a gun in his hand right now and is thinking about you as he's loading up his bullets? What the hell did you just do? And why?"

JJ seemed truly perplexed. He had done exactly what his heart had told him to do, and he honestly didn't care about the consequences. "What else could I have done?" JJ asked.

"There's a lot of other things you could have done, JJ," Kitty said.

"I'll leave those things for other men," JJ said confidently, still holding Josh's shoulder tight.

Josh said, "I think he meant it." Josh was mostly talking to himself. He added as he looked at his daddy's face. "Daddy, I don't know if I've ever seen you so...I don't know...so tranquil."

Kitty stepped closer and squinted some more. "You really have changed, JJ. I don't understand how, but you surely have."

"Yeah..." JJ smiled. "And I kind of like it."

Dylan stepped up to JJ. He looked him in the eye, and reached over and shook his hand firmly. "Thank you, Governor. That was the best wedding gift we could have ever hoped for."

"Yeah, Daddy," Josh added. "I have to agree."

JJ said, "Have you ever heard a joke and didn't get the punch line. Then later it comes to you. It was like that I guess." JJ shrugged again, then a look of curiosity flooded over his face. "Look," JJ said, pointing behind Kitty and Rhashan. "It's a monkey."

For a moment they thought JJ had gone completely nuts. His sudden change in personality was just the first symptom of a sudden mental meltdown. Then Dylan, Josh, Kitty and Rhashan looked to where JJ was pointing.

It actually wasn't a monkey, but a chimpanzee. It was ambling up toward them with a friendly smile on his face. He seemed perfectly at home with people and stepped over to Kitty and reached up and took her hand. In his other hand he was swinging something that was sparkling in the sunlight, and jingling. He looked at the others with a good-natured grin.

"Well hello there little fellow," Kitty said to the chimp, and then looked up at Josh and Dylan. "Did you two bring a chimpanzee up here?"

"No," Dylan replied. "We don't actually own a chimpanzee. I think I would have mentioned that to you Momma."

Rhashan added with a teasing tone, "I don't believe they are native to Tennessee either. And I think we have uncovered the identity of the furry man from outer space Mae's husband saw up on his roof."

Kitty had a sudden realization. "I think I may know where he came from."

JJ pointed at her. He had the same idea. "The Roy Rogers and Dale Evans' Wildlife Sanctuary."

Kitty nodded. "They built that place for abandoned and abused wild animals after we moved away. I forgot how close it was to our property. It's just over that hill." Kitty pointed to a small grove of trees on the other side of the road. She looked down to the chimp. "I think what we have here is an escapee."

"Sanctuary?" Josh asked, intrigued. "What kind of animals?"

JJ answered, "Mostly old retired animals from the circus and Las Vegas shows. Daddy used to go to school with the woman who started it and he's always contributing money to their foundation."

A thunderous gunshot echoed through the hills all around them. Then another shot followed directly after. The chimp grabbed onto Kitty's leg, and buried his face into her jeans.

Dylan looked toward the area of the hills where the shots had come from - the direction Kitty had pointed. "Is it normal to hear gunfire coming from a wildlife sanctuary?" he asked.

The chimpanzee held out the shiny, jingling object up to Kitty. She took it from him and looked it over. It was a set of keys. "Now where did you get these?"

JJ noticed them, and stepped up for a closer look. "Can I see those, please?"

Kitty handed the keys over to JJ. He examined them knowingly. Among the set of keys on the ring dangled a solid gold, diamond studded trinket. It was the world renowned emblem of the Coco Chanel double C.

"Well I'll be damned," JJ said. "It isn't often that you see one of those." JJ looked the key ring over a little closer, and with more certainty. "As the matter of fact, I personally have only seen this one once." JJ knelt down to the chimp and dangled the keys. "My little friend, I wonder if you can take me to where you got these?"

The chimp took the keys from JJ and turned to walk back toward the road. JJ stood up and looked at the others. He said, "Call it a hunch, but I think we all should follow that chimp."

3

A camouflage REI alcove wind break was set up on a hillside overlooking a rolling vast meadow. Far in the distance several elephants stood in a pond of water basking in the afternoon sunshine. Two giraffes were feeding on a high tree nearby. Zebras, camels, kangaroos, emus, ostriches, and various other wild animals (many near the end of their lives) inhabited the expansive pastureland. In enclosed areas surrounded by deep moats of water and high fences were several wild cats – lions, tigers, leopards, lynxes. Monkeys, bears, and gorillas were fenced in large cages designed to recreate their various natural habitats.

Seated underneath the wind break were Petula Fletcher and Ruby Billingsley in comfortable oak and leather Borge Mogensen hunting chairs. They both were adorned in khaki pant suits and umber-colored hunting jackets. Petula had a fox fur stole thrown around her neck. They donned broad floppy safari hats and fine leather hunting boots. Next to Ruby, in a smaller hunting chair, was Minnie Pearl. The pig, seated on a blanket in the chair, was sporting a cashmere sweater, sheepskin booties and a hunting fedora (price tag still attached). Ruby cut a slice of a pear and handed it to her much appreciative pet.

Petula had a hunting rifle in her lap and was reloading. An ice bucket, a Bormioli Rocco glass whiskey decanter filled with bourbon, and two glasses with ice, set on a sturdy wooden table between the two women. Also on the table was a silver tray covered with a variety of finger sandwiches, crackers, oysters, and a caviar assortment.

Petula stood up, leaned her rifle on the table, and refilled her glass with bourbon.

"Can I freshen up your drink, Ruby?" Petula asked.

Ruby handed her glass to Petula. "Don't mind if you do. This brisk air is causing me to have a terrible thirst."

"Don't you love it out here, Ruby?" Petula asked.

Ruby nodded unenthusiastically, then shrugged. "It beats pickin' cotton."

Petula filled Ruby's glass and then added a few cubes of ice with tongs from the bucket. "The fresh air and exotic creatures exhilarate me, Ruby. It transports me back to my excursions in South America and the African bush."

Petula swigged her drink and set the glass down on the table, grabbed her rifle and stepped out to the edge of the canopy. She eyed the terrain, and placed the rifle to her shoulder. Ruby gave Petula a disapproving glance and placed her hands over Minnie Pearl's ears. Petula fired the rifle in the direction of the elephants far in the distance.

POW!

The sound thundered from one end of the hills to the other. Neither the elephants, nor any other animals, bothered looking up. Most had been in the circus or extravagant Las Vegas shows and had endured a lot worse than a booming gunshot in their long lives. A flock of geese *were* startled and soared off into the sky. Petula fired a second shot.

POW!

She sighed and turned back to Ruby. "Did I tell you about the time I once shot an anaconda while on a steamer junket down the Amazon? It took six men to drag it to dry land and cut it open. Ruby, you will never guess what we found inside the bowels of that horrible creature."

Ruby looked tender-hearted over to Minnie Pearl. "I'm not sure I want to know."

"A boy from a local village," Petula responded. "He'd been missing for two days. The snake must have nabbed the little tike right from his bed. His sleeping blanket was still clutched in his arms."

"That is horrible," Ruby said. "I wish you wouldn't tell me those stories."

Petula nodded, "Nature is unmerciful, Ruby. Only a fool doesn't respect the power of Mother Nature. I don't understand why you won't let me show you how to shoot a gun. If you ever need to defend yourself I hate to tell you, that pig isn't going to do a darn thing."

Ruby shrugged, "Well Petula, you pulled off some kind of miracle with that banker, Mr. Ackerman. I have to admit I almost wanted to shoot him. He said it would take an act of God to keep his bank from taking my house."

"Where there's money, there's a way," Petula said. "That is just a fact of life, Ruby. And that is why I have made sure I always have a lot of it."

"Well, I had said a little prayer for someone to come along and help me and you showed up at my door."

"I have found that a little prayer backed up with some cash is a lot more likely to get answered," Petula said as she spooned a little caviar on a cracker. "Just remember what I said Ruby, where there's money there's a way."

"Okay," Ruby answered. "Where there's money there's a way." Ruby adjusted the sweater around Minnie Pearl's neck.

As Petula took a bite of her caviar cracker, a screeching chimpanzee cried out from behind nearly startling Petula to spit it out. Petula shook her head, didn't turn to look, and threw up her free hand. "I told you to not feed that stupid chimpanzee, Ruby. And now he's back, and he's never going to leave us alone."

Ruby shook her head. She pointed skittishly behind Petula. Ruby dragged her safari hat to cover her face, then slowly reached over and pulled the blanket over Minnie Pearl.

"What on earth has gotten into you woman?" Petula said to Ruby, then turned around.

JJ, Kitty (holding the hand of the frightened chimpanzee), Josh, Dylan and Rhashan were standing in a row, all with a collective look of serious disdain on their faces. The chimp screamed out and pointed accusingly at Petula. He shook the jingling key ring at her, then quickly hid behind Kitty's legs.

"What in heaven's name are you all doing here? Are those my keys?" Petula yelled out. She looked around quickly, thinking fast. "I mean, how did you find me?" She feigned a look of terror, scouring the area around her. "You have to get out of here. The people who kidnapped me are going to be back here any second." Realizing she was holding a hunting rifle she slipped it carefully behind the table.

"Kidnappers?" JJ asked.

"I was arriving home when suddenly they came from behind some bushes. I tried to escape, but they were big, strong men, with guns. They roughed me up a little, and then one of them injected me with something as I tried to fight my way free. I fell unconscious into their arms and the next thing I remember I woke up here." She looked around giving the appearance of total confusion. "Wherever here is."

"And then these men left you with a gun, booze and a tray of caviar?" JJ asked, a little at a loss.

"They are very brutal and filled with hatred, but they have been kind enough to leave a small amount of food to eat. If they see you, I don't know what they might do. They could kill us all. And way out here, who would ever know?"

"Well there is the high school kid who is sitting at the front entrance that let us in," JJ replied. "He's also not happy that you left the gate open and some of the animals got out."

Petula snapped, "I wasn't in charge of the gate. That was —" She stopped herself. "I mean, what gate?"

Minnie Pearl nosed her way out from the blanket and grunted.

"Mrs. Billingsley?" JJ asked, astonished. "Is that you?"

Petula turned and looked. She wanted to strangle that pig, and not for the first time.

Petula chimed in with a quick response, "Yes! They grabbed poor old Ruby Billingsley too. Like I said, they are very brutal. They even kidnapped her pig." She continued, "From what I have seen this was carried out by a group of criminal professionals, not some small time hoodlums." She gave JJ and Kitty a severe glare. "And I certainly hope whatever their demands were, you both followed through." She looked into the ever incredulous faces staring back at her.

"Enough Momma!" JJ said firmly. "Mrs. Billingsley, would you like to explain what is going on here?"

Ruby peaked out from her safari hat. She looked at the row of displeased eyes. JJ gave Ruby an extended accusatory glare with his baby blues. Ruby always did relish those blue eyes of his. Eyes like those come around once in a person's lifetime. It was easy to tell she was going to break.

JJ said, "Ruby."

Ruby blinked, thinking to herself, *God I love the sound of my name on his lips.*

Petula saw Ruby melting at JJ's gaze. She had to act fast.

"Ruby is drugged!" Petula called out quickly. "And dehydrated! She's too weak and debilitated to speak." Petula glared at Ruby. "The last thing she should do, if she cares anything about her life, is speak!"

"Ruby," JJ said. "You know I have always thought of you in the highest regard. Whatever my dear momma has said to you, I can see in your pretty Irish green eyes, you want to tell me the truth."

He noticed they were green! Everyone else says they're pale gray, but they really are green!

Ruby looked back and forth between JJ and Petula. It was a brutal and merciless decision for her. In the end the baby blues won out – "She made me do it. If I'm lying, may God strike me dead!" Ruby yelled out and clamped her hands in a prayer position, with fear in her eyes; not fearing a wrathful act from God, but from Petula.

Petula's eyes squinted at Ruby brimming with a slow, murderous burn.

"She gave me a lot of money. A whole lot," Ruby continued, looking back to JJ. "She needed an extra set of hands to tie her up, put on those bruise marks with my makeup kit, and take all the pictures. I had to get my nephew to drive us up here in his Jeep. He's the one who took the envelope to Kitty's house." Ruby was animated with nervous energy and singing like a canary: "The bank was going to foreclose on my house. You have to forgive me. My heart might have been strong but my pocketbook was weak. Petula took care of all my money troubles with that horrible bank man, Mr. Ackerman. If I lost my house then where was Minnie Pearl going to live? They don't allow pets of any kind at the Belle Meade Heaven's Château Retirement Center!"

A contemptuous glower seethed out from Petula's eyes. "I think if someone and her ridiculous little pig want to go shopping for new hats next week, then they might want to stop all the crazy-talk." Petula turned back to JJ and the others. "They gave Ruby some strong sedatives to keep her under control. And apparently the drugs have caused her to start hallucinating. She's very confused. More than normal." Petula, never one to give up, continued on, "Now, I know this all looks strange, but it is far too dangerous for us all to stand around talking. You have to take my word. It may look like nothing suspicious and sinister is going on here, but you just happened to walk up at the wrong time. The last thing the kidnappers said was that they were going to start cutting off our body parts and send them through the mail to demonstrate how outright serious they were." Petula quickly turned and spoke directly to Ruby, "I imagine they'll start with the pig."

Ruby grabbed Minnie Pearl from the chair and held her tightly to her chest.

"Momma, you can stop talking now," JJ said.

"Petula," Kitty said. "I was scared to death thinking something had happened to you. I have been praying to high heaven that you were okay."

"You should be praying for me, after all I have had to endure!" Petula said emphatically.

JJ said, "Momma! I'm not sure if I should call the police or just throw you in with the lions and let nature restore some balance."

"I'm an invited guest here, and this is private property you're trespassing on," Petula said, giving up angrily and defeated on her kidnapping ruse.

"This is The Roy Rogers and Dale Evans' Wildlife Sanctuary, and I am putting emphasis on 'Sanctuary'," JJ responded.

"Harriette Weston, who owns this land, and is a dear friend of your father and mine, said I was welcome to stay here as long as I needed. She understood how dire my situation had become."

"Did she mention that you can't shoot the animals?" Josh asked.

"I'm not shooting any animals," Petula said. She held up her rifle and waved it around in defiant gestures. "That pimply faced kid at the entrance wouldn't allow me to bring live ammunition in with me. They're blanks. Besides, these animals and I have more in common than any of you could understand. One minute you're leading a parade down Main Street or performing in a big Las Vegas show, then suddenly you're cast aside. When men grow older, they just get better looking and gain more respect. But as a woman, people act as if you've outlived your usefulness when you're barely middle aged." Minnie Pearl grunted. Petula glared at the pig, and continued, "And I know, you can say my ideas are obsolete," Petula unwaveringly went on, "but let me tell you, it's people like me who are going to prevent the downfall of our society. I'm not going to quietly go out to pasture, while radical reformists, who have their socialist designs on my country, come marching in. You can't see it now, but some day you will be thanking me for my undying love and patriotism for this country." Petula grabbed her drink from the table and swigged it down whole, the ice clinking in the empty glass. She glared at the group again and repeated, "You will be thanking me!"

"I know she says it only has blanks," Dylan chimed in. "But I sure wish she'd put that rifle away."

JJ asked, "Does Daddy know anything about all this?"

"Of course he does," Petula answered.

Josh's shoulders dropped. "I can't believe both my grandparents were conspiring against me. I thought that Grandpa's heart was a little bigger than that."

"Don't be so quick to put your grandpa up on a pedestal, Little J," Petula said. "You have no idea what your grandmother has had to do, what personal sacrifices I have made. Your Grandpa Cowboy wasn't on his sport yacht fishing when he collapsed into a coma and nearly died, and we had to call you home from Africa, you know. No, he was not. That's just the story I told everybody." Petula poured a fresh glass of bourbon and downed it while the others watched her, intrigued. She continued, "He was not on a sport yacht at all. He was in a strip club. He had gone to some lewd, sleazy, disgusting roadhouse sex club with his reprehensible college buddy Corky Dinger. Cowboy had mixed some sex enhancing drugs Corky bought on the Internet with his own prescription of Viagra, and then while some undocumented naked seventeen-year-old stripper was giving him a lap dance, he had a massive brain hemorrhage."

JJ stood in baffled amazement. "You told me he was on his sport yacht."

"Would you have preferred the truth?" Petula asked.

Josh's face became milky white. Everyone there, including Ruby Billingsley appeared bewildered, and were growing quite pale themselves.

Petula continued, "That's right. It's sickening isn't it? And who gave that undocumented, underage lap dancer enough cash to bring her whole family from Guatemala to the United States to keep her mouth shut? That would be me! And I cleaned up the whole mess all by myself. Why? To save our family. To save the Fletcher name. I have devoted my entire life to making Cowboy Fletcher, and you JJ, into something. To make you into someone important. And you're ready to throw it all away. Is that what you want Josh? Is that what all of you want?"

No one spoke for a minute. They all knew Petula was capable of telling lies, but in the end they all knew it was unlikely she'd make up a tale like the one they just heard. Unfortunately, it was in all likelihood the truth.

Josh said, "I want my innocence back."

Dylan took his hand. "I'm sorry you had to hear that, Josh." Dylan then added, "I'm even sorry the pig and the chimp had to hear that."

JJ broke in, "Okay, this is how this is going to go. I'm not certain how many state and local laws you've broken Momma, but I'm pretty sure it's enough to keep you behind bars for a good long while."

"You wouldn't." Petula exclaimed.

"Yes, I would," JJ said.

"Your own momma?"

"With glee," JJ replied.

Petula glared at JJ a moment, then asked obstinately, "My one and only son would have me locked away in some filthy prison?"

JJ replied without hesitation, "And everyone would live happily ever after."

"You remember the last time I was incarcerated? When I was put away for driving under the influence?" Petula was excessively serious.

"You were back home within the hour, Momma. As soon as the judge found out who you were."

"I saw enough. It is all concrete and stainless steel in those places."

"I might not get on my cell phone and call the prosecuting attorney on one condition," JJ said.

"I don't like conditions."

"You'll learn to like this one," he said. "As a wedding gift to your grandson, I think it would be nice to have you do a public service commercial where you endorse Josh's marriage."

"I don't endorse any such thing," Petula rebuffed.

"Momma, you should know that a live broadcast went out where I promised to give Josh away at his wedding tomorrow, so the gig is up. You might as well join us."

"Your political career will be over!" Petula was flabbergasted.

"Maybe," JJ said. He took Kitty's hand and puts his arm around Josh's shoulders. "We'll just have to put our faith in the good people of Tennessee and see what happens. As for you Momma. I think a little on-air educating of the public might do you good. You could learn a few things yourself. Otherwise I see a lot of concrete and stainless steel in your future."

Petula held the rifle up in an unconsciously threatening way. "I won't do it."

"Don't underestimate how angry I am with you, Momma. To keep you from going to prison, everyone standing next to me will have to lie to the police and the FBI about what we have witnessed here today," JJ said firmly. "Maybe we'll go along with a story that you were released unharmed; you'll say you refuse to press charges against your kidnappers because they showed remorse for their actions. I do think you'll do whatever it is I tell you to do, Momma. Your choices are very few indeed, the way I see it."

Rhashan cleared his throat, then said, "It really isn't my place to speak, but Mrs. Fletcher, for a short time before I started my job at a security company I worked for a year as a guard at the Tennessee Prison for Women. Attractive women, as yourself, usually ended up, how do I say this in good taste?" He thought a second. "A massive, muscular, lusty, tattooed woman will become very romantic with you. And to prove your loyalty to her, and you *will* prove your loyalty to her, you'll have to perform some act…along the lines of using a knife carved from your own toothbrush to stab one of her enemies in the dining hall. You only get one toothbrush in prison, so you'll probably keep using this toothbrush to brush your teeth even though the blood from the woman you stabbed is still stained onto the handle." Rhashan added, "And that's what happens while the lights are on."

"You only get one toothbrush?" Petula asked.

"Just one," Rhashan answered.

"You can't leave the lights on?" Petula continued. "What if I want to read, or watch CSPAN?"

"11:00 P.M. lights out for everybody," Rhashan answered. "And no CSPAN in your cell."

Petula still seemed to be stalling. She looked like she was weighing her options in her head.

Josh said bluntly, "They don't allow alcohol in prison, Grandma."

"Okay, fine. I'll make the damn public service commercial," Petula said.

"Good," JJ said thankfully.

"Wait," Kitty said. She crossed her arms and glowered at Petula. "I want you to say you're sorry." Kitty stepped forward. "To everyone here."

"I won't," Petula said out-of-hand.

"I want you to say you're sorry…" Kitty responded "…and I want to hear you say that you are proud that your grandson is marrying a Holloway." The chimpanzee clinched tighter to Kitty's leg.

JJ, Josh, Dylan and Rhashan all took a step back. The confrontation was unnerving.

"No," Petula said authoritatively. "I won't be doing that."

Kitty pried the chimpanzee from her leg and the creature ran and grabbed onto Josh's leg. Kitty kneeled down and pulled up the leg of her blue jean bottoms where a small 22 derringer handgun was strapped. Kitty snapped open the holster, took the handgun into her hand, and stood back up. "I've had a really bad week," Kitty said, as she pointed the gun at Petula, "And *this* gun is loaded with *live* ammunition."

"You wouldn't shoot me," Petula said nervously, looking around for possible escape routes.

"I'm just a dullard, stinking, common as pig tracks, hillbilly." Kitty gripped the gun tighter and aimed it closer toward Petula. "Who knows what I might do?"

Petula saw all the unfavorable looks coming from everyone. Even Ruby was giving her a look of aversion. She glared back at the small, but lethal-looking, barrel of Kitty's pistol.

Dylan stepped up, "Momma, I think maybe you should put down the gun."

Kitty said, "You might want to step back, Son. I'm shaking" She was visibly trembling. "You see, Momma's got a loaded gun, my hands are clamped very tightly to it and an accident might happen. I wouldn't want anyone to get hurt. Other than her."

Dylan stepped back. "I'm stepping away," Dylan said. "Just like you asked me to, Momma."

"We all deserve a sincere apology from her, don't you think?" Kitty said with a demented-sounding timbre. "The longer I go without hearing that apology the twitchier my trigger finger is becoming." Kitty's eyes darkened. "And the more my heart is turning to ice. When the police ask, we'll say it was one of the kidnappers that did it."

Petula began to believe Kitty might really shoot her. Everyone was starting to come to that conclusion. Kitty's finger was starting to shake more and more noticeably.

Kitty stepped even closer. "Now or never, woman."

"Jesus, okay," Petula finally yelled out. "Put that pistol down. I'm sorry."

"And?" Kitty said, still shaking.

Petula looked at Dylan and Josh. She looked back at Kitty, who appeared quite crazy to her. Petula sighed heavily. "Your son seems like he's a nice enough young man…" She paused, then said through a rigid jaw, "…and I'm proud Little J is going to marry him." Petula stared at the ground. It took all she had to muster up that last line. She then looked back to Kitty who still had the gun pointed at her. "There I said it." Petula said, glancing at Dylan. "Why anyone would need so many tattoos is beyond me, but he can't be all bad or Little J wouldn't like him so much, I suppose." Petula stared at the gun in Kitty's hands, and said, "I'm sorry, I'm sorry, I'm sorry!"

Kitty lowered her handgun. Her hot-blooded rage cooled down a few degrees. "Wow, she did it." Kitty felt consoled, her sanity returning. "I was hoping I'd have to shoot her." She walked back over to stand with Josh and Dylan. Dylan carefully took the gun from her.

Josh said to Kitty, "Thank you, Kitty. I really needed to hear my grandmother say that."

Kitty nodded. "My pleasure. I needed to hear it too."

Ruby looked at JJ pleading: "Does this mean we can go home? Minnie Pearl can't take this cool air anymore."

"You can go home Ruby," JJ said. "And don't worry. You, and Minnie Pearl, won't lose your house. Just remember, everything you heard and saw here today didn't happen."

"Thank you," Ruby said. "You can count on me, and Minnie Pearl. We'll both never speak of this whole crazy day ever again. That's a promise I know I can keep."

"Thank you, Mrs. Billingsley," JJ said.

Petula and Ruby began to gather up their belongings, Petula starting with putting the caviar in a plastic Rubbermaid container.

"You had to go and leave the gate open," Petula mumbled (in her *nearly* inaudible voice). "Why is it that I have to do everything myself?" Ruby, who was folding up Minnie Pearl's hunting chair, didn't hear a thing. She was contentedly singing to herself, "…all the world seems bright and gay. And when Irish eyes are smiling, sure, they steal your heart away…"

Kitty hugged Josh, then reached over and kissed JJ on the cheek. "I am very happy this has turned out okay, but I have to go. There's a wedding happening at my ranch in less than twenty four hours."

JJ said, "I'll stay here and help Momma get packed up. You boys help Kitty get back home." JJ hugged Josh.

"Daddy, are you sure about all this?" Josh asked. "You had a big change of heart. I'm very happy you did, but is there any chance you'll be changing back?"

JJ glanced at Kitty with a beaming smile, then back to Josh. He said, "What kind of a father would not be proud of a son like you? Right?" Then he nodded to Dylan, adding, "And I'm gaining a remarkable, talented son. Don't worry. Now go get some rest, you two. You've got a wedding to show up for tomorrow."

JJ stepped closer to Kitty and bent in close to where only she could hear him. "Thank you Ruth-Adele Holloway."

Kitty glanced up inquisitively. "And what exactly are you thanking me for?"

"I almost lost my son," JJ said. "And you tried to stop me."

Kitty wanted to say *you're welcome*, but her emotions got caught in her throat. She just returned the look of gratitude at JJ with a quiet smile.

She didn't need to say it anyway.

Come live in my heart, and pay no rent.
- SAMUEL LOVER

THE END OF THE TRAIL

1

The immense, secluded skeet shooting range located on Fletcher land was surrounded by a high pine tree line and steep rolling hills. Cowboy's daddy had the range built back in the fifties. A log barn made from Douglas fir, built by Hal Fletcher himself, housed inside it an overabundance of shotguns, rifles and handguns, and countless stacks of ammunition – all locked in a safe-room the size of a small warehouse. There was always a fully stocked bar and a kitchen with cabinets and closets filled with plenty to eat.

Petula stood on the shooting range loading her Krieghoff double barreled shotgun, joined by Cowboy, Nurse Gisele Lutkenhouse and Elliot. Cowboy was over bundled in wool blankets in his wheelchair with a cigar dangling from his clinched teeth watching his wife, who was visibly drunk (and it took a lot of George Dickel to make it visible on Petula). Elliot was slouched in a canvas folding chair next to Cowboy with a drunken glower of disappointment on his face and a fresh glass of whiskey over ice hanging loosely in his hand. Nurse Lutkenhouse, the only sober one in the bunch, was kneeling next to a skeet launching device. A grand oak table more than four inches thick and nine feet long was directly behind them. Spread out across it were six empty George Dickel bottles, four full ones (one freshly opened), an ice bucket and several fine hand-blown Glencairn whiskey glasses.

President Bob McKenzie had not made any public statements about Governor JJ Fletcher, or anything related to the Fletcher's at all. He had simply selected Senator Pete Snyder, a handsome young gun from North Carolina, for the vice presidential position. He did it fairly quietly and with not much fanfare at a press conference late Saturday night. Senator Snyder was a by-the-book conservative with little to debate about among his Republican supporters in Congress, and he would easily get the majority of votes needed to be sworn in. Petula even had to admit he was a good, and safe, choice for Bob McKenzie. Petula had no real beef with the president. JJ, with his on-air declaration of defiance, had given the man no other political choice. But The First Lady was another matter. Suzanne McKenzie had been caught early this morning by the press on her way to the Southern Baptist Church in Virginia she attended periodically with her husband.

She wasn't about to miss this Sunday! Petula had noted as she watched the TV coverage.

The First Lady only said one sentence to the myriad of microphones lurching toward her, before she swiftly made her way through the church house doors in her lemon yellow knee-length dress suit and matching pill box hat. But it was more than enough to drive the knife in and give it a good, precise twist. And Petula couldn't help but feel it was meant to serve as pay-back for the national embarrassment the Fletcher family had caused for The First Lady's husband. Wives could be merciless defenders of their spouses when their husbands had to put on the congenial, politically correct, face for the public. Petula could write the book on *that* unvarnished truth. First Lady Suzanne McKenzie had said to the reporters: "Tennessee is kind of unfamiliar territory for me, but I believe I read somewhere, that is one of those states where they marry their cousins...and what not." A thin-lipped bitter smile washed across The First Lady's face, her squinting, batting eyes looked right into the camera, and then that smile dropped like mud falling off an old tire. With that, Suzanne McKenzie turned and vanished into the church.

Nurse Lutkenhouse was handling the skeet-shoot launching machine. In place of a normal skeet Petula had ordered the reluctant Swedish woman to place the goose-boy Hummel figurine (she had bought earlier from that *snooty, cross dressing antique store owner*) into the launcher. Nurse Lutkenhouse was alarmed at the level of whiskey the others around her had been consuming, and moreover, she was deeply worried that tomorrow Petula would be furious at her for not personally calling a halt to the very thing Petula was now ordering her to do.

Nurse Lutkenhouse pleaded, "I really want to insist that we stop right now, and maybe go get some breakfast back at the main house. I can make some of those lingonberry Swedish pancakes everyone loves so much."

"Pull woman!" Petula bellowed, and wobbled to one side, then quickly stabilized herself, and held up the shotgun.

"You told me yourself how much you paid fo—"

"PULL!" Petula blurted out again.

Nurse Lutkenhouse clenched her eyes shut, held her breath, and waited. She wanted to give Petula one last chance.

Petula sputtered out, "If you'd rather, Nurse Pippi Longstockin', I could have you balance the stupid German boy and his goose on your head, and I could shoot it there instead!" Petula repeated, "I SAID PULL!"

Nurse Lutkenhouse compressed her eyes even tighter, then she released the skeet launcher. The spring lever flung the Hummel with a *whish* and a *thunk*. Surprisingly the Hummel's shape was fairly aerodynamic. The chubby little German boy and goose gracefully sailed high into the cloudless, iceberg-blue sky. As it reached its pinnacle, arching in the air, Petula aimed and fired.

KERPLOW!

Like a Fourth of July firework, the Hummel exploded into a million fragments of colorful porcelain and white powder. Cowboy, Elliot and Nurse Lutkenhouse watched with Petula as the blown-to-pieces Hummel made a beautiful display falling back to earth.

Nurse Lutkenhouse exhaled. *If Petula didn't pay me so well I would seriously consider walking away from this crazy job and going back home to Stockholm.* She stood up and went back to Cowboy, pulling the blanket up around his neck. She noticed he had written on his dry erase board:

SHOOT ME NEXT

She quickly erased the words and lightly smacked Cowboy's shoulder.

"Don't look so gloomy Elliot," Petula said as she walked back to the oak table. "He's still the governor and I still have plenty of ideas."

Elliot opened his mouth and mumbled words, but they were unrecognizable drunken babble to the others.

"Forgive me for speaking," Nurse Lutkenhouse bravely chimed in. "Everyone is so gloomy. The wedding ceremony is going to start in a little while, and I think perhaps you all may regret not going. There is still time to get there and perhaps a wedding celebration would give everyone's spirits a needed lift."

Petula rolled her eyes, laid the shotgun on the table and slammed back her glass of whiskey.

Elliot explained, his slurry words uttered like heavy syrup being poured from a bottle, "As it turns out, Gisele, my dear, no one among our little party here is invited! As a matter of fact we were told if we dared to show our faces there we would be arrested on the spot!"

"Oh," Nurse Lutkenhouse said with regret, then surrendering: "Maybe I will try some of that whiskey after all." She walked over to the table and poured a glass for herself.

"Look, this is not a defeat." Petula seemed to be energized by the challenging circumstances they all were in, although her words were still fairly garbled. "We are public servants, gentlemen, and young lady. You don't raise the white flag and give up the ship just because you took on some water. This little bump in the road is not going to derail us from our obligations, our job, and our mission of keeping the world beautiful and safe and free!"

At that moment a rabbit hopped out from a holly bush about fifteen yards away. It lifted its head to inquire about the strange people it saw across the meadow.

"Look a cute little bunny!" Nurse Lutkenhouse exclaimed. She loved animals, especially sweet little creatures like this ginger brown rabbit with a white tuft of fur under his chin.

Petula whisked up the rifle and shot. The rabbit's bloody carcass flopped dead on the ground.

"Got it!" Petula said, pleased with her successful shot.

Nurse Lutkenhouse blinked continuously like a cartoon character, unable to look away from the dead rabbit.

Petula nodded confidently. "My daddy always said, a few shots of good Tennessee bourbon steadies the aim."

2

The gate entering Kitty's Ranch was closed and locked. Rhashan had just put in the security code to set the alarm and was checking to make sure no one had managed to sneak in and hide inside the bushes at either side of the gate. He was wearing a pressed fine-looking pearl-gray suit and Italian shoes he had polished to an agreeable shine. The wedding was starting in about thirty minutes and he wanted to get back inside the barn where the ceremony was taking place. Dylan had asked him to be his Best Man and he wanted to be on time.

"Hey, you!"

Rhashan looked to see that Special Agent Derek Cooper was outside the gate pushing his face through the bars. Rhashan was disheartened.

"You, Goliath," Agent Cooper continued. "I'm with the governor's security and I just got stuck in some shitty traffic. Can you let me in?"

Rhashan slowly walked over to the desperate-looking agent. Derek took a step back to let Rhashan open the gate for him.

"No one is allowed through the gate after four thirty," Rhashan said.

"I'm not a guest. So it doesn't apply to me."

Rhashan nodded, devoid of sympathy.

"Hey man, I said I'm not a guest," Derek said. "It doesn't matter."

Agent Cooper's superior demeanor didn't improve Rhashan's feelings for the man. "It does matter to Ms. Stardust." Rhashan pulled back his suit jacket to reveal his gun. Rhashan added, "Celebrity wedding rules trump Secret Service employees who can't make it to work on time."

"You're an asshole!" Agent Cooper spat out.

"That's *Goliath* asshole to you."

* * *

Josh and JJ were the only two people in a small dressing area that had been sectioned off in the back of the Kitty's barn. Josh was wearing his dusty gray Alexander McQueen attire. JJ looked equally debonair in his charcoal gray suit. JJ wore a pair of black, *cruelty-free* cowboy boots, made by vegan designer Brice Partouche (a fashion designer Josh found who made all his cowboy boots from non-animal products). JJ and Josh were staring into a full-length antique bronze dressing mirror. Josh was having trouble getting his tie adjusted correctly. His hands were noticeably shaking.

"Daddy, I need your help here."

JJ looked over at Josh, reaching for the tie and straightening it.

"There, that looks better," JJ said.

"Am I still sweating?" Josh asked.

"No. You look great. I wish your momma was here to see you right now. She would be so proud of you." JJ looked over his son a moment. "I'm proud."

Josh's foot was tapping the floor over-anxiously. He kept fretting and looking at himself in the mirror, brushing his hair back and adjusting his suit. "I probably should have taken that Valium that Kitty's mother offered me earlier."

JJ shook his head. He stepped over to the dressing table where there was a bottle of Jack Daniel's. He poured two glasses, and handed one to Josh.

"Here, Son. This is Tennessee Valium."

Josh took the glass. JJ lifted his for a toast.

"I guess if your old man has room to give advice on your wedding day, I can say one thing I have learned is that we have a finite amount of time in this life. Never let a day go by without telling him at least once that you love him."

"I'll remember that," Josh said. They clinked glasses and downed the drinks.

Josh looked at the closed door. The whole wedding event was waiting just on the other side. He took in a deep cleansing breath. "Well, Daddy. This is the point of no return."

JJ took Josh by the shoulder and led him toward the door. JJ said, "I believe, Son, the point of no return was when you had his name tattooed on your ass."

Josh looked at his father, blushing. "Daddy? You know about that?"

JJ just smiled.

* * *

Kitty had outdone herself. The barn was decorated spectacularly. Mismatched antique chairs were set up in rows. Candelabras were stationed at all the outer areas at varying heights. The ceiling was cascading, from the top to the sides, in tiny clear lights. It created the effect of a resplendent summer night. The polished wood floor shined like glass, reflecting the thousands of tiny white lights from the ceiling above. Kitty had asked Fernando, who was in charge of the flower arrangements, to make the barn appear as if the guests had wandered into a mystical forest of wildflowers. He had more than succeeded. In every direction, among deep fern-green foliage, were flowers of every variety and color pigment imaginable. The fragrance filled and lifted the senses. In the candlelight, with the wonderful perfumes of the flowers encircling the guests, it felt like one was being transported right into heaven. A towering champagne fountain was beautifully displayed, sparkling and flowing. A woman with long marigold-yellow colored hair, in a silvery white dress that cascaded on the floor behind her, sat near the front playing a hand-crafted wooden harp.

Behind the seated guests, a dance floor had been set up for the reception immediately following the ceremony. Jamie Oliver and his team of waiters had a buffet ready, and tables had been set up around the dance floor where the French Impressionist-like vision of flowers and summer-night starlight appeared to go on forever.

Estella-Jeanne sat in the front row wearing a Tiffany-blue chiffon dress. Jewell was next to her in an ivory dress with pastel lace flowers sewn throughout, and in elbow length white gloves. Georgia, in an elegant violet dress, sat beside Jewell. Byrdie sat behind the first row with Banjo Flo and the rest of Frankie's band. Other seats were filled with more friends and family.

Rebecca C. Hooper and a cameraman were positioned at a respectful distance behind the guests. Kitty had told Rebecca to feel free to film as much as she wanted, but made her sign a release form stating that Kitty had final cut of the news footage that would be played on that evening's special event coverage. Kitty's own camera crew was documenting the event in film and photographs.

Standing at the front was Dylan, in his Alexander McQueen, smoky-gray suit, wearing black cowboy boots and a shiny-new black cowboy hat. He looked up to see JJ and Josh, the two handsome men walking down the aisle toward him. Dylan's eyes had a gentle, smoldering gaze as he watched the man he loved come down the aisle. Josh's eyes met his. Dylan smiled and winked.

Kitty was wearing an apricot, bead-sequined Francisco Costa sleeveless dress. She stood just behind Dylan, with Frankie next to her. Frankie had on a wrinkled white dress shirt with a black leather vest and a dog-eared cowboy hat. He looked like he had just rolled off the cot-bed of his tour bus and stumbled into the wedding (which was exactly what had occurred). Rhashan, Dylan's Best Man, was beside Kitty and Frankie. Kasia and Mosi were across from Dylan, smiling spiritedly. Kasia was in a multi-colored, wrap-around dress and head scarf, Mosi in a burgundy and white suit. They were serving as Josh's Best Man and Best Woman.

JJ and Josh finished their walk down the aisle and came to stand across from Dylan. Josh looked over to Kasia and Mosi, smiled and nodded, "Hello." JJ stood aside to let Josh and Dylan step up face-to-face in front of the altar. Kitty and JJ caught eyes. The look from JJ was a satisfied one. It made them both feel a peace and joy inside that had been a long time coming.

Rebecca, holding tight to a microphone, looked to her camera. She said, quietly, "Governor Fletcher's son, and the son of Country Western superstar, Kitty Stardust, are about to tie the knot in the midst of a social and political firestorm. What a couple of brave young men. And what a personal and private moment. Let's watch."

Even though Kitty stationed her a little further in the back than she had hoped for, Rebecca was bubbling over with excitement. She knew she was witnessing – and getting exclusive footage of – the celebrity news scoop of the year. Her daddy would be very proud of her.

A familiar voice broke through the sound system, in a not-so-subtle, vociferous tone: "Prepare yourselves for divine, joyous matrimonial jubilatiousness! The Reverend Shandazzle proceeding!"

Shandazzle stepped up from the back of the barn. Her presence was like a bolt of thunder. Shandazzle was wearing a skin tight black sequin dress with a white clerical collar, white leather high heels, glittering white eye shadow, and her hair in a flamingo-pink pompadour. After a quick, pristine pose, she gracefully stepped up to the altar where Josh and Dylan were waiting.

"If you have not already, please take your seats." Shandazzle spoke with spirited elatedness. "This is not a dress rehearsal, honored guests. We are on the launchpad, and the engines have been set into motion. Shandazzle's rocket ship of glorious, everlasting love is ready for takeoff! I welcome, one and all, to this beautiful, inspirational marriage between these two jaw-droppingly handsome young men."

Josh and Dylan stared with delight at Shandazzle. She gave them a blissful look back. Both the boys were nervous, yet obviously excited. "You boys ready?" Shandazzle asked. Josh and Dylan nodded. She said, "It's been kind of a rough journey getting here today. Your parents are very proud of you." She glanced at Kitty, Frankie, and JJ, who were beaming. "This is your page in history." Shandazzle looked out into the audience. "Everyone in this beautiful room has come here today to witness these two young men. They're doing something here that many of us never dreamed could ever happen." She gave Josh and Dylan an appreciative nod. Then she held her hands out and looked up, as if rays of light were streaming across her face. "Rainbows," she said, then looked back to the audience. "Rainbows are made up of many colors. Yes, they are. And does a rainbow leave any colors behind? No, it does not. They go all the way up, all colors side by side, to the top of the sky. Together. A rainbow is made up of a little rain. A little sunshine. Just like us. We all love rainbows. When the rainbow looks down at you and me, what do you think it sees? What does the rainbow observe about all of us? It sees that we are made up of all the colors too. But we have inside of us something those rainbows will never have. We have not just the ability to share our colors, we can share our love with each other too. And that sharing of love is what has brought all of us here today. Especially Josh and Dylan."

Shandazzle looked at Josh and Dylan again. She said, "Sometimes there is a bride and a groom. Sometimes there is a bride and a bride. Sometimes a groom and a groom. But whoever stands in front of me to be joined in holy matrimony, it is always love."

She looked over to JJ. "And who is here today, this lovely Sunday afternoon, to give Josh away?"

JJ smiled. "That would be me," JJ said, putting his hand on Josh's shoulder. "I am the daddy. I am truly proud to be here with my boy; to give my blessing. I have loved this young man all his life. Now I'm giving him to you, Dylan. It's time to let someone else love him. But don't think I plan on loving my boy any less."

Dylan said to JJ, "We'll share him."

JJ nodded with an agreeable smile.

Josh said, "I'm happy you're here, Daddy."

JJ replied, "Me too."

Shandazzle turned to Kitty and Frankie.

"And who might this charming couple be who plan to give Dylan away?"

"I'm Kitty. I'm Dylan's very proud Momma. And I have to say, this is the most perfect moment in my life." Kitty put her hand around Dylan's shoulder. "He's my one and only son."

Dylan took her hand and squeezed. "Thank you, Momma."

Shandazzle said, "And Frankie?"

"Oh, right. I'm that handsome devil's daddy," Frankie said, who was clearly a little drunk and stoned. "I have seen these boys grow up good friends, and now they're getting married. Dylan, Josh, just keep being friends, and loving each other and you'll be fine. You're bound to get angry at one another now and then. If you do, don't go get a gun like my third wife did." Frankie put his hand over the scar on his stomach. "Just try to work it out in a non-violent way. I feel nothing but love for you both."

"Thanks, Mr. Fairway," Josh replied.

Dylan added, "I love you, Daddy. You, and Momma."

Shandazzle motioned to the seats behind them. "The parents may have a seat."

JJ allowed Kitty and Frankie to step ahead. Kitty sat down with Frankie on her left and JJ on her right – her two old lovers. She was feeling a little nostalgic, and feeling more than a little overwhelmed with pure joy.

"Who has the rings?" Shandazzle asked Josh and Dylan.

The boys both turned around to the back of the room. They watched as the chimpanzee, from The Roy Rogers and Dale Evans' Wildlife Sanctuary, entered the aisle at the back. He was dressed in a snazzy white suit, feeling quite posh himself, as he sauntered past all the bewildered and amused faces. Kitty waved to the chimp to let him know he was doing a fine job. She held up a banana.

The chimpanzee arrived at the podium, and held out his hand to Josh and Dylan. There were two gold rings in his palm. Josh took one. Dylan, the other. Josh patted the chimp on his shoulder. The chimp went to sit in Kitty's lap. He happily took the banana and began to peel it.

Shandazzle eyed the chimp for a moment longer. "Now where was I? Oh yes, I believe our two grooms prepared some words to say to one another."

Josh looked at Dylan. They both had endured a lot of stress over the past few days to get to this point, and now it seemed almost too good to be true that they were standing here. All the stifling pressure finally seemed to drift away. Josh let out a long sigh.

Dylan looked at Josh with a generous, satisfied smile. Dylan said, "I choose you, Josh. You've been a secret in my heart for a while. But now that secret won't be hidden anymore. People, just like us, have often been forced into silence, or to be alone. But, to have you, and to not tell the world, is inconceivable to me. At times, it seemed like the price of our love was going to be too high. Thank God, you're with me on this, and we have chosen to walk down this path together. We didn't let fear push our love to the back of the bus. I knew love never had to ask for permission. It should never have to. It seems like maybe others are catching up to see us for what we are. Just a couple of guys, who happened to fall in love. And I guess we couldn't be more blessed. Josh, you are my muse; my inspiration; you're my song. You are my sunshine. I imagine you will be those things for me for the rest of my life. I choose you, Josh. And that sounds good to me. I hope that sounds good to you."

Josh grinned. "Yes, it does." He took some time to savor Dylan's face a moment. "When I was in Africa," Josh said, "I learned that a good life is determined by how many stories you have collected at the end of the road. These stories are about friends." Josh looked over to Kasia and Mosi. The two friends beamed big smiles back to him. "And these stories are about family." Josh looked at JJ. "I am sure, Daddy, it wasn't always easy doing it all alone. But you did a great job. I always knew I was loved." JJ winked at Josh, who turned back to meet Dylan's eyes. "And if you're lucky, your stories will include a best friend…" Josh said. "…a best friend who joins with you to make a new family. And to make a home. I don't know what they'll call this, but I hope they call it love. People who know me know I have a traveler's heart. I'm sure I'll always have it. But I discovered something when I found this guy. He's unrivaled." Josh smiled.

"You are my happiest place on earth. When we're old and gray, we're going to have some great stories, you and I. I can't wait to get there to tell them. They'll bring us a lot of comfort. The only way today could be more perfect is if my mother was here." Josh touched his hand over his heart. "But I think I can hear her. I know she's probably looking in, and watching over us, and will be as we go down this road making our stories together. And, if we're lucky, and I feel lucky, our journey will be filled with fields of wildflowers."

Shandazzle wiped a tear from her eye. Clearing her throat, she said, "You may now place the rings on one another's fingers."

Josh placed Dylan's ring on first, then Dylan placed the other gold ring on Josh's finger. They looked up into each other's smiling eyes. They could barely contain their joy.

Shandazzle continued, "By the power vested in me by The Church of The Angelina Jolie Spirit, based in West Hollywood, California, I pronounce you husbands forever. You may now kiss each other."

Dylan took off his cowboy hat and reached in to grab Josh around the waist. He pulled Josh close and firm and they kissed. It felt like it had been a long time coming, and they were going to savor the moment; they made the kiss last.

Josh's Great Aunt Jewell pulled a white satin handkerchief from her Judith Leiber floral-lace clutch. She carefully blotted a tear. She bent over to whisper to Georgia. "Aunt Viv was a lesbian," Jewell said. "She wore trousers, and she cut her own hair. It was quite shocking at the time. We had to keep the whole thing hush-hush because it would have brought down the whole Vienna sausage empire." She reached out to take Georgia's hands into hers. They both watched as Josh and Dylan continued kissing. "My my, times have changed."

"Yes, they have, Miss Jewell," Georgia said, holding tight to Jewell's fragile hands. "Yes, they have."

The harp player began to play the song "Beautiful" made famous by Christina Aguilera. Two young boys in white robes stepped up to the front doors and flung them open. Over twenty snow white doves were released from cages hidden behind the podium. The graceful birds flew out over the crowd. Kitty watched the doves to make certain the effect was awe-inspiring, as intended, as they flew out the front doors of the barn.

It was.

She glanced over and noticed that JJ had a tear running down his face. Kitty saw the first thing Josh did was look right over to his father, curiously. Josh appearing satisfied with what he saw. The father and son's eyes remained locked for a moment. Then Josh's face broke into a full blooming smile.

It was just as Kitty had planned.

It was beautiful.

You don't love someone for their looks, their clothes, or their fancy car, but because they sing a song only you can hear.
- OSCAR WILDE

WHEN PIGS FLY

Four Months Later

1

The Great Eagle Cherokee Burial Ground, east of Nashville on the north side of the Cumberland River, was rarely visited these days; the peaceful rolling hills were a little overgrown. The warmer spring air and recent rains had softened the ground enough for easy digging. It was just past 3:00 A.M. and a hazy overcast sky and dim crescent moon offered a much appreciated dark night for a couple of ill-equipped gravediggers. A screech owl observed the two peculiar forest night visitors with a sagacious glare.

Petula Fletcher and Buster Ragsdale had been digging the six by three foot wide hole for over two hours, trading shoveling duties every ten minutes or so because neither one was in the physical shape required to dig the grave for Petrified Ed. The only source of light under the thick grove of oak trees was a Coleman lantern. The hole was roughly four feet deep and it was nearly impossible to climb out of the grave any longer without a ladder – an item neither thought to bring.

Buster took the shovel first, then grabbed Petula by her hand and hoisted her up to the surface. They both heaved and huffed, completely short of breath. They were covered from head to toe with the rich black dirt of the burial ground.

"I'm going to be in a whole world of pain tomorrow," Petula said.

Buster agreed. "I can't tell which hurts worse, my back, my knees or the blisters on my hands, and frankly, anymore I can't tell one from the other."

"You and me both," Petula replied. She eyed the hole. "I think that's plenty deep," Petula said. She took off her gloves and wiped her hands on her shirt and jeans. She had already decided she was throwing her clothes, her shoes, the shovel, and anything associated with tonight's activities, in the fire pit out on the farm, so trying to keep clean had gone out the window long ago. She didn't really believe any noisy detective would ever be investigating this middle-of-the-night deed of theirs, but she thought it best to treat it as carefully as if it were a crime of some sort. She knew it certainly was not a crime, but she always took to heart the sage words that her old dear friend, and another strong woman she held in the highest of reverence, Patricia Nixon, once told her:

Mark my words, Petula. There's not a virtuous and noble act you could ever do that some enemy-fool and his lawyer can't fine-tune into high treason.

Buster glanced over to where Petrified Ed laid on a large fleece blanket. He was still wearing the suit Jewell had dressed him in for Thanksgiving. She decided he had looked so handsome in it that he should keep it. Buster said, "Yeah, that hole should do. I want to get Petrified Ed buried. I know it's all in my imagination, but I keep getting the feeling we're being watched."

Petula stepped over to the dead body. "Are there any words you want to say for him before we commit him back to the earth?" She was not a spiritual woman, but Petula was feeling slightly reverent for the poor old dried-up man on the ground. "I'm not good with death and those kinds of things."

Buster stepped up, took Petula's hand, and looked thoughtfully down. "Well, Mister Ed, whoever you were in life, I hope you are somewhere idyllic and peaceful now. I hope you found your way to your ancestors and your Cherokee family." Buster sighed, searching his mind for any other kind words to finalize this bizarre ceremony they'd found themselves in. "I hope your soul wasn't too frustrated during the madcap adventures your body had to endure on those Halloweens years ago. And I apologize on behalf of all those people who derived pleasure from seeing you wearing those crazy costumes that Vernon Valentine and Hal Fletcher dressed you up in. They were teenage boys and knew not what they were doing."

Looking down at the dead man on the blanket Buster remembered something. He said, "I almost forgot. Jewell wanted me to tell you how much she enjoyed sharing her Thanksgiving dinner with you." Buster reached into his pocket and took out a small piece of paper. He bent down on one knee and place it inside Petrified Ed's suit jacket pocket.

Petula asked, "What is it?"

Buster shrugged. "I'm not entirely sure. It is a note written on an old gum wrapper." Buster stood up. He said, "Jewell didn't explain. She just said she didn't need it anymore."

"Golly gee willikers, is that Petrified Ed?" said a voice from behind.

Petula and Buster spun around, both nearly tumbling over the top of the body on the ground. The surprising outburst came from Ruby Billingsley. She was standing right behind them with her pet pig Minnie Pearl standing next to her. Ruby had a small flashlight in her hand and a large turkey feather in the other.

"RUBY BILLINGSLY!" Petula yelled out. "For the love of Jesus, what on earth are *you* doing here?"

Ruby looked up innocently. "Well, I couldn't sleep. My ears were ringing. Sometimes when I can't sleep I come out here and perform necessary rituals for my ancestors. I'm nearly pure Irish, as you know, but I have a thimble full of Cherokee in me. My great grandmother was quite well known in these parts in her day. She sat on the High Council of The Clan of the Boar." She smiled down at Minnie Pearl. "I'm sure she's why I have such a fondness for the little oinkers myself."

Petula said, "Ruby!" She was getting flustered. "Buster and I were right in the middle of something, and it's important, and a little private. Maybe you could go on home and come back at a better time? Say, tomorrow. I'll give you a call later this week and you can tell me all about this little story of your famous ancestor."

Ruby shrugged. "My story's practically over. I just wanted to say that Great Granny taught me the ways of red and white magic. When I can, I come here and help troubled souls follow the trail of Kanati to the faraway western land of the dead. When my ears are ringing it means Great Granny is talking to me, telling me a soul is in some kind of trouble. Is Petrified Ed in some kind of trouble?"

Buster said quickly, "Ruby, there's no reason to think this is Petrified Ed. It could be anybody, and there's certainly no need to tell anyone what you've seen here tonight."

"Buster is right," Petula agreed emphatically. "This is just an old friend of Buster's who asked that he be buried among the Cherokee people. He asked that he be buried under the moonlight, which is why you've found us here at this late hour. Maybe you can add a little blessing yourself…with your turkey feather, and be on your way."

"Oh no. That is Petrified Ed. I'd recognize him anywhere. I was just a little girl when Hal Fletcher and Vernon Valentine took me into Hal's basement and opened up a big old freezer. And there he was inside, Petrified Ed. I remember it like it was yesterday. Hal had lots of pictures too from when he and Vernon used to dress him up for Halloween. I believe my favorite was when they dressed him up as Carmen Miranda. The Chief of the Cherokee Nation will want to know about this for sure."

"Ruby, you cannot tell anyone about this," Petula pleaded. "Not the Chief of the Cherokee Nation, not your neighbors, not your bridge playing friends, not those women you have pig play-dates with, not anyone! You see, somehow Jewell Whitecotton found Mister Petrified Ed, and if you tell anyone she will probably have to go to a nursing home, or maybe even prison." Petula exaggerated for effect. "Now you don't want poor Mrs. Whitecotton to have to go through anything like that."

Ruby thought it over. "No, I better tell the Chief. He'd understand."

Petula mused, taking a glance into the dark grave Buster and she had just dug, *one more body and a pig wouldn't take up that much more room in that hole.*

"Ruby. You cannot speak of this to anyone," Petula repeated. "And I bet there is something you'd really like, that I could maybe buy for you – again." Petula let that settle in. "We have to think of Miss Jewell. She just can't take the kind of stress something like this would cause. The doctor has made that clear."

Ruby thought all her options over. She didn't think too deeply ever, and tonight was no different. "Minnie Pearl won a black Burgundy truffle eating contest once. She beat out a Wessex Saddleback by six truffles. And boy did she love those truffles. I never could afford to buy her any more after that though. They are very expensive."

"Perfect!" Petula released a deep breath. Buster let out a relieving breath too. Petula added, "I think you should have all the truffles you and your little pig ever could want."

"Florie Pettygrove told me the best ones are in little restaurant called Chez l'Ami Jean," Ruby said enthusiastically. "She said it was just off Rue Saint Dominique. That's a little neighborhood a few blocks from the Seine."

"The Seine?" Petula asked, her eyes widened. "Like in Paris?"

"Yes," Ruby agreed. She thought she might need to explain more clearly, so Ruby added, "Paris, France."

"Well, I don't see why I can't have the nice chef there at Chez l'Ami Jean ship you all the truffles you need right here to Nashville?"

Ruby's smile wavered. She looked at Petrified Ed and shook her head. Ruby said, "I don't think they would maintain their flavor very well in a cardboard shipping box all the way from Paris, France."

Buster looked at Petula. He shook his head and added, "Maybe a nice long trip to Paris would be just the thing for Mrs. Billingsley. It might just clear her mind entirely."

Petula balked. "You know Paris has a very high crime rate…and the French are not very friendly people like we are here in Tennessee. You don't want to go all the way over there, Ruby. I'm certain the chef can have those truffles overnighted in an airtight shipping container and they'll taste just as fresh as if they were served right over there in that lovely French restaurant."

Ruby stepped closer to the body on the ground and shined her flashlight on Petrified Ed. "You are using the proper Cherokee burial shroud and a two strand apocynum cord to twine the death cloth around the body aren't you? And you anointed the corpse with white ash and tobacco, and invoked The Great Raven to protect his liver from the Black Witches? And I certainly hope you both drank the Divine Fire water and did the Talismanic Ghost Dance. If not, I'll have to have a licensed observer from the local Cherokee Tribal Council come inspect what you've done out here tonight."

"Okay, Paris, France it is!" Petula grabbed the flashlight from Ruby. "Buster is an ordained, licensed, Native American burial expert himself, so don't you worry, Ruby. Petrified Ed here is completely covered. The Hotel Raphael is a lovely hotel just two blocks from the Arc de Triomphe. I'll get you the best suite they have and you can stay as long as you want. I can get you a first class airline ticket and you can be gone as soon as you can possibly get packed."

Ruby blinked her eyes and shrugged. "Well, first class for two, right?"

"Ruby," Petula said. She pulled Ruby slightly away from earshot of Minnie Pearl, although she had no sane reason on earth to believe the pig understood a word she was saying. "I'm afraid they are not going to let Minnie Pearl sit in a first class seat on an international flight. That's just not going to happen."

Ruby took the flashlight back. She shined it on Petrified Ed. Then she shined it onto the face of Buster and Petula. "Someone once told me," Ruby said with more than a little conviction of heart, "Where there's money there's a way."

Petula regretted saying those words as much as anyone could ever regret anything in their life, but there was nothing she could do; there was no taking them back now.

Petula said, "First class, for two it is."

2

The melting snowfall fed a running mountain stream far up in the hills of Tennessee. Snow that was glistening on tree branches in the sun was thawing and dripping like raindrops to the ground. Near the stream, tiny pastel-purple wildflowers were pushing their way through the glistening frosty-white snow.

A raccoon family of six passed the stream and crossed a dirt road, and then made their way past a wooden post. Atop the post was a hand-painted population sign. It read:

ARMADILLO - POP. 5

* * *

In Mae's General Store it was very quiet, practically ghostly so. Ernie was outside holding himself steady with a cane he had whittled himself from an old chestnut tree branch. His dog Duke was loyally right at his side. Ernie was reading a note his wife and sister had posted to the front door of the store. He carefully examined it through his thick, smudgy eyeglasses.

CLOSED

GONE TO WELCOME NEW NEIGHBORS TO TOWN

"Duke, can you help me make sense of this?" The dog looked up at his old master with obedient glee, but no answer. Ernie read it over again. He shook his head. "Good God Almighty, Duke, how long was I asleep?"

* * *

The windows of the old Holloway house were warm and glowing yellow from the firelight inside. Smoke billowed out the chimney top. The snow that covered roof of the house, and the barn nearby, was dripping icicle-water on all sides.

A horse drawn cart sat next to Dylan's Land Rover and Kitty's Tesla Roadster. Mae and Calliope were removing two big stainless steel cooking pots from the back of the cart.

Josh opened the front door of the house. "Hey, they're here."

Dylan stepped out and took a lingering look. "I swear I kept saying to them you were a vegetarian. But all they kept hearing was veterinarian. I finally gave up. Unless you can find a way to talk your way out of it, tomorrow morning they're expecting you to castrate a bull."

Josh shrugged and smiled. "I'm not a vegetarian today. I have been waiting all my life to have some of this stew."

Josh and Dylan ran down the porch stairs and across the lawn. "Hey, let us help you carry those?" Josh yelled out.

"I sure hope you boys are hungry!" Mae called out to Josh and Dylan.

Calliope agreed, "You boys better be. It's Sunday. On Sunday I always make two pots."

Josh grabbed a pot from Mae. Dylan nodded, as he took the other pot from Calliope. Josh said, "Well we have a couple of guests, so I think two pots should be just fine."

The front door opened and out stepped Kitty and JJ. They were looking out to the two new arrivals with curiosity.

"Well, who have we got here?" JJ asked. "Is this the surprise guests Josh was so eager for me to meet?"

"I'll be." Kitty shook her head in amazement. "All these years. And they're still going. Mae and her sister-in-law, Rattlesnake Calliope."

JJ gave the approaching women with Josh and Dylan a lingering, inquisitive look - focusing closely on the one with beautiful blue eyes. He gave her a second look. "She is real," he finally said. "My Lord, she *is* real," he repeated with genuine fond amazement.

Kitty took hold of JJ's hand. She gave it an affectionate squeeze and glanced up into his eyes. She was glowing. "So," she asked, "when do you think we should tell 'em?"

JJ smiled confidently. "We can tell them over dinner." He snuck a quick kiss on Kitty's cheek, and winked.

JJ said, "I've got nothing to hide."

ACKNOWLEDGMENTS

THIS NOVEL WAS BORN in a screenwriting program created by Jeff Gordon called Writers Boot Camp based in Santa Monica. It was Kickstarter crowd funded. Primarily friends and family helped me meet and surpass my goal, which makes this book very special. I want to thank these people, and a few others who never lost faith in me, for their support and resounding encouragement. They made my dream come true.

Missy Anderson, Aubrie Armstrong, Midtown Beach Hut Deli, Jason Becking, Lellingby Boyce, Yvonne Birchett, Catherine Conte, Daniel Cordova, Laura Craig, Robin Cradles (best photographer in the universe, & in lesser known universes), Lynda Draper, Steve DuBois, Denise Fladager, Matthew Forrest, Ember Fox, Racheal Frederick-Vijay, Linda Eagle Gio, Andrew Hanz Gion, Julia Gitter, Haley, Lisa Hart, Stephen Hayhurst, Aubrey Johnson, JZ Knight, Susie Magnuson, Patrick Mathews, Sarah Mathews, Jenny McMullen, Megan Meier, Devon Coats Montemayor, Elizabeth Morehead, Satomi Nakajima, Sara Padama, Erika Crocker Parker, Konnie Plumlee, Eric Preyer, Erin Preyer, Mark Preyer, Rebecca Preyer, Micki Pulleyking (whose grandfather, John Weaver, baptized Porter Wagoner), Beth Rains, Ram, Mario Reza, Dale Riston, RSE gang, Jane Samuels, Bonnie Sangimino, Sophie Sears, Aleta Gio Severe, Vicky Smith, BJ Solinger, Martin Swinehart, Marilyn Taylor, Katie Thames, Traci Rich Tomlinson (for Rattlesnake Calliope), Woodstocks, Ann Wynes, and Sarah Wynes.

AND A TIP OF THE HAT TO GRANDPA ALBERT GREEN AND AUNT ALLIE MAYE for their round-the-clock supply of unsubstantiated, outlandish and fabulous tales.

FALLING UNDER THE SPELL of an extraordinary magical story; turning that first page and entering a fantastic world of new friends (and enemies); and never wanting the bewitchment to end - in other words, my love of a good book - comes from the one and only master storytelling wizard. I love you man. Thank you Stephen King.

ABOUT THE AUTHOR

J. Kent Preyer was born and raised in southern Missouri and now lives in northern California with his fiancé and two cats. Tennessee Wildflowers is his first novel.

www.ingramcontent.com/pod-product-compliance
Lightning Source LLC
Chambersburg PA
CBHW032016230426
43671CB00005B/102